Anthony Collins

A DISCOURSE OF THE GROUNDS AND REASONS OF THE CHRISTIAN RELIGION
1724

Wipf & Stock
PUBLISHERS
Eugene, Oregon

Wipf and Stock Publishers
199 W 8th Ave, Suite 3
Eugene, OR 97401

A Discourse of the Grounds and Reasons of the Christian Religion
By Collins, Anthony
ISBN: 1-59752-067-5
Publication date 1/26/2005

A DISCOURSE
OF THE
GROUNDS and REASONS
OF THE
CHRISTIAN RELIGION.

In two Parts:

The first containing some CONSIDERATIONS on the Quotations made from the Old in the New Testament, and particularly on the Prophesies cited from the former and said to be fulfill'd in the latter.

The second containing an EXAMINATION of the SCHEME advanc'd by Mr. WHISTON in his *Essay towards restoring the true Text of the Old Testament, and for vindicating the Citations thence made in the New Testament.*

To which is prefix'd an Apology for free debate and liberty of writing.

Who hath also made us able Ministers of the New Testament, not of the Letter, but of the Spirit; for the Letter killeth, but the Spirit giveth Life. 2 Cor. iii. 6.

Omnia a *MOSE* ordinata enumerans, ostendere possem figuras & notas & *denunciationes* esse eorum quæ CHRISTO eventura erant, eorumq; qui in ipsum ut crederent præcogniti fuerant, atq; item eorum quæ CHRISTUS ipse erat facturus. JUSTINI MARTYRIS *Opera*. p. 261.

Sin dixerint post adventum Domini salvatoris & prædicationem Apostolorum libros Hebræos fuisse falsatos, cachinnum tenere non potero: Ut Salvator, & Evangelistæ, & Apostoli ita testimonia protulerint, ut Judæi postea falsaturi erant!
HIERON. *Oper*. tom. 3. p. 64. c. 6. in ISAIAM.

LONDON. MDCCXXIV.

PREFACE

TO THE

READER:

CONTAINING,

An Apology for Mr. WHIS-TON's *liberty of writing.*

HE title of my book, and the contents, which I shall place at the end of this preface, will sufficiently explain the subject and method thereof, and make all further preliminary to those ends needless.

But

But it may not be improper to endeavour to prevent a misconstruction and false inference, which the second part, which more particularly concerns Mr. WHISTON, may perhaps occasion.

It is very possible, that in opposing the opinions of that ingenious and learned gentleman, I may be undesignedly instrumental in raising up against him the passions of some readers; who may think, that the opinions he maintains, are such, as should not be allow'd to be advanc'd or defended; and that he ought to suffer in his person or fortune for maintaining them. Wherefore, to clear my own intention, and to prevent, as far as I can, such thoughts in my readers minds against my adversary, I will here offer a few particulars by way of apology for his liberty of writing; which, in my opinion, is not only justifiable in itself, but highly becoming a *Man*, a *Christian*, and a *Protestant*, and especially a *Clergyman*, *a Scholar* and a *Philosopher*.

1. In matters of opinion, it is every man's natural right and duty to think for himself, and to judge upon such evidence as he can procure to himself, after he has done his best endeavours to get information. Human decisions are of no weight in this matter. Another man has no more right to determine what Mr. WHISTON's opinions shall be, than Mr. WHISTON has to determine what another man's opinions shall be. It seems amazing to consider; how one man can presume he has such right over another; and how any man can be so weak as to imagine another has such right over him. *Suppose,* says (*a*) STILLINGFLEET, *a man living in the times of the prevalency of Arianism, when almost all the guides of the Church declar'd*

(*a*) Stillingfleet's *Answer to several Treatises, &c.* pt. 1. p. 152.

declar'd in favour of it, when several great Councils oppos'd and contradicted that of Nice, *when Pope* LIBERIUS *did subscribe the* Sirmian Confession, *and communicated with the* Arians, *what advice would you give such a one if he must not exercise his own judgment? Must he follow the present guides? Then he must join with the* Arians. *Must he adhere to the* Nicene *Council. But there were more numerous Councils which condemn'd it. What remedy can be suppos'd in such a case, but that every person must search and examine the several doctrines, according to his best ability, and judge what is best for him to believe and practise?*

2. As it is every man's natural right and duty to think, and judge for himself in matters of opinion; so he should be allow'd *freely* to *profess* his opinions, and to endeavour, when he judges proper, to *convince* others also of their truth; provided those opinions do not tend to the disturbance of society. For

For unless all men be allow'd *freely* to *profess* their opinions; the means of information in respect to opinions, must in great measure be wanting, and just inquiries into the truth of opinions almost impracticable; and by consequence our natural right and duty to to think and judge for ourselves must be subverted, for want of materials, whereon to employ our minds. A man, by himself, can make no great progress in knowledge. He is like to the (*b*) young man at *Chartres* in *France*, who, being deaf and dumb from his birth till the age of four and twenty, took in but few ideas; and who, tho' he had good natural parts, yet, for want of communication with others, did not even make such inferences from the comparison of those ideas, as were very obvious and might be expected from him. A single man is

---

(*b*) Histoire de l' Academie Royale des Sciences An. 1703. p. 22, 23. de l'Edition d' Holland.

is unable, by his own strength, to take in the compass of things necessary to understand his own opinions fully; and besides, a man is indispos'd to use his own strength, when an undisturb'd laziness, ignorance, and prejudice give him full satisfaction as to the truth of his opinions. But if there be a *free profession* or communication of notions; every man will have an opportunity of acquainting himself with all that can be known from men; and many, for their own satisfaction of mind, will make inquiries, and, in order to know the truth of opinions, will desire to know all that can be said on any side of a question.

Unless men are allow'd to endeavour to *convince* others of the truth of their opinions; all *teaching* must be laid aside, and men will be hinder'd from doing the greatest act of humanity and charity for one another. For no man can *teach* others, but by endeavouring to *convince* them:

them: nor ought any one to *teach* another any thing, but that whereof he himself is perswaded, nor can any man have any other rule of *teaching* truth, but his own sentiments.

If such liberty of *professing* and *teaching* be not allow'd, *error*, if autoriz'd, will keep its ground: and *truth*, if dormant, will never be brought to light; or, if *autoriz'd*, will be supported on a false and absur'd foundation, and such as would equally support error ; and, if receiv'd on the foot of *autority*, will not be in the least meritorious to its professors.

Nor are these all the ill consequences flowing from the disallowance of this *liberty :* for nothing has been a greater source of mischief among men, than the violent means, that have been us'd, and, indeed, are necessary to be us'd to destroy such original and fundamental rights and duties of men as to *think and judge* for themselves, to *profess* what they *believe* true, and
to

to *teach* what they *believe* true to others.

3. Whoever desires that truth should take place, should be well-pleas'd to have all men of learning, penetration, and integrity, publish their opinions. For such men are the most capable of finding out truth themselves, and of setting it in a due light before others. Would not every man of understanding and honesty be glad to know the most intimate thoughts of such men, as HOOKER, HALES, CHILLINGWORTH, MEDE, WILKINS, WHITCHCOT, MORE, CUDWORTH, SPENCER, TILLOTSON, BACON, FALKLAND, SELDEN, MILTON, MARSHAM, BOYLE, TEMPLE, and LOCKE, (for example) and be sorry, that such like men ever have been, or are, under any restraints from speaking their minds; and wish, that they might speak their minds on all important questions in philosophy and theology, like Mr. WHISTON; who has not many superiors

in

in learning and penetration, and seems superior himself to most in integrity? Is it not ridiculous, that men of the greatest integrity and capacity should be under any discouragement from making inquiries after truth, and under any difficulties for publishing writings in consequence of their inquiries; and that none can safely speak in matters of speculation, but the blind followers of the blind, or the interested followers of the interested?

4. Not to permit and encourage ingenious, learned, and honest men to profess and defend their opinions, when different from ours, is to distrust the truth of our own opinions, and to fear the light. Such conduct *must*, in a country of sense and learning, increase the number of *unbelievers*, already so greatly complain'd of; who when they see matters of opinion not allow'd to be profess'd and impartially debated, justly think they have foul play, and therefore reject

reject many things as false and ill-grounded, which otherwise they might receive as truths. And it must do so especially, when it is consider'd, what a numerous clergy we have; who are all bred scholars, and have literature chiefly in their hands, and are many of them men of great parts, learning, and leisure; who understand, and practise all the arts of perswasion, and have the common people (I mean the common people as to understanding) devoted to them; who can never want able men among themselves (to say nothing of their followers and dependants), either in the way of banter or seriousness, poetry or prose, dialogue or discourse, declamation or argument, to answer and expose whatever can be alledg'd in behalf of falshood by men, who cannot pretend to match them, without truth on their side; and who have the sole privilege of speaking frequently to the people

from

from the *(c) pulpit*, where, as Mr. *Whiston* observes, they may *dogmatically assert, and earnestly press* what they *would hardly venture at all to justify elsewhere, in any learned conversation*, or as BOILEAU expresses it, *C'est là que bien ou mal on a droit de tout dire*. *(cc)*

5. The grand principle of *men* consider'd as having a relation to the *Deity* and under an obligation to be *religious*, is that they ought to consult their *reason*; and of *Christians*, and *Protestants*, that they ought to consult *the scriptures as the rule of their faith and practise*. But how can these, which are practical principles, be duly put in practise; unless we be at liberty, at all times and in all points, to consider and debate with others, (as well as with ourselves) what *reason* and *scripture* say, and to *profess* and *act openly*, according to what we are convinc'd they say?

(c) *Papers relating to Mr.* Whiston's *cause*, &c. p. 170.
(cc) *Sat.* I. V. 149.

say? How can we be better inform'd than by using the best means of information; which consists in consulting *reason* and *scripture*, and calling in the aid of others? Of what use is it to consult *reason* and *scripture* at all, as any means of information, if we are not, upon conviction, to follow their dictates? And what *principles* of religion are men to *profess* (which all say must be) *openly*, and act upon, but those, whereof they are convinc'd?

6. Clergymen, by being devoted to the service of *truth*, and to preach the *gospel* of *truth*, are under a particular obligation to inquire into the mind of God, and to impart the discoveries they make to the world, and, as successors of the apostles, *to go and teach all nations*. And they cannot act more effectually against the design of their own profession, than either by being silent as to the discoveries they make, or by preaching and writing contrary to their own light;
to

to say nothing of their obligations as men, to assist their neighbours, by putting them in the right way, and to deal sincerely with all men. Will any *layman* be so stupid and foolish as to say, that he desires and expects it of the *clergy*, that they should knowingly *deceive* him, and lead him on in an erroneous way? Will any of the clergy be so abandon'd as to say, that they ought thus to *deceive* the *laity*; tho' the laity themselves should desire it, and be pleas'd to be thus *deceived*? And yet this ought to be the state of the case, if *clergymen* are not to declare, what they take to be the will of God, to the people.

7. Nothing can tend more to the *true honour* of the *clergy*, than that they should have *full liberty*, that is, that they should be under no impediments in their inquiries after truth, nor in the least suffer for teaching what they believe true.

For those learned clergymen; who for want of this liberty are now o-
blig'd

blig'd (as a great divine (d) justly complains) *to turn themselves to the Heathen Historians, Poets, Orators, & Philosophers; to spend ten or twelve years upon* HORACE *or* TERENCE; and to *illustrate billet-doux's or drunken catches, explain obscene jests, and make happy emendations of passages, that a modest man would blush at*; such learned clergymen, I say, would then apply their *sagacity and labour* more HONORABLY, as well as more virtuously and religiously, *to the study of* religion and *the scriptures*. I say, more HONORABLY; because, such application is *honourable* in itself, and any other is *dishonourable* in them, whatever degree of (e) *reputation* it may now give them.

And at the same time, other learned clergymen, who may think it their duty to inquire after religious truth, will be under no temptation of professing to believe,

---

(d) Hare's *Diss.* and *Discourag.* p. 28.
(e) Ib. p. 29.

to believe, what they believe not, but may then act the *honourable* part of sincerity.

And as this proposal tends to the *HONOUR* of all the *clergy*, so it cannot be against the *interest* of *any*: and it will be greatly for the *interest* of *such*, who think themselves oblig'd in conscience to profess opinions, which happen to be contrary to those receiv'd, and whose case seems to be worthy of consideration; for they will then be in no danger of losing preferment on account of their integrity.

8. Men have no reason to apprehend any ill consequence to truth (for which alone they ought to have any concern) from *free debate*; but on the contrary to apprehend ill consequence to truth from *free debate* being disallow'd. For truth propos'd to the understanding is like light to the eye: it must distinguish itself from error, as light does itself from darkness. And while *free debate* is allow'd, truth will never want a professor thereof,

nor

nor an advocate to offer some plea in its behalf: and it can never be wholly banish'd, but where human decisions, back'd with power, carry all before them.

Would *Transubstantiation* pass in *France* without an attack made upon it, if men could *freely* write against it? Would truth suffer there, if that doctrine were allow'd to be a subject of debate? Could that doctrine keep the ground it now has there, under *free debate*? Would its falshood, set forth in the utmost light, have no effect on the understandings of the polite and ingenious French nation? Nay, is there any thing, that keeps up that absurdity, and stifles the light of truth, but autority? And are not the popish ecclesiasticks so sensible of the force of truth, and so particularly fearful of losing that *pearl of great price*, the darling doctrine of *Transubstantiation*, that no man can with safety, where they have influence, to

his

his person, fortune, and reputation, call it in question.

Did *popery* get any ground in *England* by the liberty the papists had in the reign of king JAMES the *second* to publish whatever they pleas'd in behalf of their religion? On the contrary, was not *popery* more expos'd to scorn and contempt by being the subject of debate, than if nothing had been wrote in behalf of it?

Does *protestantism* decay in *Holland*, where not only the papists themselves print what apologies and controversial treatises they please, but where the booksellers print all manner of popish books, for which there is any demand, and by consequence chuse such books chiefly, which the papists themselves deem most strenuously written?

9. If men did but consider, what infinite variety of religions have prevail'd, and do now prevail in the world; what variety of notions and practises have prevail'd, and do pre-

vail in the same country; what revolutions of opinions there have been among christians, and how greatly divided they have always been, and now are in sentiment, and how much departed every sect thereof is from their primitive institution; what a small part of the world is possess'd by christians, and how very inconsiderable a part is possess'd by any one set of christians, and what little figure the church of *England* (whose members are infinitely divided in sentiment from one another) makes upon the globe; what monstrous absurdities prevail in most places, and what excessive ignorance every where; and how this state of things has endur'd among men, who have been and are chiefly conducted by *autority* and compell'd by *force*; it should seem, that *autority* and *force* are so far from being the way to put an end to error, or make men wiser, that they have contributed to encrease the errors and follies of men. And if this be be so, I must conclude for the necessity of introducing *free inquiry, profession,* and *debate*; which cannot make men more erroneous and foolish than they are; and seems to be the only way to make men less erroneous and more wise than they are; and does in fact make men less erroneous and more wise in every country, according to that degree of it, which prevails.

A sacred author tells us. (f) *Wisdom is glorious and never fadeth away; and is* EASILY SEEN *of them that love her, and* FOUND *of such as* SEEK *her, in making herself first known unto them. He that seeketh her early shall have no great travels: for he shall find her sitting at his door. To think therefore on her is perfection of wisdom, and whoso watcheth for her shall quickly be without care. For she goeth about seeking such as are worthy of her, sheweth herself favourably unto them in the ways, and meeteth them in every thought.* So that if men were not put out of their way by

---

(f) Wisdom 6. 12.—16.

by *autority*, but were allow'd to *seek*, or would of themselves *seek* truth, they could not fail of finding her.

10. If it be said, that *it is necessary to peace and quiet in the state, that there should be no debates about speculations; and that all men should square their principles and practises by what they find receiv'd in their country*; then let not men pretend any concern for *truth*, and against *falshood*; for this removes *truth* and *falshood* out of the question. Let them then set up for *hobbism* or *popery*; which by force and an inquisition, perhaps, may keep all things quiet, as well as, certainly, most, if not all, men ignorant. But in reality, the allowance of *free debate* is the method to obtain a more solid and lasting *peace* (*peace* flowing from temper and principle) than that mere *outward form* of *peace*, which is sometimes obtain'd by force and an inquisition. For if debates are *free*, that is, if no man gets or loses by maintaining

par-

particular opinions, the grand motives which make men disturb one another about opinions will cease; and they will insensibly fall into a *due temper of mind* (which force can never procure) and will be no more angry with one another on account of different sentiments, than for different features of their faces, or for different proportions of their bodies.

Besides, *free debate* tends to shorten and lessen the number of controversies. Many points, notwithstanding the present warm contests, and learned books written *pro* and *con* about them, are so plain, that they would not then bear a long debate: many others would be dropp'd, when it was seen, that they were too obscure for the learned to master: and all points of speculation whatsoever would be dropp'd among the vulgar; who, when speculations cease to be recommended them as objects for their zeal, and are neither matters of faction or interest, will concern themselves no more about them, than they do about mathematicks or other matters, whereof they are incapable of understanding any thing.

A learned (g) author gives us the following account of the state of religious controversy in *Greece* and the parts about it, as it is set out by ancient authors, until the days of SOCRATES. He says, *There were as many religions almost as men; for every man's religion was his fancy; and they had most credit and autority, that could best invent, and make best shew. Among so many religions there were no controversies, but very good agreement and concord; because no reason us'd either to examine or to disprove. There was no talk among men, but of dreams, revelations, and apparitions: and they that could so easily fancy, had no reason to mistrust or to question the relations of others, tho' never so strange, which were so agreeable to their humours or dispositions;*

(g) Casaubon of Enthusiasm, p. 6.

fitions; and by which themselves were confirm'd in their own suppos'd enthusiasms.

After the days of SOCRATES, *Greece* for a long time abounded in philosophers, who were divided into all possible sentiments concerning the most important points of speculation, and disputed with each other and wrote books without number and without controul in behalf of their schemes. And the variety and altercation among them whetted and improv'd the wits of *Greece*, insomuch that *Athens* by their means became the theatre of learning and politeness, and was visited by great numbers of foreigners, who, either as travellers or students sent thither by their parents and guardians, came to be instructed by the philosophers. Nor did their different notions, under the liberty allow'd, ever disturb the civil government; but on the contrary kept the men of sense in good humour, gave them entertainment

at their repasts and parties of pleasure, where the chief diversion often was to debate with temper and civility questions of speculation; wherein they imitated the philosophers themselves, who, tho' they wrote in behalf of their several opposite sentiments, have not left a book behind them wrote with the least spirit of rancour or malignity. There was little or nothing got or lost by maintaining opinions; and therefore men were not at all concern'd to impose their opinions on one another, nor were they angry for dissent in opinions any more than for disagreement in fortune, or taste, or about beauty in a mistress; nor was there any application made to gain the common people to bawl in behalf of any set of notions; which, as they understood not, so they left wholly to the men of learning and sense. How unlike is this to the state of things among us christians; whose religion exceeds the religion of these old
Greeks,

Greeks, as much as they exceeded us in practise. Our disputes with one another, for want of impartial liberty, make convulsions in government, involve neighbourhoods in feuds and animosities, render men impolite, and make conversation among friends, of different sentiments, often disagreeable? Into what feuds did the city of *Hambourg* run (to omit a thousand other instances) on occasion of a dispute between *two ministers*, whether in the *Lord's prayer*, the first words should be translated *Our Father*, or *Father Our*; under whom the citizens were work'd up into great heat and flame against one another, and at length divided themselves into parties that fought daily in the streets? Nothing of which could happen under liberty and a free debate; to which it is absolutely necessary (as I before observ'd) that no man get or lose by maintaining either side of a question. There would then be nothing to raise or feed the spirit of contention:

tion: *enthusiasm*, like love and other passions, would spend itself by free vent and amicable collision: *knavery* would want its spur: and *gross nonsense*, when unsupported by *enthusiasm* and *knavery*, would sink and fall by being inquir'd into and expos'd; for as a true sense of things is only to be got from trial and experience, or comparison; so let such trial be made, and the difference between things will soon be seen, and the right measure of all things of consequence to us will soon be found out.

While *Rome* was in the height of its glory for arms, learning, and politeness, there were *six hundred different religions* (h) profess'd and allow'd therein. And this great variety does not appear to have had the least ill effect on the peace of the state, or on the temper of men; but on the con-

---

(b) *Lipsius* de Magn. Rom. l. 4. c. 5.

contrary, a very good effect: for there is an entire silence in history about the actions of those ancient different professors, who it seems, liv'd so quietly together as to furnish no materials for an *Ecclesiastical History*, such as christians have given occasion for, which a reverend divine (*i*) thus describes. *Ecclesiastical History*, says he, *is chiefly spent in reciting the wild opinions of hereticks* (that is, in belying hereticks); *the contentions between emperors and popes; the idle and superstitious canons, and ridiculous decrees and constitutions of pack'd councils, their debates about frivolous matters, and playing the fool with religion; the consultations of synods about augmenting the revenues of the clergy, and establishing their pride and grandeur; the impostures of monks and fryars, the schisms and factions of the church; the tyranny, cruelty, and impiety of the clergy;*

(*i*) Edward's *New Discoveries*, &c. p. 40, 41.

clergy; insomuch that the excellent GROTIUS, (k) says "He that reads ecclesiastical history reads nothing but the roguery and folly of bishops and churchmen."

In fine, matters were happily (l) ballanc'd among the antient *Greeks* and *Romans*. "Reason had fair play; politeness prevail'd; learning and science flourish'd; and wonderful was the harmony, temper, friendship, charity and peace, which arose from the contrarieties allow'd among them. Enthusiasm and superstition being mildly treated, and let alone, never rag'd to that degree, as to occasion wars, or bloodshed, or persecutions, or devastations in the world."

Are not the *United Provinces*, remarkable for *liberty* and *peace*? There all men, how different soever in notions, live in such peace and friendship

---

(k) *Grotii* Epistolæ, p. 22.
(l) Shaftsbury's *Letter of Enthusiasm*.

ship with one another, as is unknown to men of the same religion in other countries; where some foolish question about the antiquity and autority of *hair, teeth, tears, milk, rags, handkerchiefs, smocks, bones*, and other *relicts*, or about the immaculate conception of the virgin, or about habits and dress, about (*m*) *the manner of men's holding their fingers when they cross themselves*, and such like mere ceremonies, or about metaphysical speculations (some of which are as little understood by the disputants themselves as by the vulgar) is fuel for the most uncharitable contention. There the *lyon* and the *lamb*, I mean, the *Papist* and the *Mennonite*, lye down in peace together; the first forgetting his wonted rage, and the latter preserving that innocence, which he was born with, and which liberty and experience have cultivated in him. (*n*) *It is hardly to*
be

(*m*) Perry's *State of Russia*, p. 153.
(*n*) Temple's *Observat. on the Netherlands*, p. 205. &c.

be imagin'd, says Sir W. TEMPLE, *how all the violence and sharpness, which accompanies the differences of religion in other countries, seems to be appeas'd or softned* in the United Provinces, *by the general freedom which all men enjoy, either by allowance or connivance; nor how faction and ambition are thereby disabled to colour their interested and seditious designs with the pretences of religion, which has cost the christian world so much blood for these last hundred and fifty years. No man can here complain of pressure in his conscience; of being forc'd to any publick profession of his private faith; of being restrain'd from his own manner of worship in his house, or oblig'd to any other abroad: and* WHOEVER *asks more in point of religion, without the undisputed evidence of a particular mission from heaven, may be justly suspected, not to ask for God's sake, but for his own; since pretending to sovereignty, instead of liberty, in opinion, is indeed pretending the same in autority too. But in this commonwealth, no man having any reason to complain of oppression in conscience; and no man having hopes, by advancing his religion, to*

form

form a party, or break in upon the state, the differences in opinion make none in affections, and little in conversation, where it serves but for entertainment and variety. They argue without interest and anger; they differ without enmity or scorn; and they agree without confederacy. Men live together, like citizens of the world, associated by the common ties of humanity, and by the bonds of peace, under the impartial protection of indifferent laws, with equal encouragement of all art and industry, and equal freedom of speculation and enquiry; all men enjoying their imaginary excellencies and acquisitions of knowledge, with as much safety as their more real possessions and improvements of fortune. And as in other places, 'tis in every man's choice with whom he will eat or lodge, with whom go to market, or to court; so it seems to be here, with whom he will pray or go to church, or associate in the service and worship of God; nor is any more notice taken or more censure pass'd of what every one chuses in these cases, than in the other.

[xxxiv]

I believe the force of commerce, allian‑ces, and acquaintances, spreading so far as they do in small circuits, (such as the Province of Holland*) may contribute much to make conversation and all the offices of common life so easy, among so different opi‑nions, of which so many several persons are often in every man's eye; and no man checks or takes offence at faces or customs or ceremonies, he sees every day, as at those he hears of in places far distant, and perhaps by partial relations, and comes to see late in his life, and after he has long been possess'd by passion or prejudice against them. However it is, religion may possibly do more good in other places but it does less hurt here; and where-ever the invisible effects are the greatest and most advantageous, I am sure the visible are so in this country, by the continual and undisturb'd civil peace of their go‑vernment for so long a course of years; and by so mighty an increase of their people, wherein will appear to consist chiefly the vast growth of their trade and riches, and consequently the strength and greatness of their state.*

I will conclude this article with an observation of our most judicious and learned (p) Archbishop. *Whilst instead of examining, says he, impartially, where the truth lyes, men magisterially assume to themselves an autority to denounce anathema's against their brethren, who would convince them of their deviations; it is in vain to hope, that either truth should prevail, or* PEACE *and Unity be establish'd among us. But would they once be perswaded to remove this obstacle out of the way; would they know themselves to be but men, and as such expos'd to the same frailties and infirmities with others; would they impartially search after truth, out of the alone certain and infallible rule of it, the word of God; why should we despair, but that the light of the glorious gospel of* CHRIST *might*

(p) Wake's Pref. before *Sure and honest means for the conversion of* Hereticks, p. 6.

might so shine upon us, as to guide our feet into the way of PEACE.

11. The advantage of *free debate* to society is infinite. It is not only the way to true religion, and to *true peace*, but the way to *knowledge* and *arts*, which are the foundations of politeness, order, happiness, and prosperity; as ignorance is the foundation of brutality, disorder, misery, and declension in society It is the way to make men honest and sincere in the profession of religion (as imposition is only the way to make men knaves and hypocrites); and that will introduce *honesty* in other respects, which is the *best policy*, and the *best* improvement of *man*.

12. The bulk of men do, I confess, reason and practise very differently from what I have asserted and defended. Most men, conscious of their own weakness, see plainly, that they are unable, by any application to inquiries, to judge for themselves in many points. Thence they conclude

clude they ought to be govern'd in their belief by the judgment of others. Then they take up with such guides, as some chance or other directs them to; who not only form their opinions for them, but make them zealous for those opinions.

Upon which way of reasoning and practise, I will only observe; that *zeal* and *ignorance* are a most absurd and ridiculous composition in the same persons; and that these men most manifestly determine the point before them wrong, by taking sides in matters, wherein, as understanding nothing, they have no concern, and should not pretend to have any opinion at all. Would it not be excessively ridiculous to see ignorant people zealously engag'd for or against propositions (as led by different guides chosen at a venture) in *Astronomy*, whereof they neither do, nor can understand any thing? And is it less ridiculous for ignorant people zealously to concern themselves about other matters, (as led by guides chosen at a venture) whereof they know as little?

13. Men have very different tempers and capacities from one another, *naturally*; have very different educations; do improve themselves very differently by study, according to their different capacities, application, and opportunities; have different interests, passions, and infirmities, by which they are influenc'd and acted; and are all fallible, not only in matters that depend upon *reason*, but in understanding the *scriptures*, which tho' true in themselves, and deliver'd to us by divine inspiration, are in many places too obscure for men to be certain of their meaning.

Hence a foundation is laid for unavoidable differences of opinion among men; which differences are greatly encreas'd by the *dogmatick discipline* that is infinitely more promoted and prevalent than those *disciplines*

ciplines, which teach men to doubt and distrust the truth of matters propos'd to them: and God himself, by forming men as he has done, and by placing them in their present circumstances, seems to have design'd, that they should not agree in opinion; or, at least, seems not to have design'd, that they should agree.

What then can any violent attempt or project to hinder men from differing in opinion from one another be, but an attempt to subvert the common state of human nature and the design of God; and not less ridiculous, romantick, and impossible to succeed, than an attempt to hinder speech, or to make all men of the same size or height, or to quell the natural passion of love, or to build a tower up to heaven?

And must not the men of this project be perfect DON QUIXOTS, and the greatest *fanaticks*, in setting about and pursuing so unaccountable a work?

If some *great genius* would but give an account of the actions of these men (who may be properly call'd *Saint-errants*) in the *Life and Adventures* of some renown'd persecuting *Prince* or *Ecclesiastick*, who has spent his time in promoting and establishing unity and uniformity in whimsies, dress, and forms; as the great CERVANTES has done of *Knight-errantry*, in the *Life and Actions* of DON QUIXOT, who spent his time in *adventures* to free the world of monsters, and to tame giants, and all in honor of DULCINEA DEL TOBOSO, whom, tho' homely and agreeable only to his deprav'd taste, all the world should be obliged to bow down before and to admire, as a consumate beauty: he might give us a more useful and entertaining work than CERVANTES has done. *Saint-errantry* is a more common and natural enthusiasm than *Knight-errantry*, which was an enthusiasm, but of yesterday and of small duration and extent; and therefore *Saint-errantry*

rantry has furnish'd materials in almost all ages, and infinite materials in particular ages, which are recorded in *history*, but especially in *ecclesiastical history*.

But till a new CERVANTES arises and performs this work, I would recommend the *History* of DON QUIXOT, as in some measure suited and appplicable to *Saint-errantry*, to be read in conjunction with *ecclesiastick historians*. For the principle of enthusiasm being the same in the *Saint*, as in the *Knight*, and producing like effects; the reader may, by comparing things, and by an easy application in many cases, take DON QUIXOT for a *Termagant Saint*, and a *Termagant* Saint for a DON QUIXOT.

14. It may be objected to Mr. WHISTON, that he has advanc'd a multitude of paradoxes about very important matters, many of which are founded on very slight appearances of probability; and, in particular, that he calls in question the integrity of

our

our present copies of the Old Testament, which he supposes corrupted to that degree by the Jews in respect to some of the quotations made from thence by the apostles, as to make their reasonings from, and use of, those quotations, seem *weak* and *enthusiastical.*

To which I answer,

That Mr. WHISTON acts the part of an honest man and lover of truth, by thus proposing his *conjectures* and *sentiments*, and putting points of consequence in the way of examination, and is so much better than all other such learned divines as himself, as he exceeds them in the liberty he takes of proposing his *conjectures* and *sentiments:* that the method, whereof he sets us an example, tends to the information of all men of sense, and both encreases the number of capable judges, and renders the learned themselves better judges than they were before: that, in particular, the Old Testament will appear so undoubtedly ly genuine and uncorrupt in the respect abovemention'd, when the question is debated, that it must unavoidably gain ground as a genuine and uncorrupt book, in that respect, in the minds of all intelligent men, who are not wedded to an *hypothesis*: and that it ought to be consider'd; that Mr. WHISTON proposes his *scheme* (o) of a corrupted Old Testament, as the best and only method of defending christianity, which, according to him, had a rational dependance on the Old Testament before it was corrupted; and that he apprehends, that the *scheme* or supposition of an uncorrupted Old Testament really destroys the truth of christianity, and gives the Deists, Jews, and Infidels, a just subject of triumph over it, which, according to him, is now in an (p) *irreconcileable State* with, and depends not on, the present

---

(o) *See also his* Advertisement *before his* Supplement *to his* Essay, &c.
(p) Whitton's, *Essay*, &c. p. 263.

sent Old Testament: whereby this matter amounts to no more than a question between christians contending for the truth of christianity against unbelievers, viz. which is the best method of defending christianity, whether by supposing the Old Testament corrupted, or uncorrupted.

But Mr. WHISTON himself, in few words, makes a just and true defence for liberty, and also a noble proposal in behalf of *truth* and *christianity*, when he says, (q) *I wish that all unbelievers were openly allow'd and invited to produce their real arguments, substantial objections, and considerable doubts, without molestation; as being perswaded,* says he, *they are capable of satisfactory answers and solutions.* For it is sufficient, that all the unbelievers arguments can be answer'd. The *answers* and *solutions* mention'd by Mr. W. which are now want-

---

(q) Whiston's *Reflections on the Disc.* of *Free-thinking*, p. 6.

wanting, would, if produc'd, greatly weaken the cause of unbelievers; who can now pretend to have *real arguments*, and *substantial objections* unanswer'd, and *considerable doubts* unsolv'd; and clamor, because they have not liberty to speak for themselves; and who have a pretence to say, that their adversaries, conscious of the weakness of their own cause, dare not let them speak or write against it. And Mr. W. is very far from being singular in thinking, that it would be a benefit to allow infidels to publish their objections against christianity.

GROTIUS, in a letter to PEIRESKI, says, (r) *I send you, most noble Sir, some passages taken out of the writings of* PORPHYRY, *by the defenders of the christian religion, from whence you may easily see, how many things might have been produc'd out of his books for the purpose of christanity, if we had them*

them entire; those books especially, which he wrote against the christians, wherein he put many weapons into our hands that might be employ'd against himself and the pagans. As to the poison contain'd in those books, sufficient antidotes were to be had out of many apologetick writings of the ancient christians, and especially out of the books of ORIGEN *against* CELSUS, *and of* CYRIL *against* JULIAN. *Wherefore I should esteem it a publick benefit to have those books in the hands of such men who are willing and able to use them.*

(s) *It were* MUCH TO BE DESIR'D, says the great JOSEPH SCALIGER, *that we had the books which* PORPHYRY *wrote against the christian religion.*

LE CLERC (t) says, that *the thirty books of* EUSEBIUS *against* PORPHYRY, *are the greatest loss that could be in*
re-

(s) *Scaligerana* Art. *Porphyrius.*
(t) *Le Clerc* Bib. Univ. Tom. 10. p. 493.

[xlvii]

respect to the works of EUSEBIUS; *for by them we might have learn'd the objections of the ablest philosopher of his time against the christian religion, and the answer of the most learned bishop of his age.*

The late Bishop (*u*) LOYD says, *Tho' some of our aeists complain of the loss of* PORPHYRY'S *books against the christian religion, yet they may be assur'd for their comfort, they will not want the help of our learned men to bring them to light. We want them indeed on many accounts; but especially, to shew them, that as they have* PORPHYRY'S *malice, so if they had his great learning too, both these joyn'd together would not hurt the christian religion. As for his arguments, it cannot be imagin'd, that there was any thing of strength in them, more than what* JULIAN *the apostate took into the work, that he writ afterwards on that subject.*

(*u*) Loyd's *Chron. Account of* Pythagoras, &c. p. 21.
(*x*) Ib. p. 23.

subject. And to our comfort, as well as the deists, that work is not lost.

The church of Rome, says, (y) Dr. Sherlock, will not suffer her people to dispute their religion, or to read heretical books, nay not so much as to look into the bible itself. But we allow all this to our people, as that which God not only allows, but requires, and which all considering men will allow themselves, whoever forbids it.

Dr. Nichols and other learned divines have writ many elaborate works, in behalf of christianity, by way of *dialogue:* wherein they introduce *deists* and *scepticks*, who must be suppos'd to argue for their several *hypotheses* with the same strength *real deists* and *scepticks* do; for it is not to be imagin'd, that the authors of those dialogues, (who could not but know that the nature of dialogue requires a true representation of characters,

---

(y) Sherlock's *Preservative against Popery*, Part 1. p. 3.

racters, and that justice is due to all men) should be so illiterate and unfair, as to make their *Dialogist-Deists* and *Scepticks* talk booty, and in concert with the *Orthodox Dialogist*, in order to establish the author's own opinions.

In fine, the reverend Dr. JENKIN should seem to be of the same sentiment with the great men before-mention'd, when he says, (*z*) that *all the arguments brought against christianity are so weak and insignificant, that they rather make for it.* For I cannot suppose him willing to have christianity depriv'd of any *arguments* that *make for it*, and especially of *arguments brought* by the adversaries of *christianity against it*, that *make for it*.

15. The greatest enemies to liberty of debate in matters of religion do allow certain religious questions to be publickly debated: and pursuant

---

(*z*) Jenkin's *Pref. to Reas: of Christ. Rel.* Vol. 1. p. 36.

suant thereto, there are ever some religious debates on foot, even in those countries, where agreement in doctrine and uniformity in worship are the chief objects of the care of the magistrate, the church, and the inquisition, and of the zeal of the beggars; which four, when united in a common polity, make the strongest band imaginable against the just liberties of mankind. On the other side the greatest contenders for liberty of debate in matters of religion do contend for some restraints upon that liberty, and think, that there are certain propositions, which ought not to be call'd in question, as being necessary to be profess'd for the support of peace and order in society, or at least not deny'd.

Both parties must therefore allow, that there is a *just medium* between restraint and liberty.

This *medium*, from the great importance of the matters constantly depending on it to society, should seem
not

not very difficult to fix and determine in most cases. And it seems to me so plainly to discover itself, that almost any man, if plac'd in proper circumstances, would judge rightly and truely how far or in what particulars, men should have liberty in religion, and consequently wherein they should be restrain'd.

Let, for example, a member of the church of *England* (whom I will suppose perswaded, that he himself is oblig'd in conscience publickly to profess the doctrine of the church of *England*) go successively into countries of *Presbyterians*, *Papists*, *Mahometans*, and *Heathens*: and by finding out the reasonable liberty which he wants himself, he can hardly fail of finding out the reasonable liberty of men.

He cannot but think: that he ought to be allow'd publickly to profess his religion among the *Presbyterians*; tho' they may esteem him *superstitious*, or *fanatical*, or *factious*, for making a separation from their *establish'd*

blish'd church about ceremonies and matters of discipline: that he ought to be allow'd to profess his religion publickly among the *Papists*; tho' they may esteem him an *heretick* and *scismatick*, and a destroyer of all order and uniformity, for pretending to make the scriptures, interpreted by his own judgment, his rule of faith, and for denying the autority of the church: that he ought to be allow'd to profess his religion publickly among the *Mahometans*; tho' they may deem him impious, for denying the divine inspiration of the *Alcoran* and the autority of MAHOMET, and an *idolater* for worshiping the Son and the Holy Ghost, each as supreme God, as well as the Father: and that he ought to be allow'd to profess his religion publickly among the *Heathens*; tho' they may call him *atheist*, as the heathens did the primitive christians, either for asserting the *Unity of a deity*, with whom they were unacquainted, or for denying the existence

stence of their *plurality of gods*. Moreover, it cannot be doubted, but that he will be ready to own to these several parties, from whom he expects liberty, that he ought to allow the like liberty, in the like circumstances, for the like matters.

Here then is *the liberty*, contended for, settled from an obvious and common case, and from the fundamental principle of morality, of *doing as men would be done unto*.

It is not to be suppos'd, that men should in many cases make perfect laws much less in this matter of *liberty*, which the *powerful sects* commonly think they have a right to destroy in the *less powerful*: yet *our Statesmen* seem to have understood the matter in great perfection, and to have establish'd a most excellent *constitution* in *Carolina*, one of our plantations. There, driven by the nature of things, they acted according to the rules of equity and good sense, and have rivall'd the *Dutch*, and even the *Chinese*, in their political (*a*) *Constitutions*.

16. Opinions, how erroneous soever, when the effect of an impartial examination, will never hurt men in the sight of God, but will recommend men to his favour. For impartial examination in the matter of opinions is the best, that a man can do towards obtaining truth: and God, who is a wise, good, and just being, can require no more of men than to do their best, and will reward them, when they do their best; and he would be the most unjust being imaginable, if he punish'd men who had done their best endeavour to please him. Besides, if men were to be punish'd by God for mistaken opinions, all men must be damn'd; for all men abound in mistaken opinions.

On the other Side, opinions, how true soever, when the effect of education, or tradition, or interest, or passion,

---

(*a*) See *Fundamental Constitutions* of Carolina, *in a* Collection *of Pieces of Mr.* Locke.

passion, or any thing else besides impartial examination, can never recommend a man to God. For those ways have no merit in them, and are the worst a man can take to obtain truth; and therefore may be objects of forgiveness, but never of reward, from God.

Let not therefore any man deny Mr. WHISTON the liberty of professing and proposing his opinions on account of the dangerousness of error to his soul; who, as far as we can judge, seems, by his conduct, both to do his best endeavours to obtain truth and to recommend himself to God, and to decline the worst methods of obtaining truth, and the most unacceptable to God.

17. If the question of the reasonableness of the *open profession and defence* of what men take to be the *truth*, in opposition to prevailing opinions, was to be determin'd by *autority*, I think Mr. WHISTON may lay claim to the best *autority*, and has only the worst against him.

He has the autority of JESUS CHRIST, who oppos'd the false traditions receiv'd in the Jewish church of his time; of the apostles, who travell'd throughout the world, preaching down the receiv'd notions both of Jews and Gentiles; of the fathers of the church before the empire became christian, who in their famous *apologies* written to emperors and senates, and in their other writings in behalf of christianity, have with the utmost freedom attack'd all that the heathens esteem'd sacred; of the noble army of martyrs in all ages, of the several christian countries, that send missionaries abroad to convert Heathens, Jews, Hereticks, and Mahometans, and of those countries, that hospitably receive the said missionaries; of all countries, that allow toleration; of all true christians and protestants; of our first reformers from popery; of the greatest philosophers and wisest men of all times, who have either openly profess'd fefs'd their fentiments, or elfe have by their moderation and temper, or by their oppofing perfecution, or by their arts of concealment, fufficiently fhown, what *liberty* they would have been glad to have taken themfelves, and would have allow'd to others; of all men, who judge for themfelves; and in fine, of all bigots, impofers, perfecutors, and enemies of liberty themfelves; for, as TILLOTSO^N (*b*) fays, *there is one feafon and nick of time, wherein they will allow any of the people to examine and inquire into matters of religion, and that is when they would gain a man to their religion*

And who have been or are the men, that make up the *autority* on the other fide? The *interefted*, the *politicians*, the *hypocrites*, the *bigots*, the *enthufiafts*, and the *ignorant*; who, all wanting reafon to fupport their opinions, either make *decifions* themfelves, or are govern'd by the decifions of others.

(*b*) Tillotfon's *Serm. Vol.* 13. *p.* 333.

18. I will conclude this *apology* for Mr. WHISTON with the passage of a great prelate of our church.

"Autority is the greatest and most irreconcileable enemy to *truth*, and *argument*, that *this world* ever furnish'd out, since it was in being. All the *sophistry*, all the color of *plausibility*, all the *artifice* and *cunning* of the subtilest *disputer* in the world, may be laid open, and turn'd to the advantage of truth, which they are design'd to hide, or to depress. But against *autority* there is no defense. It is *autority* alone which keeps up the *grossest errors* in the countries around us. And where *truth* happens to be receiv'd for the sake of *autority*, there is just so much diminish'd from the love of truth, and the glory of reason, and the acceptableness of men to God, as there is attributed to *autority*.

"It

" It was *autority*, which crush'd
" the *noble sentiments* of SOCRATES,
" and *others*, in the heathen world;
" and prevented the reception of
" them among men. It was *autority*
" which hinder'd the voice of the
" *son* of *God* himself from being
" heard; and which alone stood in
" opposition to *his* powerful *argu-*
" *ments*, and his divine *doctrine*;
" whilst it was a more moving que-
" stion, among the people, to ask,
" *Do any of the Pharisees, or Doctors*
" *of the Mosaick Law believe in him?*
" than to ask, *whether ever man spake*
" *or liv'd, or work'd wonders like him*;
" and whilst *excommunication*, or be-
" ing put out of the *synagogue*, was
" the *mark* set upon those who
" should embrace his religion. It
" was *autority* among *heathens*,
" which afterwards put all the stop
" to CHRIST's profession, which *this*
" *world* could put. And when
" *christians* were increas'd into a *ma-*
" *jority*; and came to think the same
                               " method

"method to be the only proper one,
"for the advantage of *their* cause,
"which had been the enemy and
"destroyer of it: *then*, it was the
"*autority* of *christians*, which, by
"degrees, not only laid waste the
"honor of *christianity*, but well
"nigh extinguish'd it from amongst
"men. It was *autority*, which
"brought in all that merciless heap
"of useless and burthensome foppe-
"ries; prayers in an unknown
"tongue; prayers to multitudes of
"beings; and the whole load of
"*absurdities* and depravations of the
"religion, under which the christi-
"an people were in captivity, till
"they became gross and weighty
"enough at last, to break the props
"that supported them. It was *auto-*
"*rity*, which would have prevented
"all *reformation*, where it is; and
"which has put a barrier against it,
"where-ever it is not. It was *hu-*
"*man autority* in *religion*, which a-
"lone set up itself against the begin-
"nings

" nings of this *Church* of *England*
" itself: and which alone now con-
" tests with it the *foundation* upon
" which it stands. This *autority*
" was at first exercis'd in *little* by
" *those*, who were so far from pre-
" tending to such *enormities*, as it
" afterwards arriv'd at, that they
" would have detested and abhorr'd
" the thought of them. And so it
" will be, for ever, and every where.
" The calling in the Assistance of
" *mere autority*, even against *errors*,
" or trifles in religious matters, at
" first, will by insensible degrees come
" to the very same issue, that it has
" been ever hitherto seen to end in.
" And how, indeed, can it be ex-
" pected, that the *same thing*, which
" has in all ages, and in all coun-
" tries, been hurtful to *truth* and
" *true religion*, among men, should
" in any age, or in any country, be-
" come a friend and guardian of
" them; unless it can be shewn that
" the *nature* of *mere autority*, or the

" *na-*

" *nature* of *man*, or *both*, are intire-
" ly alter'd from what they have
" hitherto been. For it is not in
" *religion*, as it is in the *civil con-
" cerns* of *human life*. The *end* of
" *human society* is anſwer'd by *out-
" ward behaviour*, and *actions*; which
" therefore, ought to be reſtrain'd
" and govern'd by *civil autority*. But
" the *end* of *religion*, and of the *chri-
" ſtian religion*, in particular, is *de-
" ſtroy'd*, juſt in proportion to the
" *influence* of *great names*; and to
" the effect of *worldly motives*, and
" *mere autority* of men, ſeparated
" from the *arguments* of *reaſon*, and
" the *motives* and *maxims* of the
" *goſpel* itſelf."

THE

THE CONTENTS.

	Page
Introduction	1

PART I.

Of the Grounds and Reasons of Christianity.

I. *That Christianity is founded on Judaism, or the New Testament on the Old* — 4

II. *That the Apostles ground and prove Christianity from the Old Testament* — 5

III. *That the Old Testament is the Canon of Christians* — 13

IV. *That it is a common and necessary method for new Revelations to be built and grounded on precedent Revelations* — 20

V. *That the chief Proofs of Christianity from the Old Testament are urg'd by the Apostles in the New Testament* — 26

VI. *That*

The CONTENTS.

VI. *That if those Proofs are valid, Christianity is invincibly establish'd on its true foundation* id.

VII. *That if those Proofs are invalid, then is Christianity false* 31

VIII. *That those Proofs are Typical or Allegorical Proofs* 39

IX. *The nature of Typical or Allegorical Proofs, and Reasoning.* 50

X. *The nature of Allegorical Reasoning further shewn by application of it to several particular instances cited from the Old and urg'd in the New Testament* 61

XI. *An Answer to an Objection, that,* the Allegorical Reasonings of the Apostles were not design'd for absolute proofs of Christianity, but for proofs AD HOMINEM, to the Jews, who were accustomed to that way of reasoning 79

The CONTENTS.

PART II.

Containing Considerations on the scheme which Mr. Whiston sets up in opposition to the allegorical scheme.

I. *Mr.* WHISTON's *scheme represented; which consists chiefly in maintaining; that the Hebrew and Greek of the Old Testament agreed in the times of* JESUS *and the apostles; that the apostles cited exactly and argu'd literally from the Greek or Septuagint translation; and that since their times both these copies of the Old Testament have been corrupted by the Jews, which makes it seem as if the apostles had not argu'd literally from the Old Testament; and in proposing, by various means, to restore the text thereof as it stood in the days of* JESUS *and his apostles* 97

II. *That it is incredible, that the Old Testament should be so corrupted as Mr.* WHISTON *asserts* 103

III. *That to suppose the Old Testament so corrupted as Mr.* WHISTON *asserts, is to give up christianity to Jews and Infidels* 111

IV. *That*

The CONTENTS.

IV. *That Mr.* Whiston *is not able to restore one prophetical quotation made out of the Old in the New Testament, so as to make that literally apply'd which now seems allegorically apply'd* 120

V. *That the Jews have not corrupted the Old Testament in respect to the passages cited from thence in the New* 131

VI. *That the Septuagint version was not in the days of* Jesus *and the apostles, agreeable to the hebrew text* 162

VII. *That the* Samaritan Pentateuch *is not an uncorrupt copy of the books of* Moses, *and originally deriv'd from the first separation of the ten tribes themselves in the days of* Jeroboam 184

VIII. *That the apostles did not always quote the Septuagint version* 209

IX. *That the means, whereby Mr. W. proposes to restore the true text of the Old Testament in respect to the citations made from thence in the New, will not reach that end* 215

The CONTENTS.

X. *Typical or allegorical reasoning defended against Mr. Whiston; wherein is a digression that compares together the allegorical scheme and Mr. Whiston's literal scheme, and that proves his literal scheme false and absurd*   227

XI. *That Mr.* WHISTON's *first proposition is subverted by his book*   270

The CONCLUSION.

Containing an account of Mr. WHISTON *himself*   273

A great mathematician, philosopher, and divine   id.

A most acute person   id.

A good christian   274

The reverse of most other divines   276

A zealous member of the church of England   277

Deficient in judgment   278

The CONTENTS.

Has taken all proper methods in his power to promote what he thinks to be the truth — 279

His conversation and its effects — 281

His projects — 282

His temper — 284

His service to the church of Scotland — 284

THE
GROUNDS and REASONS
OF THE
Christian Religion, &c.
IN A
LETTER to a Divine of *North Britain*.

Reverend SIR,

OU seem extreamly surpriz'd upon having occasionally heard of Mr. WHISTON's *Essay towards restoring the true text of the Old Testament*; which title, according to you, implies a most *anti-christian paradox*, who have *always* believ'd, with the greatest part of protestants, that *the text of the Old, as well as New Testament, has been the peculiar care of providence, and constantly preserv'd pure and uncorrupted.* And I am no less surpriz'd, that you should desire some account of that book; who very lately would have thought such curiosity to be an evil inclination and temptation of the devil; who never enquir'd after any books

written by our episcopal divines, but those of Dr. JOHN EDWARDS of *Cambridge*; and who us'd to detest *anti-trinitarian* more than *popish authors*, as introducing not only equally dangerous errors in doctrine, but the use of *reason* and *private judgment*, which utterly subvert all *church autority*, the sole foundation of *unity* and *uniformity* in matters of religion.

But, it seems, *curiosity*, the effect of liberty, sense, and learning, begins to reach even the divines of *Scotland*; who of all protestant divines, are most tenacious of their *orthodoxy*; and who are no less charm'd with the *pure* doctrine and *holy* discipline receiv'd from their ancestors of the reformation, than we are with *the beauty of holiness* in our *Common-Prayer-Book*, which was first compos'd one hundred and seventy four years ago by the (*a*) *aid of the Holy Ghost*, and has, since that time, been (*b*) *five* times reform'd! and consequently, *theology* (than which nothing is more naturally changeable, and which neither art nor power, nor discipline, could ever long fix or ascertain among Heathens, Jews, Christians, or Mahometans) may soon receive a new form

in

(*a*) Act *for establishing the Liturgy in the 2d of* Edward the Sixth. 1548.
(*b*) Nichols's *Preface to Commentary on the Common-Prayer.*

in the *kirk*, as it daily does in all other churches.

You defire alfo fome account of Mr. WHISTON himfelf, and would know what fort of a man, or monfter, he is, of whom you hear fo much, when you meet your brethren in *presbyteries* and *fynods*; who, upon mere reports, reprefent him under the various characters, of ignorant and learned, rich and poor, ferious and mad, heretick and atheift, churchman and papift, arian and focinian, and almoft every thing but *calvinift*, *presbyterian* and *athanafian*.

To gratify, therefore, your curiofity in the beft manner I am able, I fend you Mr. WHISTON's book itfelf; together with *fome Confiderations* on the fubject-matter of it, and fome *remarks* on his *fcheme*, *project*, or *theory*; which I clofe with an account of the gentleman himfelf.

PART

Part I.

Of the Grounds and Reasons of Christianity.

I.

That *Christianity is founded on Judaism, or the New Testament on the Old.*

CHRISTIANITY is founded on Judaism, and the New Testament on the Old; and Jesus is the person said in the New Testament to be promis'd in the Old, under the character of the Messias of the Jews, who, as such only, claims the obedience and submission of the world. Accordingly, it is the design of the authors of the *New*, to prove all the parts of christianity from the Old Testament, which is said to contain (c) *the words of eternal life*; and to represent Jesus and his apostles, as (d) *fulfilling*, by their mission, doctrines, and works, the pre-

---

(c) John 5. 39.
(d) Matt. 5. 17.

predictions of the *prophets*, the historical parts of the Old Testament, and the *Jewish law*; which last is expresly said to (*e*) *prophecy* of, or tipify, christianity.

II.

That the Apostles ground and prove christianity from the Old Testament.

ST. MATTHEW proves several parts of christianity from the Old Testament; either by shewing them to be things foretold therein as to come to pass under the gospel-dispensation, or to be agreeable to, or founded on, the notions of the Old Testament.

Thus he proves (*f*) MARY's being *with child by the Holy Ghost*, and the *angel's* telling her she *shall bring forth a son, and shall call his name* JESUS, and the other circumstances attending his miraculous birth; JESUS's (*g*) birth at *Bethlehem*; his (*h*) flight into *Egypt*; the (*i*) slaughter of the infants; (*k*) JESUS's dwelling at *Nazareth*; the (*l*) preaching of JOHN *the Baptist*; JESUS's (*m*) leaving *Nazareth* and dwelling at *Capernaum*, in the borders of *Zabulon* and *Napthali*; his (*n*) *casting* out *devils*, and

healing

(*e*) Matt. 11. 13. (*f*) Ib. 1. 18, 23. (*g*) Ib. 2. 5, 6. (*h*) v. 15. (*i*) v. 17, 18. (*k*) v. 23. (*l*) Ib. 3. (*m*) Ib. 4. 13. (*n*) Ib. 8. 16, 17.

healing the *sick*; his (*o*) *eating with publicans and sinners*; his (*p*) *charging* those he heal'd, *that they should not make him known*; his (*q*) *speaking in parables*, that the Jews might not *understand* him; his (*r*) sending his disciples to fetch an *ass and a colt*; the (*s*) *childrens crying in the temple*; the (*t*) lawfulness of taking *corn* in the fields, when *an hungred*, on *the sabbath-day*; the (*u*) *resurrection of the dead*; (*w*) JESUS's being betray'd by JUDAS, and his apprehension; and (*x*) JUDAS's returning back the *thirty pieces*, (the reward he had for betraying JESUS) and the priest's *buying the potter's field* with them, and his *hanging* himself.

JESUS himself is represented as proving the truth of christianity thus: he, (*y*) joining himself, after his resurrection, to *two of his disciples*, who *knew him not*; and finding out their mistakes about his person, whom they *now* took not to be the MESSIAS, because he had been *condemn'd to death*, and *crucify'd*; and observing their disbelief of his resurrection, which had been reported to them by *certain women* of their acquaintance, upon the credit of *angels*; (*z*) *said unto*

(*o*) Matt. 9. 11—13.   (*p*) Ib. 12. 16—21.
(*q*) Ib. 13. 13.   (*r*) Ib. 21. 2—7.   (*s*) v. 15, 16.
(*t*) Ib. c. 12.   (*u*) Ib. 22. 31, 32.   (*w*) Ib. 26.
54, 56.   (*x*) Ib. 27. 5—10.   (*y*) Luke 24.
15—22.   (*z*) v. 25—27.

[7]

unto them, O fools, and flow of of heart, to believe all that the prophets have spoken! Ought not CHRIST *to have suffer'd these things, and to enter into his glory? And beginning at* MOSES, *and all the prophets, he expounded unto them, in all the Scriptures, the things concerning himself.*

FABRICIUS *says,* Hic (*a*) sermo ejus a multis non immerito anxie desideratus, & a LUCA fortasse auditus, nusquam extat.

But our learned (*aa*) *Mede* has endeavour'd to supply this loss, by *pointing out those very scriptures which our Saviour expounded to his disciples.*

Again, he discours'd to all his disciples, putting them in mind, that before his death, he told them, that (*b*) *all things must be fulfill'd, which were written in the law of* MOSES, *and in the prophets, and in the psalms concerning him*; adding, *thus it is written, and thus it behoveth* CHRIST *to suffer, and to rise from the dead the third day; and that repentance and remission of sins should be preach'd in his name among all nations, beginning at* Jerusalem.

When the people of several nations were (*c*) *amaz'd* at the apostles speaking in their several tongues; and when many *mock'd*

the

(*a*) *Fabricii* Codex Apocryphus, Nov. Test. *p.* 322.
(*aa*) *Mede*'s 13th Disc.
(*b*) *Luke* 24. 44, 46, 47.   (*c*) *Acts* 2. 12.--16.

the apostles, saying, they were *full of new wine*; St. PETER makes a speech in publick, wherein, after saying, *they were not drunken, because it was but the third hour of the day*, he endeavours to shew them, that *this was spoken of by the prophet* JOEL; and he concludes, with proving the *resurrection* of JESUS from the *psalms*.

St. PETER and St. JOHN tell the people assembled at the temple, that (*d*) *God had shew'd by the mouth of all his prophets, that* CHRIST *should suffer*; and also that JESUS *should come again*.

St. PETER, to justify his preaching to the Gentiles, concludes his discourse with saying, (*e*) *To* JESUS *give all the prophets witness, that through his name, whosoever* (that is, Jew or Gentile) *believeth in him shall receive remission of sins*.

St. PAUL also endeavours to prove to the Jews, in the synagogue of *Antioch*, (*f*) that the history of JESUS was contain'd in the Old Testament, and that he and BARNABAS were *commanded*, in the Old Testament, to preach the *gospel to the Gentiles*.

On occasion of a (*g*) dispute among the christians, whether the Gentile converts were to be *circumcis'd after the law of* MOSES, and to observe the other parts of the Jewish law;

(*d*) Acts 3. 18, 20—24. (*e*) Ib. 10. 43.
(*f*) Ib. 13. (*g*) Ib. 15.

law; a council of *apostles* and *elders* was held at *Jerusalem*, wherein, after *much disputing*, and speeches made by PETER, BARNABAS, and PAUL, JAMES concludes the point from the Old Testament (citing AMOS and MOSES;) from whence, in all probability, all their arguments were taken; the things in debate being such as had long before been matters of controversy among the Jews in relation to their *proselytes of the gate*; some Jews being so narrow as to think circumcision and a strict observance of all the laws of MOSES necessary in all who pretended to be *proselytes* to them; and others requiring a conformity from *proselytes* in such matters only as should keep them at a distance from all idolatrous practices. And JAMES, suitably to the latter more gentle determination and common practice of the Jews in relation to their *proselytes of the gate*, infers, that the Gentile-converts to christianity, were to be bound by no other laws of MOSES, but those which requir'd the *abstinence from pollutions of idols, and from fornication, and from things strangled, and from blood*; the practice of those things having too great a connection with heathen idolatry, and rendering men too impure for society with *christians*, who were now the real and true Jews. Upon which the assembly came to a determination to that effect, and or-

der'd

der'd *letters* to be written to notify the same to all concern'd.

The *Bereans* are highly extoll'd for (*h*) *searching the scriptures*, that is, the Old Testament, *daily*, in order to find out, whether *the things* preach'd to them by the apostles *were so* or no; who, if they had not prov'd those *things*, that is, christianity from the Old Testament, ought to have been rejected by the *Bereans*, as teachers of false doctrine.

St. PAUL, when accus'd before AGRIPPA by the Jews, said, (*i*) *I stand and am judg'd for the hope of the promise made of God unto our fathers*, that is, for teaching christianity or the true doctrine of the Old Testament: and to this accusation he pleads guilty, by declaring in the fullest manner, that he taught nothing but the doctrine of the Old Testament. (*k*) *Having, therefore,* says he, *obtain'd help of God, I continue unto this day, witnessing both to small and great, saying none other things than those which the prophets and* MOSES *did say should come: that* CHRIST *should suffer, and that he should be the first who should rise from the dead, and should shew light unto the people and to the Gentiles.*

St. PAUL says, (*l*) JESUS *rose again the third day, according to the scriptures*, that is, according

---

(*b*) Acts. 17. 11. (*i*) Ib. 26. 6. *See* Ib. 25. 19, &c. *and* 23. 29. (*k*) Ib. 26. 22, 23. (*l*) 1 Cor. 15. 4.

according to the Old Testament: and he is suppos'd to ground this on the history of the prophet JONAS, who was three days in a whale's belly, and then came out.

But most divine is St. PAUL's argument in his *Epistle* to the *Galatians*, to prove christianity to the Jews from the Old Testament. (*m*) *Tell me, says he, ye that desire to be under the* LAW, *do not ye hear the law? For it is written, that* ABRAHAM *had two sons; the one by a bond-maid, the other by a free-woman. But he who was of the bond-woman was born after the flesh; but he who was of the free-woman was by promise. Which things are an* ALLEGORY; *for these are the two covenants; the one from the mount* Sinai, *which gendereth to bondage, which is* Agar. *But this* Agar *is mount* Sinai, *in* Arabia, *and answereth to* Jerusalem *that now is, and is in bondage with her children. But* Jerusalem, *which is above, is free, which is the mother of us all. For it is written,* (*n*) *rejoyce thou barren that bearest not; break forth and cry, thou that travailest not; for the desolate hath many more children than she which hath an husband. Now we, brethren, as* ISAAC *was, are the children of the promise. But as then he that was born after the flesh persecuted him that was born*

(*m*) Gal. 4. 21—   (*n*) Isa. 54. 1.

born after the spirit, even so it is now. Nevertheless, what says the scripture? (o) *Cast out the bond-woman and her son, for the son of the bond-woman shall not be heir with the son of the free-woman. So then, brethren, we are not children of the bond-woman, but of the free. Stand fast, therefore, in the liberty, wherewith* CHRIST *hath made us free, and be not intangled again with the yoke of bondage.*

In fine, St. PAUL, throughout his *Epistles*, reasons in the same divine manner from the Old Testament, which, according to him, (p) *was able to make men wise unto salvation*; asserting himself, and others, to be (q) *ministers of the New Testament*, as being *ministers not of the letter, but of the spirit*, of the law, that is, of the Old Testament spiritually understood; and endeavouring to prove, especially in his (r) *Epistle to the Hebrews*, that christianity was contain'd in the Old Testament, and was imply'd in the Jewish *history* and *law*, both which he makes *types* and *shadows* of christianity.

The grand and fundamental article of christianity was; that JESUS of Nazareth *was the* MESSIAS *of the Jews, predicted in the Old Testament.* And how could that
appear,

(o) Gen. 21. 10, 12. (p) 2 Tim. 3. 15.
(q) 2 Cor. 3. 6, 14. (r) Heb. 8. 5. & 10. 1. *See also* Col. 2. 16, 17.

appear, and be prov'd, but from the Old Teſtament?

In a word, the books of the Old Teſtament were the ſole *canonical ſcriptures*, and the ſole *ſcriptures* during the life of JESUS, and for near thirty years after his death, (tho' chriſtianity had by that time made a (*s*) mighty progreſs:) and from them did the moſt primitive fathers, BARNABAS, POLICARP, CLEMENS ROMANUS, IGNATIUS, and JUSTIN MARTYR, as well as the apoſtles and authors of the books of the New Teſtament, declare and endeavour to prove chriſtianity to the world: with all whom the church of *England* concurs in ſentiment, when ſhe ſays, that (*ss*) *in the Old Teſtament everlaſting life is offer'd to mankind by* CHRIST.

III.

That the Old Teſtament is the Canon of Chriſtians.

INdeed, to ſpeak properly, the Old Teſtament is yet the *ſole true canon of ſcripture* (meaning thereby a *canon* eſtabliſh'd by thoſe who had a *divine* autority to eſtabliſh a *canon*, and in virtue thereof did eſtabliſh

---

(*s*) Maſſueti Annot. in Iræneum, *p.* 43, &c.
(*n*) *Article the* 7*th.*

blish a *canon*) as it was in the beginning of christianity. For the books of the New Testament are all *occasional* books, as Mr. Whiston (*t*) has clearly shown, and not a *digest or system of laws for the* (*u*) *governing the church*; and I add, were not join'd together in one body or collection, nor declar'd by any *human* autority to be all *canonical*, till the seventh century, when the controversy about the last book of canonical scriptures, so call'd, (*w*) *seems to have been brought to an end*, as says the reverend Mr. John Richardson, our most learned defender of the *canon of the New Testament*. They are christian books, and contain proofs of christianity from the Old Testament; but contain christianity itself, no otherwise, than as explaining, illustrating, and confirming the christianity taught in the Old Testament. They all seem, what (*x*) Grotius expresly says of the books of Luke, *piously and faithfully written, and upon subjects of great concern to salvation, and therefore made* Canonical *by the church*. Which was plainly an accidental event, and did

---

(*t*) Whiston's *Essay on the Apostol. Constitutions*, p. 159. —164.

(*u*) See Hare's *Sermon of Church Autority*, p. 44.

(*w*) Richardson's *Canon of the New Testament vindicated against* Toland, p. 17.

(*x*) *Grotii*—Votum pro Pace, &c. Oper. Theologic. Tom. 3. p. 672, 673.

did befal thofe books (*y*) gradually, and after long difputes about their autority, and might have befel other pious books, which tho' deem'd fcripture, and declar'd (*z*) *canonical* by the ancients, have been fince rejected, as fpurious and apocryphal.

It is alfo to be obferv'd, that our Saviour, who affures us, that he came to (*a*) *fulfil the law and the prophets*, and not to *deftroy* the religion of the Jews, (many of whom were, long before the coming of CHRIST, deem'd (*b*) real *Chriftians*, and equally to believe the *gofpel* or chriftianity, with thofe who were converted by the apoftles) left nothing in writing to eftablifh his *new law*, if it may be fo call'd, which was not properly a *new law*, but Judaifm (*c*) explain'd, and fet in a due light. In a word, Jews and Chriftians had one and the fame *canon of fcripture* ; nor would there have been any difference between them, or any feparation of the latter from the former, with whom

---

(*y*) Nye's *Defence of the Canon of the New Teftam.* p. 122.
Floyer's *Pref. to the Propheties of* Efdras, p. 3.
(*z*) *Laft Apoftolick Canon.*
(*a*) Matt. 5. 17. *Simon*, Supplement aux Ceremonies des Juifs, *p.* 28, 29.
(*b*) Gal. 3. 8. Heb. 11. *See* Barlow's *Remains*, p. 577---593.
(*c*) *See* Selden de Synedriis, l. 1. c. 8. p. 225.

whom they continu'd many years in communion after the death of JESUS, if the Jews had understood the spiritual sense of their own books, as declar'd and explain'd to them by the apostles, who (*d*) *said none other things* to any, *than those which the prophets and* MOSES *did say*.

In fine, JESUS and his apostles do frequently and emphatically style the books of the Old Testament the *Scriptures*, and refer men to them as their *rule* and *canon:* And St PAUL says, (*e*) *After the* [Christian] *way, which ye call heresy, so worship I the God of my fathers, believing all things that are written in the law and the prophets.* But no new books are declar'd by them to have that character: Nor was there (*f*) *any new canon of scripture, or any collection of books of scripture made, whether of gospels or epistles, during the lives of the apostles;* as is confess'd by the knowing in antiquity, and particularly by our learned GRABE and MILL, who, latest of all authors, have search'd, and that with great diligence, into these matters. And if JESUS and his apostles have declar'd no books to be *canonical*, I would ask, who did, or could

---

(*d*) Acts 26. 22. (*e*) Ib. 24. 14. (*f*) *Grabe* Spicil. *Sec.* 1. p. 320. *Millii* Proleg. ad Nov. Testam. p. 23.

could afterwards declare, or make any books *Canonical?* If it had been deem'd proper, and ſuited to the ſtate of chriſtianity, to have given or declar'd a *new canon* or *digeſt of laws*, it ſhould ſeem moſt proper to have been done by JESUS, or his apoſtles, and not left to any after them to do; but eſpecially not left to be ſettled long after their times, by weak, fallible, factious, and intereſted men, who were diſputing with one another about the genuinneſs of all books bearing the names of the Apoſtles; and contending with one another about the autority of very different books.

I have given theſe ſhort hints concerning the *true canon of Scripture* of chriſtians, not only as they relate to my argument, but as *conſiderations*, which put an end to all the controverſies of chriſtians about the *canon of Scripture*, and which may alſo ſerve to ſet Mr. WHISTON right; who (*g*) adds, to the preſent books of the New Teſtament, the two *epiſtles of* CLEMENT *to the Corinthians*; (both which, after having been wholly loſt for ſeveral hundred years, were but lately recover'd, and that but imperfectly, eſpecially the ſecond); the *doctrine of the apoſtles* (a book loſt, which Mr. *W.* (*h*) imagin'd

---

(*g*) Whiſton's *Eſſay on the Apoſtol. Conſtit.* P. 33, 74, 67, 68, 71.

(*h*) Ib. Advertiſement *before* Primitive Chriſtianity.

gin'd he had found); the *epistle* of BARNABAS; the *pastor* of HERMAS; the (*i*) *second book of apocryphal* ESDRAS; the *epistle of* POLYCARP; and the *larger epistles* of IGNATIUS; and who seeing plainly, that the books of the New Testament are *no system of laws for the governing the church*, nor design'd for that purpose; and being perswaded, that christians ought to have such a *system*, sets up that manifestly forg'd modern book of the *apostolick constitutions*, as containing that system, tho' (*k*) doubtful as to the antiquity of some of its parts, *interpolated* in others, and *first published in the middle of the fourth century*. Which book has, indeed, the *form* of a *law*, and pretends it self to be the work of *all the apostles assembled* together at *Jerusalem*; tho' (*l*) *inconsistent* in many instances with the books of the New Testament, and that by the confession of Mr. WHISTON (*m*) himself, who says that such inconsistency is *a plain character, peculiar to the original and genuine records of christianity, and at least equally*

(*i*) *See* Floyer's *Preface to Prophesies of* Esdras, p. 3.

(*k*) Whiston's *Essay on Apost. Const.* p. 233 —— 236. 122, 673, &c. 150.

(*l*) Smalbroke's *Pretended Authority of the Apostol. Constitut. confuted.*

(*m*) Whiston's *St.* Clement, *and St.* Irenæus's *Vind. of the Apost. Const.* p. 5. *See also Proceedings in Convoc.* p. 103.

equally true of the four gospels, and the rest of our present canonical books, compar'd with one another; and that the *constitutions* are *the most authentick and exact* of the two, *and that the present copies of the Gospels are rather to be corrected by them than the contrary.*

I will finish this article with observing, that tho' Mr. WHISTON calls the books of the New Testament *scriptures,* and *canonical scriptures,* according to the common language of christians: yet it is apparent, that he cannot think them *divinely inspired* books, or of that autority which other christians do. For he not only thinks them to have been (*n*) alter'd and chang'd, and to be contradictory to one another; but that the authors themselves may be (*o*) mistaken: and he corrects a *disorder* of LUKE's making; wherein he acts like the famous JURIEU, who (*p*) *puts in order,* as he says, *those things which the Holy Ghost had plac'd in disorder.* Nor does Mr. WHIS-

TON

(*n*) Whiston's *Proceedings in Conv.* p. 87, 99. Id. *Pref. to Letter to* Earl of Nott. p. 35, 36. Id. *Chron. and Harmony,* p. 100. Id. *St.* Clement *and St.* Irenæus's *Vind.* &c. p. 5. Id. *Proceed. in Conv.* p. 103. Id. *Essay towards Restor.* &c. p. 119. and *Essay on Revelations,* p. 129, 135.

(*o*) Id. *Chron. and Harm.* p. 100.

(*p*) Jurieu Accompl. des Prophet. Vol. 1. p. 111.

TON herein much differ from many other great divines; who seem to pay little deference to the books of the New Testament, the text whereof they are perpetually mending in their sermons, commentaries, and writings, to serve purposes; who pretend (*pp*) *we should have more of the true text by being less tenacious of the printed one*, and in consequence thereof, presume to correct by critical (*q*) *emendations*, several *capital places* in the *sacred writers*; and who, by requiring men's assent to, and urging the belief of, traditional explications of scripture, and of catechisms, creeds, confessions of faith, and such like compositions, which men, under penalties every where, are oblig'd to believe the scripture supports, do virtually set aside the autority of the scripture, and place those compositions in its stead.

IV.

That it is a common and necessary method for new revelations to be built and grounded on precedent revelations.

THIS method of introducing christianity into the world by building and grounding it on the Old Testament, is agreeable

---

(*pp*) Hare's *Clergyman's Thanks to* Phil. Lipsiensis, &c. p. 37.
(*q*) Id. *Scripture Vindicated*, &c. p. 150.

able to the (*r*) common method of introducing *new revelations* (whether real or pretended) or any *changes* in religion, and also to the *nature of things*. For if we consider the various *revelations*, and *changes* in religion, whereof we have any tolerable history, in their beginning, we shall find them for the most part to be grafted on some old stock, or founded on some preceding *revelations*, which they were either to supply, or fulfil, or retrieve from corrupt glosses, innovations, and traditions, with which by time they were incumber'd: and this, which may seem matter of surprize to those, who do not reflect on the changeable state of all things, has happen'd; tho' the old *revelations*, far from intending any change, engraftment, or new dispensation, did for the most part declare they were to last *for ever*, and did forbid all alterations and innovations, they being the *last dispensations* intended.

This *grafting on old stocks*, we see by experience to be the case of all the *sects*, which alike and according to the natural course of things, rise up in the several great and domineering religions of the world. Nor is it less true of the domineering religions themselves; some of which

---

(*r*) Stanhope's *Charron of Wisdom*, l. 2. c. 5. p. 103, &c.

we know to have been originally, but such *sects* themselves.

Thus the mission of Moses to the *Israelites* suppos'd a (*s*) former revelation of God (who from the beginning seems to have been constantly giving a succession of dispensations and revelations) to their ancestors: and (*t*) many of the religious precepts of Moses were borrowed, or had an agreement with the religious rites of the heathens, with whom the *Israelites* had correspondence, and particularly with the religious rites of the *Egyptians*, (who upon that account seem (*u*) confounded with the *Israelites* by some pagans, as both their religious rites were equally, and at the same time (*w*) prohibited by others;) to whose religious rites the *Israelites* seem to have been (*x*) *conformists* during their abode in *Egypt*; not excepting (*y*) Joseph himself, who by his post in the administration of the government, his match with the prince or *priest* of *On*'s daughter, made up by Pharaoh him-

---

(*s*) Exod. 3.
(*t*) Simon. Hist. Crit. du Vieux Test. p. 50. *Spencer* de Legibus, &c. *Stanhope*'s Dissert. in Charron *of Wisdom*, Vol. 2. p. 93, 97. *Marsham* Canon Chronicus, &c. p. 181.
(*u*) *Strabo*, l. 16, & 17.
(*w*) *Taciti* Annales, l. 2. *Sueton.* in Tiber.
(*x*) Jos. 24. 14. Amos 5. 26. Acts 7. 43.
(*y*) Gen. 41. 40, 45. Ib. 42. 15, 32. Ib. 44. 5.

[23]

himself, his manner of *swearing*, his *eating* with the *Egyptians*, his practise of heathen *divination*, and, above all, by his political conduct, seems to have been a most true member of, and convert to, the establish'd church of *Egypt*.

The mission of ZOROASTER to the *Persians*, suppos'd the *religion of the* Magians; which (z) *had been for many ages past, the antient national religion of the* Medes *as well as* Persians.

The mission of MAHOMET suppos'd *christianity*, as that did *judaism*.

And the (a) *Siamese* and (b) *Brachmans*, both pretend, that they have had a *succession of incarnate Deities* among them, who, at due distances of time, have brought new revelations from heaven, each succeeding one depending on the former; and that religion is to be carry'd on in that way for ever.

And if we consider the *nature of things*, we shall find, that it must be (c) difficult,

if

(z) *Prideaux*'s *Connect*. Vol. 1. p. 214. *Pocock*, *Spec. Hist*. Arab. p. 147—149.

(a) *Gervaise*, Hist. de Siam, 3d. pt. c. 1. *Tachard*, Voyage de Siam, Vol. 1. p. 396, &c.

(b) *Delon* Des Dieux Orient, p. 10——30. Philos. Transac. Ann. 1700. p. 734, &c.

(c) *Charron of Wisdom*, l. 2, c. 5.

if not impossible, to introduce among men (who in all civiliz'd countries are bred up in the belief of some reveal'd religion) a reveal'd religion wholly new, or such as has no reference to a preceding one: for that would be to combat all men in too many respects, and not to proceed on a sufficient number of principles necessary to be assented to by those, on whom the first impressions of a new religion are proposed to be made.

Perfect novelty (*d*) is a great and just exception to a religious institution; whereof religious sects of all kinds have been so sensible, that they have ever endeavour'd to give themselves, in some manner or other, the greatest antiquity they well could, and generally the utmost antiquity. Thus St. Luke says, that (*e*) *God spake of the Redeemer by the mouth of all his prophets, which have been since the world began.* St. Paul defends himself and the christian religion from the charge of novelty, when he says, (*f*) *after the way, which ye call heresy, so worship I the God of my fathers, believing all things that are written in the law and the prophets;* declaring hereby, that christianity was so far from being *heresy*, or a new opinion, that it was the
doctrine

(*d*) Defensio S. *Augustini* contra *J. Phereponum.* p. 185, 187.
(*e*) Luke 1. 70.
(*f*) Acts 24. 14.

doctrine of the Old Testament. And christian (*g*) divines date the *antiquity* of christianity from the time of *the fall of* ADAM, asserting; that CHRIST was then *promis'd* in these words, (*h*) *the seed of the woman shall break the serpent's head*, which they say contain (*i*) *the gospel in miniature*; and that, from that time, men have been sav'd by faith in the said *promise* of CHRIST to come, who was (*k*) *the Lamb slain from the foundation of the world*; CHRIST's (*l*) death *looking backward as well as forwards*.

And an eminent divine thinks he can with great probability settle the precise time, when the christian *covenant* began. He says, (*m*) that ADAM was created on the sixth day at nine in the morning; that he *fell* about *noon*, that *being the time of eating*; and that CHRIST was *promis'd about three a-clock in the afternoon*.

So that the truth of christianity depends, as it ought, on antient revelations, which are

---

(*g*) Taylor's *Preservat. against Deism*, p. 213, &c. Whiston's *Sermons and Essays*, p. 59——78. Stillingfleet's *Sermons*, fol. p. 187.
(*h*) Gen. 3. 15.
(*i*) Taylor, Ib. and Beveridge *on the Articles of the Church of* England, p. 138.
(*k*) Heb. 9. 24, 25, 26. Ib. 11. 7, 13.
(*l*) Tillotson's *Sermons*, Vol. 5. p. 66, 67.
(*m*) Lightfoot's *Works*, Vol. 2. p. 1324.

are contain'd in the Old Testament, and more particularly and immediately on the *revelations* made to the *Jews* therein.

V.

That the chief proofs of christianity from the Old Testament, are urged by the apostles in the New Testament.

HOW christianity depends on those *revelations*, or what *proofs* are therein to be met withal in behalf of christianity, are the subjects of almost all the numerous books written by divines and other apologists for christianity; but the chief and principal of those *proofs* may be justly supposed to be urged in the New Testament by the authors thereof; who relate the history of the first preaching of the gospel, and were themselves, either apostles of JESUS, or companions of the apostles.

VI.

That if those proofs are valid, christianity is invincibly establish'd on its true foundation.

THOSE proofs have in some measure been already produc'd by me. And if they are valid proofs, then is christianity strongly and invincibly established on its true founda-

foundations. It is eſtabliſh'd on its true foundations; becauſe JESUS and his *apoſtles* grounded chriſtianity on thoſe *proofs*: and it is ſtrongly and invincibly eſtabliſhed on thoſe foundations; becauſe a *proof* drawn from an *inſpir'd book*, is perfectly concluſive; and *prophecies* deliver'd in an inſpired book, are, when fulfilled, ſuch, as may be juſtly deem'd (*n*) *ſure* and *demonſtrative* proofs; and which (*o*) PETER *prefers* as an argument to the miraculous atteſtation, whereof he himſelf and two other apoſtles were witneſſes, given by God himſelf to the miſſion of JESUS CHRIST. His argument ſeems as follows. " Laying this foundati-
" on, that propheſy proceeds from the
" Holy Ghoſt, it is a ſtronger argument,
" than a miracle, which depends upon ex-
" ternal evidence and teſtimony.

Beſides, according to our (*p*) Saviour, MOSES *and the prophets* are, not only without further miracles, but tho' miracles ſhould be wrought in oppoſition to them, a ſufficient foundation of faith.

In building thus on *propheſy* as a principle; JESUS and his *apoſtles* had the concurrence of all ſects of religion among the *pagans*;

(*n*) *Origen* contr. *Celſ.* p. 34.
(*o*) 2 Pet. 1. 19. *See* Whitby in locum. *Whiſton's* Lect. p. 4.
(*p*) Luke 16. 31. Mat. 24. 23, 24. Mark 13, 21, 22.

gans; who (*q*) universally built their religions on *divination*; and also made a great part of their religion to lie in the practise of that *art*. They learnt that *art* in *schools*, or under discipline, as the *Jews* did (*r*) *prophesying* in the *schools* and *colleges of the prophets*; where the learned DODWELL says, *the candidates for prophesy were taught the rules of divination practis'd by the pagans, who were skill'd therein, and in possession of the art long before them*. Besides, this miraculous gift of prophesy, among the *Jews*, was not occasional, but a common matter of fact, and a standing proof of the divine autority of *judaism*. For, suitably to the words of MOSES, (*s*) *a prophet will the Lord God raise up unto thee like unto me; to him shall ye hearken*; (which imply an (*t*) establishment of an order and succession of prophets in analogy to the heathen diviners) there were great (*u*) numbers of prophets among them; who not only in the most important affairs of government, but in the discovery of (*w*) *lost goods*,

---

(*q*) *Cicero* de Divinatione.

(*r*) Bull's *Sermons*, p. 419. Wheatley's *Schools of the Prophets*. Dodwel's *Letter of Advices*, &c. p. 214, &c.

(*s*) Deut. 18. 15, 18.

(*t*) Dodwel, *Ib*. Stillingfleet's Orig. Sacræ, l. 2. c. 4. n. 1.

(*u*) Ib. n. 2. *Burnet*, Archæol. p. 43, 44.

(*w*) 1 Sam. 9. 6, 20. 1 Kings 14. 2, 3. 2 Kings 8, 10. 1 Sam. 9. 7, 8.

goods, and in *telling fortunes*, shew'd their divine inspiration; and who were paid for it by those who consulted them, either in *victuals* or *money*, or *presents*. Whereby the meanest person in *Judea* had the opportunity of having this miracle wrought for him, whenever he had occasion; which therefore we may easily judge must have been a common indisputed matter of fact; for the frequent wants of the people must have made them often attend the *prophets*, as the livelihood the *prophets* got by it must have caused them to have made constant use of their divine faculty.

It may also be justly supposed, that the divine power of *interpreting dreams*, (which was a prophetick science pretended to in all nations) prevalent among the *Jews*, gave daily occasion to numbers of people to have their *dreams interpreted*, which were usually thought to signify some good or evil that was to befal them, and were commonly interpreted in relation to things to come.

Lastly, *Prophesies fulfilled*, seem the most proper of all arguments, to evince the truth of a revelation, which is designed to be universally promulgated to men. For a man, for example, who has the Old Testament put into his hands, which contains *prophesies*, and the New Testament, which contains their completions, and is once satisfy'd, as he may be with the greatest ease, that the

Old

Old Testament existed before the New, may have a compleat, internal, divine demonstration of the truth of christianity, without long and laborious inquiries. Whereas, arguments of another nature, such, for instance, as relate to the autority and genuinness of books, and the persons and characters of authors and witnesses, require more application and understanding than falls to the share of the bulk of mankind; or else are very precarious in themselves, as we may judge by the representation of the state of primitive antiquity given us by our most learned Divines. The pious and learned Bishop *Fell* says, (x) *Tanta fuit primis sæculis fingendi licentia, tam prona in credendo facilitas, ut rerum gestarum fides graviter exinde laboraverit; nec orbis tantum terrarum, sed & dei ecclesia de temporibus suis mythicis merito queratur.* Bishop STILLINGFLEET says, (y) that *antiquity is most defective, where it is most useful, namely in the time immediately after the apostles.* And Dr. HICKES says, (z) that *there were in the apostles times as many, and as great heresies, and schisms, as perhaps have been since in any age of the church.* So that

---

(x) *Fell,* in præmissa Monit. Confess. suppos. Cypriani.

(y) *Stillingfleet*'s Irenicum, p. 296.

(z) *Hickes*'s *Apol. Vind. of the Church of England,* p. 124.

that setting aside the before-mention'd internal proofs from *prophesy*, (which are apostolical proofs, and sufficient of themselves) christianity should seem, by this representation of its primitive state, to be destitute of other or external arguments; and nothing should seem more false and more remote from the original state of things, than the assertion of the reverend Mr. REEVES, (*a*.) *that if christianity be a cheat, 'tis a cheat,* [so prov'd or contriv'd] *that we are bound to embrace and follow.*

VII.

That if those proofs are invalid, then is christianity false.

ON the other side, if the proofs for christianity from the Old Testament be not valid; if the arguments founded on those books be not conclusive; and the *prophesies* cited from thence be not fulfill'd; then has christianity no just foundation: for the foundation on which JESUS and his apostles built it is then invalid and false. Nor can *miracles*, said to be wrought by JESUS and his apostles, in behalf of Christianity, avail any thing in the case: for *miracles* can

never

(*a*) *Reeves's Apol.* Vol. 2. p. 137.

never render a foundation valid, which is in itself invalid; can never make a false inference true; can never make a *prophesy* fulfill'd, which is not fulfill'd; and can never mark out a MESSIAS, or JESUS for the MESSIAS, if both are not mark'd out in the Old Testament. Besides, *miracles*, said to be wrought, may be often justly deem'd false reports, when attributed to persons, who claim an autority from the Old Testament, which they impertinently alledge to support their pretences. God can never be suppos'd *often* to permit miracles to be done for the confirmation of a false or pretended mission; and if at any time he does permit miracles to be wrought in confirmation of a pretended mission, we have directions from the (*b*) Old Testament not to regard such miracles; but are to continue firm to the antecedent revelation confirm'd by miracles, and contain'd in the Old Testament, notwithstanding any miracles; which (in the opinion of some divines, (*c*) *as splendid gifts as they are, are no demonstrations of the truth*, but) under the circumstance of attesting something contrary to an antecedent revelation, confirm'd by miracles, are certainly no proofs of the truth. No new revelation, however prov'd by

---

(*b*) Deut. 13. 1, 2.   (*c*) Hickes's *Apol. Vind. of the Church of* England, p. 23, 24. *Stillingfleet*'s Orig. Sacræ, l. 2. c. 5. n. 7.

by miracles, ought ever to be receiv'd, unless it confirms, or does not contradict the preceding standing true revelation.

Moreover, *(c) Those among the* Jews, who expected a MESSIAS or *Deliverer* (for all the *Jews* did not *(d)* in our Saviour's time, and perhaps none before the captivity) ever expected a real or temporal *deliverer*. Such the *(e)* apostles before the death of JESUS expected he would be. Such they expected he would be after his resurrection, when they asked him, whether *(f) at this time* he would *restore again the kingdom of* Israel; in which notion he seems to leave them, by not setting them right as to the *restoration of the kingdom of* Israel; but taking their notion for granted, he only answers as to the *time*, by telling them, that it was not *for them* to know *the time*, when he would restore the kingdom of *Israel*: and all the primitive christians were, for a considerable time after the ascension of JESUS, in the vulgar error of expecting him to come in the clouds, and reign personally and triumphantly upon earth in *a kingdom that was at hand*. The *Jews* expected a MESSIAS, who was to change their miserable condition into a happy one, and to govern them by their own law,

D with-

(*c*) Luke 2. 38.   (*d*) *Le Clerc*, sur l'endroit,
Ib. *Hist. Eccl.* p. 4.   (*e*) Luke 24. 21.
(*f*) Acts 1. 6. *See* Tillotson's *Sermons, Vol.* 10. p. 126.

without the least imagination of a mere *(g)* spiritual deliverance or any alteration of their divine law, (which they thought was *(h) to be eternal*) in virtue of a new legislative power conferr'd on him by God. Pursuant to which they thought the person and doctrines of JESUS to be so far from being held forth in the Old Testament, that they *(i) knew not whence he was*, and look'd on him to be in many respects different from the CHRIST they expected from *thence*; and thought *(k) no greater contradiction could be form'd, nothing in nature or terms more irreconcilable, than affirming the same person to be* CHRIST *(that is, a triumphant prince) and to be crucify'd.* Wherefore the numerous and wonderful miracles wrought by JESUS, tho' equal *(l)* to what the *Jews* expected from their MESSIAS, were no proofs to them, that he was the MESSIAS. They did not take him for the MESSIAS on *(m)* account of them; but on the contrary they procur'd him to be crucify'd for pretending to be the MESSIAS, *(n) not knowing the Lord of glory*, from his miracles.

Nor

(g) Scripta Judæi apud *Limborchii* Amic. Collat. p. 76, 115.
(h) *Whitby's* Note on Gal. 4. 21.　　(i) John 9. 29.
(k) Stanhope's *Boyl. Lect. First Sermon for* 1700. p. 7, 8.
(l) John 7. 31.
(m) Luke 2. 34.　　(n) Acts 3. 17.

Nor had his miracles any effect on his own (*o*) *brethren*, and *kindred*, and *family*, who seem to have been more incredulous in him, than other Jews. Nor had they the effect, which naturally they should seem fitted to produce, among his immediate followers, and disciples: some of whom did not (*p*) *believe in him*, but *deserted* him, and particularly had no *faith* in him, when he spake of his *sufferings*; and thought he could (*q*) not be the MESSIAS, when they saw him suffer; notwithstanding his miracles and frequent declarations to them, that he was the MESSIAS. And the Jews were so rooted in their notion of a temporal deliverer, even after the resurrection and ascension of JESUS, and the progress of christianity grounded on the belief of JESUS to be the MESSIAS, that they have in all times of distress, and particularly in the (*r*) apostolical times in great numbers follow'd *impostors*, who have set up for the MESSIAS with force and arms, as the way to *restore the kingdom of* Israel. So that the Jews, who mistook in this most important matter, and after the most egregious

manner

(*o*) Mark 6. 4. John 7. 5. (*p*) Ib. 6. 64, 66. Mark 8. 31. (*q*) Luke 24. 21. (*r*) *Joseph.* Antiq. l. 20. c. 2. & 6. Ib. De bello Jud. l. 3. c. 23. l. 7. c. 30. *Lent* De Pseudo Messiis. *Vandale* Dissert. de Origine Idol, &c. p. 227, &c. Tillotson's *Sermons*, Vol. 13. p. 116--119, 151.

manner the meaning of their own books, might, 'till they were set right in their interpretations of the Old Testament, and were convinc'd from thence, that JESUS was the MESSIAS, as justly reject JESUS asserting his mission and doctrine with *miracles*, as any other Person, who, in virtue of miracles, would lead them into *idolatry*, or into any other real breach of the *mosaick law*. And the Gentiles, who ought regularly to be converted to Judaism, before they could become christians, and ought to ground their christianity on the Old Testament, had a right to the same satisfaction; and might want it (as (s) CELSUS did) no less than the Jews, whom they might perhaps allow to understand their own books better than the apostles, who manifestly put new interpretations upon them, and those not agreeable to the obvious and literal meaning of those books, and contrary to the sense of the Jewish nation. And for this both Jews and Gentiles might plead the example of the apostles; who, at first, did, like other unbelieving Jews, expect a temporal prince, and did disbelieve JESUS to be the MESSIAS on account of his sufferings, notwithstanding his *miracles*; who continu'd in those thoughts till they came to understand the spiritual sense

---

(s) *Origen* contra Celsum, p. 78, 343.

sense of the *scriptures*, which they receiv'd, partly by conversation with JESUS after his *death*, and partly by (*t*) inspiration; and who might seem to act an inconsistent part, in interpreting the scriptures in so many respects about JESUS as they did, according to the traditional rules and explications of the Jews, and yet rejecting their traditional explication in respect to the temporal kingdom of their MESSIAS.

In fine, the *miracles* wrought by JESUS are, according to the gospel-scheme, no absolute proofs of his being the MESSIAS, or of the truth of christianity.

Those *miracles* were prophesy'd of in the Old Testament, like the other matters of the gospel; and therefore they are no otherwise to be consider'd as proofs of those points, than as fulfilling the sayings in the Old Testament, like other gospel-matters and events, or (as a *Boylean* lecturer well expresses it) (*u*) *as comprehended in, and exactly consonant to the prophesies concerning the* MESSIAS. In that sense they are good *proofs*, and in that sense only: for, as I have before observ'd, if JESUS is not the person prophesy'd of as the MESSIAS in the Old Testament, his miracles will not prove him to be so, nor prove his divine mission. And in that sense only

---

(*t*) Acts 26. 22.   (*u*) Stanhope's *Boyl. Lect.* 1701. *Serm.* 8. p. 29.

[38]

only Jesus himself urges his miracles to prove his being the Messias. For when (*w*) John the *baptist, who had heard in prison of the works* or miracles of Christ, but yet doubted whether he was the Messias, as perhaps expecting, like other Jews, and like the apostles themselves, a temporal prince, and one who would deliver him from his prison, sent two of his disciples to him, to know, whether he was the Messias, or they *were to look for another*; Christ declares himself to be the Messias, by *shewing*, that the (*x*) characters of the Messias as extant in the prophets manifestly agreed to him in these words, (*y*) *Go and shew* John *again those things, which you do hear and see: The blind receive their sight, and the lame walk, the lepers are cleans'd, and the deaf hear, the dead are rais'd up, and the poor have the gospel preach'd unto them. And blessed are they who shall not be offended in me.* Which characters consist of two parts, first in doing *miracles*; and secondly, in appearing in a *low* state, and *teaching the poor* (which last was much mistaken by, and gave great *offence* to the Jews; for as to the first, the Jews (*z*) agreed to it.) Neither

---

(*w*) Matt. 11. 2, 3. Vid. *Hammondum* & *Clericum in locum*.

(*x*) *See* Hammond, *who cites* Isaiah, *as referr'd to* ch. 29. 18, 19. & 21. 1. & 35. 5, 6.

(*y*) Matt. 11. 4--6.   (*z*) John 7. 31.

ther of which would, of itself, be sufficient to prove JESUS to be the MESSIAS, without the other; nor both together, but as they are the characters of the MESSIAS in the prophets.

VIII.

That those proofs are typical or allegorical proofs.

OF the *strength* or *weakness* of the proofs for christianity out of the Old Testament we seem well qualify'd to judge, by having the Old and New Testament in our hands; the first containing the proofs of christianity, and the latter the application of those proofs. And we should seem to have nothing more to do, but to compare the Old and New Testament together.

But these *proofs* taken out of the *Old*, and urg'd in the *New* Testament, being, sometimes, either not to be found in the *Old*, or not urg'd in the *New*, according to the literal and obvious sense, which they seem to bear in their suppos'd places in the *Old*, and therefore not proofs according to scholastick rules; almost all christian (*a*) com-
mentator's

(*a*) Origen, Eusebius, Jerom, (*who says directly to* Pammachius, *that the Passages alledg'd by* Paul, *out of*

[40]

mentators on the bible, and *advocates* for the christian religion, both antient and modern, have judg'd them to be apply'd in a secondary, or typical, or mystical, or allegorical, or enigmatical sense, that is, in a sense different from the obvious and literal sense, which they bear in the Old Testament.

1. Thus for example, St. MATTHEW after having given an account of the conception of the virgin MARY, and of the birth of JESUS, says, *(b) all this was done that it might be fulfill'd, which was spoken by the prophet, saying,* " Behold a virgin " shall be with child, and shall bring forth " a Son, and they shall call his name IMMANUEL."

---

of the old Testament, aliter in suis locis, aliter in Epistolis Paulinis sonant) Cyril, Chrysostom, Austin among the Antients. *And among the Moderns*, Sextus Senensis *in* Bibl. Sancta; Glassius *in* Philologia Sacra; Grotius *in* Vetus *and* Nov. Test. & sicut at *in* Isa. 53. 1. *in* Psal. 22. 1. *and in* Matt. 1. 22; *Cuneus* dans sa Republique des Hebreux, l. 3. c. 8. Vol. 1. p. 376; *Simon* Hist. Crit. du V. T. p. 97, 98.— Hist. Crit. du Nov. Test. c. 21. & 22.—Suppl. aux Ceremonies des Juifs. p. 7; Jenkins's *Reasonab. of the Christian Religion;* Nichols *Conference with a Theist*. Vol. 3d. White *on* Isaiah; *Dupin* Dissert. Prelim. sur la Bible, l. 1. c. 10; and *Le Clerc* Bib. Choisie, Vol. 27. p. 388.—399. *See* WHISTON's *Confession of this Matter in* Essay, &c. p. 92.
 (*b*) Matt. 1. 22, 23.

[41]

MANUEL," But the words, as they stand in ISAIAH, (*c*) from whom they are suppos'd to be taken, do, in their obvious and literal sense, relate to a *young woman* in the days of AHAZ, king of *Judah*, as will appear by considering the context.

(*d*) When REZIN, king of *Syria*, and PEKAH, king of *Israel*, were confederates in arms together, against *Ahaz*, king of *Judah*; ISAIAH the prophet was sent by God first to comfort AHAZ and his nation, and afterwards to assure them by a *sign* or miracle, that his enemies should in a little time be confounded. But AHAZ refusing a *sign* at the prophet's hands, the prophet said, (*e*) *The Lord shall give you a sign: Behold a virgin* (or (*f*) *young woman*) *shall conceive and bear a son, and shall call his name* IMMANUEL. *Butter and Honey shall be eat; that he may know to refuse the evil, and chuse the good. For before* (*g*) *the child shall know to refuse the evil and chuse the good, the land shall be forsaken of both her kings.* And this sign is accordingly given AHAZ by the prophet, who (*h*) *took two witnesses*, and in their presence *went unto* the said virgin or young woman, call'd the (*i*) *prophetess*, who in due time *conceiv'd*
and

(*c*) Isa. 7. 14. (*d*) c. 7. (*e*) v. 14---16. (*f*) *Vide* Erasmum *in* Matt. c. 1. v. 30. (*g*) *See* Isaiah 8. 4. (*h*) Ib. v. 2. 18. (*i*) v. 3.

and bare a son, who was nam'd (*k*) IMMA-
NUEL; after whose birth, the projects (*l*) of
REZIN and PEKAH were soon confounded,
according to the *prophesy* and *sign* given by
the prophet.

And the prophet himself puts it past dispute, by express words, as well as by his
whole narration, that his own child was the
sign mention'd, when he says, (*m*) *Behold I
and the children, whom the Lord hath
given me, are for signs and for wonders in
Israel; from the Lord of hosts, that dwel-
leth in mount Sion.*

This is the plain drift and design of the
prophet, literally, obviously, and primarily
understood; and thus is he understood by
one of the most judicious of interpreters, the
great GROTIUS. Indeed, to understand the
prophet as having the conception of the virgin MARY and birth of her son JESUS literally and primarily in view, is a very great
(*n*) *absurdity*, and contrary to the very in-
tent and design of the *sign* given by the prophet. For the *sign* (*o*) being given by the
prophet to convince AHAZ, that he brought
a message from the Lord to him to assure
him that the two kings should not succeed
against

(*k*) *See* Grotius *in* Matt. 1. 22.   (*l*) Isa. 8. 8, 10.
Ib. 7. 14. & 8. 4.   (*m*) Ib. v. 19.   (*n*) *White*
in hunc locum, & Pref. p. 20.   (*o*) Isa. 7. 14. & 8. 4.

against him; how could a virgin's conception and bearing a son seven hundred years afterwards, be a *sign* to AHAZ, that the prophet came to him with the said message from the Lord? And how useless was it to AHAZ, as well as absurd in itself, for the prophet to say, (*p*) *Before the child*, born seven hundred years hence, shall distinguish between *good* and *evil, the land shall be forsaken of both her kings*? which should seem a banter instead of a sign. But a prophesy of the certain birth of a male child, to be born within a year or two, seems a proper *sign*; as being not only what could not with certainty be foretold, except by a person inspir'd by God; but as immediately or soon coming to pass, and consequently evidencing itself to be *a divine sign*, and answering all the purposes of *a sign*. And such a *sign* is agreeable to the divine conduct on the like occasions. God gave (*q*) GIDEON and (*r*) HEZEKIAH immediate *signs* to prove, that he spoke to them; and that the things promis'd to them should come to pass. Had he given them remote *signs*, how could they have known, that the *signs* themselves would ever have come to pass? And how could those *signs* evidence any thing? Those *signs* would have

---

(*p*) Isa. 8. *v.* 15, 16.   (*q*) Judg. 6.
(*r*) 2 King. 20.

[44]

have stood in need of other *signs* to manifest, that God would perform them in time.

This prophesy therefore not being fulfill'd in Jesus according to the literal, obvious, and primary sense of the words, as they stand in Isaiah; it is suppos'd, that this, like all the other prophesies cited by the apostles, is (s) fulfill'd in a secondary, or typical, or mystical, or allegorical sense; that is, the said prophesy, which was then literally fulfill'd by the birth of the prophet's son, was again fulfill'd by the birth of Jesus, as being an event of the same kind, and intended to be signify'd, either by the prophet, or by God who directed the prophet's speech. I say, *like all other prophesies cited by the apostles*, not only upon having myself particularly consider'd all those prophesies, but upon what I find asserted by an eminent divine, who says, (t) *'Tis possible in the consideration of single prophesies to find out some other person or event*, (besides Jesus and the matters relating to him) *to which these might be adapted without great violence to the text*. And this suppos'd *allegory* or *obscurity* (which indeed reigns in all prophesies that ever were, whether Pagan, Jewish, Christian, or Mahometan, that have
ex-

(s) *Le Clerc* Bib. Univ. Tom. 20. p. 54.
(t) Stanhope's *Boyl. Lect. Serm.* 7. 1701. p. 27.

exifted before the events to which they have been referr'd) is fo far from being made matter of objection, that the neceffity (*u*) thereof is contended for, in order to make the prophefies of the Old Teftament reach the *end* for which they were defign'd. The great clearnefs of prophefies has ever been deem'd a mark among intelligent people, whether believers or unbelievers in prophefy, that they have been made after the event; and thus from their great clearnefs, as well as from other topicks, almoft all criticks now condemn the prefent collection of *Sybilline oracles* as forg'd.

If the reader defires farther fatisfaction, that the literal, obvious, and primary fenfe of this prophefy relates to Isaiah's own fon, or not to Jesus, I refer him to (*w*) Grotius; to (*x*) Huetius (who confirms his explication with the autority of Eusebius, Basil, Jerom, Cyril, Theodoret, and Procopius;) (*y*) to Castalio; (*z*) to Episcopius; to (*a*) Curcellæus; to (*b*) Hammond;

(*u*) Montagu's *Acts and Monuments*, &c. c. 2. Sect. 2. &c. *Auguftin* De Doctr. Chriftian. l. 2. c. 5. *Stanhope*, lb. p. 11—32. Jenkins's *Reafon. of Chrift*. Vol. 2. p. 159—170. (*w*) *Grotius* in Matt. & Ifaiam,
(*x*) *Huetii* Demon. Evang. p. 352—355. *Huetiana*, p. 206. (*y*) *Caftalionis*, Biblia.
(*z*) *Epifcopii* Inftit. l. 3. c. 13. Sect. 14.
(*a*) *Curcellæi* Inftit. p. 220.
(*b*) *Hammond's* Annotations, &c.

Hammond; to (c) Nichols; to (d) Simon; to (e) Le Clerc; to (f) Lamy; to (g) Kidder; (who, tho' he endeavours in many pages to prove the words of Isaiah applicable to the birth of Jesus in their literal sense, yet confesses there *are very considerable difficulties in the matter*, and after all is forc'd to have recourse to *type* and *allegory*); to our learned and ingenious commentator (h) White; and even to (i) Mr. Whiston himself, who shows the words of Isaiah not to be applicable to Jesus's birth in their literal sense, according to the present text of Isaiah; which is deem'd by all christians, but himself, the *true text* of Isaiah.

2. Again, St. Matthew gives us another prophesy, which he says was *fulfill'd*. He tells us, that Jesus was carry'd into *Egypt*, from whence he return'd after the death of Herod, (k) *that it might be fulfill'd which was spoken of the Lord by the prophet, saying*, "Out of *Egypt* have I call'd my son." Which words being word for word in Hoseah, (l) and no where else to be found in

---

(c) *Nichols's* Confer. with a Theist, Vol. 3.
(d) *Simon* Hist. Crit. du N. Test. c. 21.
(e) *Le Clerc* Nov. Test.
(f) *Lamy* Harmon. p. 36.
(g) Kidder's *Dem. of the Messias*, Vol. 2. p. 285--313. p. 292, 309, &c.
(h) White's *Comment. on* Isaiah.
(i) Whiston's *Essay*, &c. p. 229, &c.
(k) Matt. 2. 15.   (l) Hos. 11. 1.

in the Old Testament, are suppos'd to be taken from thence; where, according to their obvious sense, they are no prophesy, but relate to a *(m)* past action, and that to the calling the children of *Israel* out of *Egypt*; as, I think, is denied by few. This passage therefore, or, as it is stil'd, *prophesy* of Hoseah is said by learned men to be mystically or allegorically apply'd in order to render Matthew's application of it just; and they say, all other *methods of some learned men to solve the difficulties* arising from the citation of this prophesy, *have prov'd unsuccessful*.

3. Matthew says, *(n)* Jesus *came and dwelt at* Nazareth, *that it might be fulfill'd, which was spoken by the prophets, saying,* "He shall be call'd a *Nazarene*." Which citation does not *expresly* occur in any place of the Old Testament, and therefore the Old Testament cannot be literally fulfill'd therein.

4. Jesus says of John the *Baptist*, *(o) This is the* Elias *that was for to come*: Wherein he is suppos'd to refer to these words of Malachi, *(p)* "Behold, I will send you Eli-
"jah the prophet, before the coming of the
"great

(m) See Whiston's *Lect.* p. 12. Ib. *Essay*, &c. p. 88, &c. *Simon* Hist. Crit. du N. Test. c. 21. p. 260. *Cunæus* Rep. des Heb. Vol. 1. p. 376. *Huetii* Dem. Evang. p. 730. *(n)* Matt. 2. 23. *(o)* Matt. 11. 14. *(p)* Mal. 4. 5.

[48]

"great and terrible day of the Lord;" which, according to their literal sense, are a prophesy, that ELIJAH or ELIAS was to come in person, and therefore were not *literally* but *mystically* fulfill'd in JOHN the *baptist*.

5. Again, JESUS (*q*) cites this prophesy of ISAIAH, (*r*) "By hearing, ye shall hear and shall not understand;" and he assures us, that it was *fulfill'd* in his time in those to whom he spoke in *parables*; tho' it is manifest, that, according to the literal sense, it relates to the obstinate *Jews*, who liv'd in the time of ISAIAH.

In fine, the prophesies cited from the Old Testament by the authors of the New, do so plainly relate, in their obvious and primary sense, to other matters than those which they are produc'd to prove; that to pretend they prove, in that sense, what they are produc'd to prove, is, (*s*) *to give up the cause* of christianity to *Jews* and other *enemies* thereof; who can so easily show, in so many undoubted instances, the Old and New Testament to have no manner of connection in that respect, but to be in an (*t*) *irreconcileable state*.

Nay

(*q*) Matt. 13. 34, 35.   (*r*) Isa. 6. 9.
(*s*) *Cunæus* Rep. des Hebr. l. 3. c. 8. Vol. 1. p. 372, &c. *Simon* Bibl. Crit. Vol. 4. p. 513. Ib. Hist. Crit. du Nov. Test. c. 21, & 22.
(*t*) Whiston's *Essay*, &c. p. 282.

Nay, this inconsistency is shown to their hands by the most learned men of the Christian Church; who, according to Mr. WHISTON, (*u*) have taken no small pains to show, that the apostles arguments from the Old Testament are not grounded on the literal sense thereof. *Grotius* (*w*) shows this of most, if not all, of the prophesies and citations quoted from the Old in the New Testament. DODWEL (*x*) in a posthumous work, does (with the learned (*y*) Sir JOHN MARSHAM) refer even the famous prophesy in DANIEL about the *weeks* to the times of ANTIOCHUS EPIPHANES; wherein he shows, that the *expressions* taken from thence by (*z*) CHRIST, and urg'd by him as foretelling the destruction of *Jerusalem* by the *Romans*, have only in *a secondary sense a respect to that destruction*. And that famous passage in the pentateuch, (*a*) *A prophet will the Lord God raise up unto thee, like unto me; to him shall ye hearken*; (which some interpret literally to mean JESUS CHRIST, and which (*b*) LUKE in two places refers to as spoken

---

(*u*) Whiston's *Essay*, &c. p. 92. Ib. *Lectures*, p. 13, 19, 20, 38, 47, 48.
(*w*) *Grotius* in Novum Testamentum.
(*x*) Apud *Brookesby's* Dodwel's Life, p. 508.
(*y*) *Marsham* Canon Cronicus, &c. p. 568——576.
(*z*) Matt. 24.
(*a*) Deut. 18. 15, 18.
(*b*) Acts 3. 22. & 7. 37.

spoken of JESUS CHRIST) is *generally* (c) *understood*, and particularly by GROTIUS and STILLINGFLEET, to signify in its *immediate sense a promise of a succession of prophets*; to the judicious reasonings of which last author, on this occasion, I refer the reader. Which conduct of these eminent divines and advocates for christianity can only be owing to the plainness of the case itself; which (d) Mr. WHISTON himself acknowledges is such in divers instances, that, taking the present Old Testament for genuine, it is impossible to account for those citations on any other foundation than on the allegorical scheme.

IX.

The nature of typical or allegorical proofs and reasoning.

IN order therefore to understand the full force of the *proofs* for christianity, it is necessary to understand the nature and rules

---

(c) *Vandale* Diss. de Origine Idololat. &c. p. 187. *Simon* Hist. Crit. du N. Test. p. 227. Id. Apologie contre le *Vassor*, p. 127. *Grotius* in locum. *Stillingfleet*'s Orig. Sacræ, l. 2. c. 4. n. 1. p. 100. Dodwel's *Letters of Advice*, &c. p. 214.

(d) Whiston's *Lectures*, p. 226, 227. Ib. 256. Ib. *Essay*, &c. p. 92.

rules of typical, myſtical, and allegorical reaſoning. Which is what I ſhall now endeavour to explain to the reader.

To ſuppoſe that an author has but one meaning at a time to a propoſition (which is to be found out by a critical examination of his words) and to cite that propoſition from him, and argue from it in that one meaning, is to proceed by the common rules of grammar and logick; which, being human rules, are not very difficult to be ſet forth and explain'd. But to ſuppoſe paſſages cited, explain'd, and argu'd from in any other method, ſeems very extraordinary and difficult to underſtand, and to reduce to *rules*. Accordingly, notwithſtanding it is ſuppos'd by the learned interpreters of the New Teſtament and the ſeveral chriſtian apologiſts, that the apoſtles apply'd the paſſages they cite out of the Old Teſtament to their purpoſes after a typical, or myſtical, or allegorical manner; and notwithſtanding, both ancients and moderns do almoſt univerſally make application of paſſages of the Old Teſtament (to ſay nothing of their manner of interpreting the New Teſtament, and the *revelation* of St. JOHN in particular) in ſome ſuch manner, not only as to matters, that relate to the goſpel of JESUS, but to the matters and events of all times: yet the *rules* of thus applying paſſages of ſcripture ſeem not underſtood by many of thoſe perſons, who contend, that

[52]

the apostles us'd that method, or who use it themselves. For I find it lamented by a *Boylean Lecturer*, that (*f*) *the* Jewish *Traditions or* Rules *for interpreting scripture, which had been received among the ancient* Jewish *Rabbins*, and were followed by the apostles in their interpretations of the Old Testament, were *lost*. And so lately as 1708, I find in the reverend Dr. Jenkin the following passage: He, on occasion of St. Stephen's giving an historical account of several matters contrary to what we read in the Old Testament, and arguing before the *Sanedrin* from thence, says, that (*g*) St. Stephen *would never have produced any thing out of the Old Testament before the Sanedrin, nor would St.* Luke *have recorded it soon after, if it had been capable of any disproof or confutation, whatever difficulties at this distance of time there may appear to us to be in it. And so in all other cases we may depend upon it, that the apostles, and other disciples, who had such demonstrative evidence for the conviction of unbelievers, by a constant power of miracles, would never make use of any arguments to the* Jews *from the Old Testament, but such as they well knew, their adversaries*

(*f*) Stanhope's *Boyle's Lect. Serm.* 8. 1701. p. 23.
(*g*) Jenkin's *Reasonab. of the Christ. Relig.* Vol. 2. p. 320.

ries could never be able to disprove or deny. For there were then certain methods of interpretation, as we may learn from JOSEPHUS, *(h) which are* now lost; *and they disputed from acknowledg'd maxims and rules: the only difference and matter of dispute, was in the application of them to the particular case; however our ignorance of things, then generally known, may now make it difficult to reconcile some texts of the New Testament with those of the Old from whence they are cited.*

But since that time, the learned SURENHUSIUS, professor of the *Hebrew* tongue in the *illustrious school* of *Amsterdam*, has made an ample discovery to the world of the *rules* by which the apostles cited the Old Testament, and argued from thence, in a (*i*) *treatise*; wherein the whole mystery of the apostles applying scripture in a secondary or typical, or mystical, or allegorical sense seems unfolded. I shall therefore state this matter from SURENHUSIUS; who himself gives the *substance*, as well as the *occasion* of his work, in his *preface*.

(*h*) *Joseph.* De Bello, Jud. l. 3. c. 14.
(*i*) Tractatus in qno secundum Veterum Theologorum Hebræorum formulas allegandi, & modos interpretandi, conciliantur loca ex V. in Nov. Test. allegata. Amstel. 1713. p. 712.

He says, (k) "That when he considered
"the various opinions of the learned about
"the passages of the Old Testament quoted
"in the New, he was *filled with grief*, not
"knowing where to set his foot, and being
"much concerned, that what had been done
"with good success upon profane authors,
"could not be so happily perform'd upon the
"sacred.

He tells us, "That having had frequent
"occasions to converse with the *Jews*, (on
"account of his application to *Hebrew* li-
"terature from his youth) who insolently re-
"flected on the New Testament; affirming
"it to be plainly corrupted, because it sel-
"dom or never agreed with the Old Testa-
"ment, some of whom were so confident in
"this opinion, as to say, they would profess
"the christian religion, if any one could
"reconcile the New Testament with the Old;
"he was the more *griev'd*, because he
"knew not how to apply a remedy to this
"evil. But the matter being of great im-
"portance, he discours'd with several learn-
"ed men about it, and read the books of
"others, being perswaded, that the authors
"of

(k) *For this Extract out of* SURENHUSIUS, *I am for the most part obliged to the learned and ingenious Monſ.* De la Roche ; *from whoſe* Memoirs of Literature *I have in great measure taken it.*

" of the books of the New Testament had
" writ nothing, but what was suited to the
" time, wherein they liv'd, and that Christ
" and his apostles had constantly follow'd
" the method of their ancestors. After he
" had long revolv'd this *hypothesis* in his
" mind, at last he met with a Rabbin well
" skill'd in the *Talmud*, the *Cabala*, and
" the *allegorical books* of the Jews. That
" Rabbin had once embrac'd the christian
" religion, but was again relaps'd to Juda-
" ism, on account of the idolatry of the pa-
" pists, yet not perfectly disbelieving the *in-*
" *tegrity* of the New Testament. Mr. Su-
" renhusius ask'd him, what he thought
" of the passages of the Old Testament, quoted
" in the New, whether they were rightly
" quoted or not ? and whether the Jews had
" any just reason to cavil at them ? And at
" the same time he propos'd to him two or
" three passages, which had very much ex-
" ercis'd the most learned christian commen-
" tators. The Rabbin having admirably ex-
" plain'd those passages, to the great surprize
" of our author, and confirm'd his explica-
" tions by several places of the (*l*) *Talmud*,
" and by the writings of the Jewish com-
" mentators and allegorical writers ; Mr.
" Surenhusius ask'd him, what would be
" the best method to write a treatise, in or-
" der

(*l*) See Scaligerana, p. 265.

"der to vindicate the passages of the Old
"Testament which have been quoted in the
"New? The Rabbin answer'd, that he
"thought the best way of succeeding in
"such an undertaking, would be to peruse
"a great part of the *Talmud*, and the alle-
"gorical and literal commentaries of the
"most ancient Jewish writers; to observe
"their several ways of quoting and inter-
"preting scripture; and to collect as many
"materials of that kind, as would be suffi-
"cient for that purpose. Mr. *S.* took the
"hint immediately: he read several parts
"of the *Talmud*; he perus'd the jewish
"books above-mention'd, and observ'd eve-
"ry thing that might be subservient to his
"design. And having made a large col-
"lection of those materials, he put all his
"*Theses* into order, and digested them into
"four books: The first whereof treats *of
"the forms of quoting, illustrating, and
"reconciling the scriptures*, in 59 *The-
"ses*: The second treats *of the manner of
"quoting*, in 20 *Theses*: The third treats *of
"the manner of interpreting*, in 25 *Theses*.
"And the fourth treats *of the manner of ex-
"pounding and reconciling the genealogies*,
"in 35 *Theses*." Then he proceeds in a
fifth book to explain and justify all the
quotations made from the Old Testament in
the New, by his foregoing *Theses*.

As

As to the *forms of quoting*, which is the subject of his first book, he says, "that in order to vindicate and reconcile any passage of the Old Testament quoted in the New, one must in the first place observe, what *form of quoting* the apostles made use of; because from thence one may immediately know, why they alledge the following words in a certain manner, rather than in another, and why they depart more or less from the *Hebrew* text. Thus a different sense is imply'd in each of the following *forms of quoting* used by the sacred writers of the New Testament: *it has been said: it is written: that it might be fulfill'd which was spoken: the scripture says: see what is said: the scripture foreseeing: is it not written: wherefore he says: have you never read: what says the scripture; as he spoke*, &c. Besides, he says, it ought to be consider'd, why in those quotations God is introduc'd under the name of *Lord* or *God*, or *Holy Ghost*, and sometimes the writer himself, or the scripture; and likewise, why the persons or things in question are introduc'd speaking. Lastly, it ought to be observ'd, when and why a passage of the Old Testament is alledg'd in the New without any previous form of quoting; and why some traditions, and history almost forgotten, are sometimes "occa-

"occasionally brought in, as if they made
"a part of scripture?" In the second book,
which treats *of the manner of quoting*, he
shows, "that the books of the Old Testa-
"ment have been dispos'd in a different or-
"der at different times, and have had diffe-
"rent names, which is the reason, why a
"writer or a book, is sometimes confound-
"ed with another in the New Testament."
Besides, he produces several reasons, "why
"the sacred writers of the New Testament
"might, and even were oblig'd to alledge
"the passages of the Old Testament other-
"wise than they are express'd in the original,
"*viz*. because the ancient *Hebrew* doctors
"affirm'd, that in the time of the MESSIAS
"some obscure and difficult passages of
"scripture should be clear'd, and the im-
"propriety of words mended, the intricacy
"of the stile remov'd, words dispos'd in a
"better order, and a mystical sense drawn
"out of the literal, that the vail being taken
"away, truth might plainly appear to every
"body. The author infers from thence,
"that the Jews cannot reasonably find fault
"with the apostles for putting a spiritual
"sense upon several passages of the Old Te-
"stament." In the next place he shows,
"that the jewish doctors take a prodigious
"liberty in quoting the scripture, and gives
"us several instances of it." The last is very remarkable, and made Mr. SURENHU-

sius very angry with the seeming absurdity of the Rabbins. But, says he, " when " I saw St. PAUL do so too, my anger was " appeas'd."

In the third book, which treats *of the manner* of interpreting the scriptures, he shows, " how the authors of the *Gemara*, " and the ancient allegorical writers, and " others, interpreted the scripture in such a " manner, as to change the mean literal " sense of the words into a noble and spiritual " sense. To that end the jewish doctors " used *ten ways* of citing and explaining " the Old Testament;" which for their curiosity and importance, I shall here recite at large after my author.

1. The first is, " reading the words, not " according to the points plac'd under them, " but according to other points substituted in " their stead; as we see done by PETER, " *Acts* 3. 3; by STEPHEN, *Acts* 7. 43; " and by PAUL, 1 *Cor.* 15. 54; 2 *Cor.* 8. " 15; and *Heb.* 3. 10; & 9. 21; & 12. 6."

2. The second is, " changing the letters, " whether those letters be of the same organ " (as the jewish grammarians speak) or no; " as we see done by PAUL, *Rom.* 9. 33; " 1 *Cor.* 11. 9; *Heb.* 8. 9; and 10. 5; and " by STEPHEN, *Acts* 7. 43."

3. The third is, " changing both letters " and points; as we see done by PAUL, *Acts* " 13. 41; and 2 *Cor.* 8. 15."

4. The fourth is, " adding some letters and
" taking away others."

5. The fifth is, " transposing words and
" letters."

6. The sixth is, " dividing one word into
" two."

7. The seventh is, " adding other words
" to those that are there, in order to make
" the sense more clear, and to accommodate
" it to the subject they are upon; as, is ma-
" nifest, is done by the apostles throughout
" the New Testament."

8. The eighth is, " changing the order of
" words; which he shews to be done in
" many places of the New Testament."

9. The ninth is, " changing the order of
" words, and adding other words; which
" are both done by the apostles in citing
" passages out of the Old Testament."

10. The tenth is, " changing the order of
" words, adding words, and retrenching
" words; which is a method often us'd by
" PAUL.

Thus by a most lucky accident of Mr. Su-
RENHUSIUS's meeting and *conference* with a
learned allegorical *Rabbin*, are the *rules*,
by which the apostles cited and apply'd the
Old Testament, discover'd to the world; to
which they had been for several ages lost, as
has been observ'd from the rev. doctors STAN-
HOPE and JENKIN, above-mention'd. Which
confe-

conference seems not, in its nature and consequence, much unlike that between LUTHER and the *devil*. LUTHER reports himself to have had frequent conferences with the devil; in one of which he pretends he receiv'd from him the *arguments* for the *abolition of the sacrifice of the mass*, which he urges in his book, *De Abrog. Miss. Privat.* The *Rabbin* establishes christianity; and the *devil* protestantism!

X.

The nature of allegorical reasoning further shewn by application of it to several particular instances cited from the Old Testament and urg'd in the New Testament.

TO compleat this account of the nature of mystical or allegorical reasoning, I shall conclude with showing, how my author applies some of the *Theses* laid down by him in his three first books to the prophesies cited above by me as not *literally*, but *mystically* fulfill'd.

1. The first prophesy is contain'd in these words of MATTHEW, (m) *all this was done, that it might be fulfill'd, which was spoken by the prophet, saying,* " behold a virgin
" shall

(m) Matt. 1. 22, 23.

"shall be with child, and shall bring forth a
"son, and they shall call his name Immanuel."

Mr. Surenhusius (*n*) observes, that Matthew urges the quotation from the prophet, as *a confirmation of what is said*, just before (*o*) by the angel to Joseph. *As if the angel had said*, "what I have said to you "concerning your wife Mary being with "child by the Holy Ghost, ought not to ap- "pear so wonderful and unheard of a thing "to you; for it was foretold of the Lord, "by the prophet Isaiah, that a virgin should "be with child without the concurrence of "a man, whose off-spring should be call'd "Immanuel. This passage ought not to "have been unknown to you, but since you "did not know it, I refer you to it, and bid "you carefully consider it, that you may "more easily apprehend the unusual concep- "tion of your wife Mary, and take her "home to you." And he proves this to be the sense from *the form of quoting*. For he observes, that *the form of words* "that "it might be fulfill'd which was spoken," *often (p) signifies, according to the gemarick doctors*, "that it might be confirm'd which "is said." *So that the sense of the place is*
as

(*n*) *Surenhusius*, p. 150, 151.   (*o*) Matt. 1. 20.
(*p*) Thesis 2da de formulis allegandi.

as if the evangelist had said, "By this means, by what has now happen'd in MARY, is confirm'd this place of ISAIAH, where it is foretold, that a virgin shall conceive without the concurrence of a man." And he adds, that *the design of the evangelist was not to oppose the Jews, and prove to them, that* JESUS *was the true* MESSIAS; *but to shew to those, who did believe* JESUS *to be the true* MESSIAS, *how the whole divine (q) oeconomy of former times, having always the* CHRIST, *as it were, in view, had form'd all things to resemble him.* Which *notion* (r) my author supposes to have prevail'd always among the Jews, and makes to be the general key, whereby to understand all the Old Testament, and especially this prophesy before us, which he explains at large by this key, as we shall see by and by. So that the reader may observe how the *virgin's conception* in *Isaiah*, as apply'd by MATTHEW, relates to the virgin MARY in an allegorical sense, *viz.* as a *type*, like all the ceremonies of the *law*, and the passages of *history* in the Old Testament, which are all deem'd *types* of JESUS, as representing beforehand what he was to go through and ordain; and, in particular,
like

(q) 1 Pet. 1. 20.   2 Cor. 10. 11.   Gal. 4.   Eph. 1.
(r) *Surenhusius*, p. 159, 160.

like (s) SARAH's *conception* in her old age of ISAAC, which by the ancients and moderns is made a type of the virgin MARY's conception of JESUS; like (s) ABRAHAM offering up ISAAC, which was a type of CHRIST's being offer'd up on the cross; like (s) ISAAC's carrying the wood on his shoulders, which was a *type* of CHRIST's carrying his cross; and like the (s) lifting up of the brazen serpent in the wilderness, which was a *type of* CHRIST's being lifted up on the cross.

But this most important prophesy being, as it lies in ISAIAH, and as it is referr'd to the conception of the virgin MARY, subject to very great difficulties, and much objected to by the Jews (all whose objections Mr. SURENHUSIUS endeavours to answer and obviate at large), I shall draw the substance of what he says into an explication and defence of the whole prophesy, setting down the words of ISAIAH in one column, and SURENHUSIUS's explication and defence in another.

ISAIAH 7. 1--16.	SURENHUSIUS, p. 150--165.
And it came to pass in the days of AHAZ, *the son of* Jo-	'In the days of AHAZ, 'king of *Judah*, REZIN 'king of *Syria*, and PE- 'KAH

(s) Lesley's *Truth of Christ. demonst.* p. 132, 133. Jenkin's *Remarks on* Whiston's *Sermons*, p. 54. Ib. *Reasonableness of Christ. Rel.* Vol. 1. p. 235.

ISAIAH.	SURENHUSIUS.
THAM *the Son of* UZZIAH, *King of Judah, that* REZIN *the King of Syria and* PEKAH *the Son of* REMALIAH, *King of Israel, went up to Jerusalem to war against it. And it was told the house of* DAVID, *saying, Syria is confederate with Ephraim. And his heart was moved, and the heart of his people as the trees of the wood are moved with the wind. Then said the Lord unto* ISAIAH, *Go forth now to meet* AHAZ, *thou and thy son* SHEAR-JASHUB, *at the end of the conduit of the upper pool, in the high way of*	‘KAH King of *Israel* be-‘sieg'd *Jerusalem*. Up-‘on the dread which this ‘occasioned to AHAZ ‘and his people, ISAIAH ‘is commanded by the ‘Lord to bid AHAZ take ‘courage and not fear; ‘for that their design a-‘gainst *Judah*, and to ‘dethrone him, should ‘not succeed. But AHAZ ‘doubting about the mat-‘ter, the Lord sent ISAI-‘AH again with this mes-‘sage, Ask thee a sign ‘as a proof that I come ‘to you from the Lord. ‘But AHAZ refusing a ‘sign, ISAIAH says to ‘the house of DAVID, ‘the Lord shall give ‘you a sign. Behold a ‘virgin is with child, ‘or shall miraculously ‘conceive the MESSIAS, ‘seven hundred years ‘hence, and call his ‘name JESUS, (IMMANU-‘EL and JESUS being of ‘the

SURENHUSIUS.	ISAIAH.
'the same import) who 'tho' born miraculously, 'shall live upon the com-'mon food of the coun-'try. By which it is 'manifest, that the house 'of DAVID shall not be 'destroy'd, nor *Jerusa-*'*lem* come under the 'power of DAMASCUS, 'before the birth of the 'MESSIAS; and there-'fore you, AHAZ, have 'nothing to fear from 'those enemies, for *Je-*'*rusalem* or the house of 'DAVID, if you will 'consider, that the MES-'SIAS is to arise out of 'that house. For if the 'house of DAVID is to 'continue till the birth of 'the MESSIAS, neither of 'these two, nor any of 'the enemies of that 'house shall prevail a-'gainst it. And as cer-'tainly as the MESSIAS 'is to be born in a mira-'culous manner of a vir- 'gin	*of the fullers field: and say unto him, Take heed and be quiet: fear not, neither be faint-hearted; for the two tails of these smoaking fire-brands, for the fierce anger of* RE-ZIN *with Syria, and of the son of* REMALIAH: *be-cause Syria, Ephra -im, and the son of* REMALIAH *have taken evil counsel against thee, say-ing; Let us go up against Judah, and vex it, and let us make a breach therein for us, and set a King in the midst of it, even the son of* TA-BEAL. *Thus saith the Lord God, it shall not stand, neither shall it come*

ISAIAH.	SURENHUSIUS.
come to pass. For the head of Syria is Damascus, and the head of Damascus is Rezin; *and within threescore and five years shall Ephraim be broken, that it be not a people. And the head of Ephraim is Samaria, and the head of Samaria is* Remaliah's *son: if ye will not believe, surely ye shall not be establish'd.*	'gin of the house of David, 'so certainly will the house 'of David be preserv'd 'from whence he is to 'spring, and that for the 'sake of him, who is to be 'Immanuel, God and 'Man in one person, and 'to reconcile men to God, 'and God to men. By all 'which the connection ap- 'pears, and the reason of 'the sign is plain, *viz.* that 'the Jews might consider 'the promise of the Messi- 'as, which was confirm'd 'to them by so many mira- 'cles and prophesies, that 'it could not reasonably be 'call'd in question by them. 'For that promise being 'steadily believ'd by them, 'was a security to them, 'that the house of David 'should not be destroy'd 'before that time. And
Moreover the Lord spake again unto Ahaz *saying, Ask thee a sign of the Lord thy God, ask it either in the depth,*	'thus the prophet put A- 'haz under a necessity ei- 'ther not to credit God's 'promise of his own safety,
or	' of

SURENHUSIUS.	ISAIAH.
'or to be guilty of impiety, in disbelieving the fundamental promise given to the jewish nation concerning the MESSIAS in time to be born of the house of DAVID. To the objection, that it does not follow from hence, that *Jerusalem* and AHAZ would now be preserv'd from the power of those two kings, which yet was the chief end of the sign; since the house of DAVID might continue till the times of the MESSIAS, and *Jerusalem* might be taken, and AHAZ made captive, and live as such; it is answer'd, first, that the primary design of God was to preserve the house of DAVID, which God often evinces, by the promise of the MESSIAS. Secondly, that from this general promise an argument may thus be drawn for the preservation of AHAZ and his people 'from	*or in the height above. But* AHAZ *said, I will not ask, neither will I tempt the Lord. And he said, hear now, O house of* DAVID, *Is it a small thing for you to weary men, but will ye weary my God also? Therefore the Lord himself shall give you a sign. Behold, a virgin shall conceive, and bear a son, and shall call his name* IMMANUEL. *Butter and honey shall he eat, that he may know to refuse the evil and chuse the good. For*

ISAIAH.	SURENHUSIUS.
For before the child shall know to refuse the evil and chuse the good, the land that thou abhorrest shall be forsaken of both her kings.	'from their enemies. If God 'is not only true in his pro-'mise of a MESSIAS, but 'powerful enough to pre-'serve the house of DAVID 'till the times of the MES-'SIAS, he ought to be 'deem'd sufficiently true 'and powerful to fulfil his 'promise in preserving A-'HAZ and his people from 'the power of these two 'kings. And this may 'more strongly be conclu-'ded (for tho' absolutely 'speaking, the promise of 'the MESSIAS might be 'fulfill'd without it, yet 'hypothetically it could 'not, because God propo-'sed that as the means of 'performing his promise; 'for whosoever designs an 'end, designs some means 'to effect it) after this man-'ner. He who is willing 'to give, and can give, 'and certainly will give 'in time, *more*, he is wil-'ling to give, and can give,

and

'and will give *less*. But the preservation of the house of DAVID, to the times of the MESSIAS, and bringing him into the world at a fix'd time, is a greater and more excellent good than the preservation of AHAZ and his people: if therefore God would fulfil that promise, much more would he fulfil this. Besides, it was (*a*) customary for the prophets to confirm the truth of all other matters by alledging the promise of the MESSIAS, which was the basis and foundation of them. Lastly, the promise of the MESSIAS comprehended in it, that *the land should be forsaken* by the two kings; and therefore both a MESSIAS to be born of a virgin, and present deliverance, were promised to the Jews by the prophet.

II. The

(*a*) Isaiah 9. Jer. 23.

II. The second prophesy mentioned by me was, *Out of Egypt have I called my son; which* MATTHEW *applies* (*b*) to JESUS's coming out of *Egypt,* and introduces with the same *form of quoting* used in the preceeding prophesy, *that it might be fulfilled which was spoken of the Lord by the prophet, saying.*

1. First, Mr. *S.* (*c*) says, that it appears by the form of quoting used, that the words of HOSEAH, which relate primarily to the children of *Israel's* being called out of *Egypt,* are *confirm'd* by JESUS's coming out of *Egypt;* that is, the coming of the children of *Israel* out of *Egypt* was a type or figure of JESUS's coming out of *Egypt;* and so the latter confirm'd the former.

2. Secondly, he says, the jewish doctors are used to detach passages from their connection, and put a sense upon them, which has no relation to what goes before or follows after, as he shows in *Thesis 9.* l. 1.

3. Thirdly, the words of the prophet are, (*d*) *when Israel was a child, then I loved him, and called my son out of Egypt.* By which my author thinks, that the prophet marks out the time of the coming of CHRIST, and may be thus understood. " When the " people of *Israel* were in their infancy as " to

---

(*b*) *Surenhusius,* p. 182, 183.
(*c*) Ib. & l. 1. Thes. 2.   (*d*) Ib. 183, 184.

" to light (which happen'd in the time of
" our Lord, when religion was wholly
" corrupted by false traditions) God called
" his son out of *Egypt* to preach the gos-
" pel in *Judea*." And *this answer*, he
*thinks ought to satisfy the Jews, being
suited to the manner of explaining scripture used by the old jewish doctors*, *whom*
MATTHEW *followed*. But if this last be not
deem'd satisfactory, Mr. *S.* has another way
of drawing out the *allegorical sense*, which
he wants for his purpose, or would find out:
and thus he interprets MATTHEW citing the
prophet. " You Jews know, that the pro-
" phet HOSEA says, *when Israel was a*
" *child, then I loved him, and called my*
" *son out of Egypt*; which words seem, ac-
" cording to their letter, to relate to the
" children of *Israel*: but I will explain
" them to you in a more useful manner,
" which is by you call'd *allegory*. I grant
" indeed, that the children of *Israel* (*e*) may
" in a sense be call'd the son of God or of
" the Lord: but if you can believe it, that
" very JESUS CHRIST, who was born a-
" mong you at *Bethlehem*, he, I say, is
" properly the son of God, who almost in
" the same manner as the children of *Israel*
" were oblig'd to go into *Egypt* on account
" of

(*e*) Exod. 4. 22. Jer. 31. 9.

[73]

"of the famine, was oblig'd to go thither
"to avoid the tyranny of HEROD. So that
"you may see, for the confirmation of your
"faith, that this did not befal the MESSIAS
"by chance, but by divine appointment, as
"it happen'd formerly to your fathers. Wherefore the prophet said, that the Lord *call'd*
"*his son out of Egypt*, and that at a time
"when you in respect of true religion were in
"a state of infancy. Besides the *form of quoting* used on this occasion, *that it might be*
"*fulfill'd which was spoken of the Lord by*
"*the prophet*, always (*f*) refers to a mystical sense hid under the literal one. But to
"say all in a word, the people of *Israel* were
"the first born adopted son of God, and Je-
"sus was the natural son of God.

III. The third prophesy mentioned by me, as not literally fulfill'd, is contain'd in these words, (*g*) *And he came and dwelt in a city call'd* Nazareth, *that it might be fulfill'd which was spoken by the prophet*, "He shall "be call'd a *Nazarene.*" Which prophesy is found by SURENHUSIUS in three places of the Old Testament, and very ingeniously explain'd by him; tho' it seems not to occur any where.

[1.] First, he observes, (*h*) that the prophets not only foretold things by *types* and *allegories*, but by *enigmas*. They foretold
things

___

(*f*) L. 3. Thes. 14. (*g*) Matt. 2. 23.
(*h*) *Surenhusius*, p. 195———204.

things by the former, when the things themselves were imply'd without any change of words; and they foretold by *enigmas* when the things were to be found out by a change of words: and when a prophesy of one or the other sort was accomplish'd, the jewish doctors used to say, *that it might be fulfill'd which was spoken.* This being so; ISAIAH (*i*) having foretold, that the MESSIAS should dwell in *Galilee*, it was almost the same thing as if he had said, the MESSIAS should dwell at *Nazareth*, which was a city of *Galilee*. It being thus foretold that the MESSIAS was to dwell at *Nazareth*, it is thereby imply'd that he should be intituled to, or call'd by the name *Nazarene*: for, tho' he was never call'd a *Nazarene*, yet being intituled to that name by dwelling at *Nazareth*, it was prophesy'd, *He shall be call'd a Nazarene*; to be call'd by a name being all one as to be intituled to a name. This enigmatical prophesy therefore of the MESSIAS's being to dwell in *Galilee*, rightly understood, was as much as to say, *He shall be call'd* (or be intituled to the name) *Nazarene*; which was fulfill'd by JESUS's dwelling at *Nazareth*.

[2.] Secondly, he conceives MATTHEW alluded also to this passage of ISAIAH, (*k*) *And there shall come forth a rod out of the stem*

(*i*) Isaiah, c. 9.
(*k*) Isaiah 11. 1. See *Lightfoot's* works, Vol. 1. p. 498.

[75]

stem of JESSE, *and a branch* (Netser) *shall grow out of his roots.* Where the argument lies in the word *Netser*; which is by the *hebrew* doctors call'd, *An argument drawn from the similitude of words, without regard had to the sense of the place*; the term *Netser*, approaching to, and therefore *enigmatically* signifying *Nazarene*. So that JESUS's dwelling at *Nazareth*, which intituled him to the name *Nazarene*, fulfill'd the prophesy, *He shall be called a Nazarene*, or Netser.

[3.] Thirdly, he cites another (*l*) text, wherein the MESSIAS is called *Tsemah*, that is to say, *a branch.* Now the word TSEMAH having the same signification with *Netser*; *Netser* may be put in the room of *Tsemah*, whereby the prophet may be said to call the MESSIAS *Netser*, which is to call him *Nazarene*.

These texts of the Old Testament are some of those, which my author, after the jewish doctors, supposes reserv'd for explanation till the times of the MESSIAS; when the *enigmas* contain'd in them were to be unridled, or the prophesies contain'd in them were to be shown to be fulfill'd.

IV. The next prophesy cited by me as not fulfill'd literally, but mystically and allegorically, is contain'd in our Saviour's (*m*) making JOHN the *Baptist* to be the ELIAS prophesy'd

---

(*l*) Zach. 6. 12.   (*m*) Matt. 11. 14.

phesy'd of as *to come* before the MESSIAS. My author (*n*) says, there was a tradition among the Jews, that ELIAS was to come before the MESSIAS; and becauſe he was not come, they could not believe the MESSIAS was come. Jeſus knowing this, told them that JOHN the *Baptiſt* was the ELIAS; who was very juſtly to be deem'd ELIAS, as having the (*o*) virtues of ELIAS. And to confirm this interpretation, my author refers to *(p)* one of his *Theſes*, where he ſhows, that, by proper names, the Jews did not always mean thoſe very perſons who are ſo nam'd, but thoſe who reſemble them in their lives and actions.

V. As to the propheſy of ISAIAH cited by JESUS *(q)* as fulfill'd in the Jews of his times, *By hearing ye ſhall hear, and ſhall not underſtand*; *that*, according to my (*r*) author, is fulfill'd as typifying, like all the jewiſh hiſtory, ſomething to happen in the times of the MESSIAS. For the ignorance and obſtinacy of the Jews being the ſame, in our Saviour's time as in the time of the prophet ISAIAH, was the *anti-type* to the *type*, or the completion of ISAIAH's propheſy.

Thus I hope, I have given ſuch a ſtate of the caſe from (*s*) SURENHUSIUS, as may qualify

---

(*n*) *Surenhuſius*, p. 329–331.   (*o*) *See* Luke 1. 17.
(*p*) 15 Theſ. de modis interpretandi.   (*q*) Matt. 13. 34, 35.   (*r*) *Surenhuſius*, p. 241, 242.
(*s*) *See* Ockley's *Letter at the end of* Wotton's *Preface to Miſcellaneous Diſcourſes,* &c.

lify the readers to judge of that *scheme* and its *rules*, which the apostles follow'd in arguing from the Old Testament, and to understand the force of the apostles arguments, which were grounded thereon. But if not; I refer them to the *Treatise* itself of SURENHUSIUS; wherein the most ingenious and learned author has set in the justest light the *rules* of reasoning used by the Jews, and follow'd by the apostles, and shown the pertinency of all the quotations made by the apostles from the Old Testament, according to those *rules*; and consequently has truly defended christianity, by showing how the apostles grounded it on the Old Testament, beyond what any author ever did before him. It is indeed possible, that in the application of the jewish *rules* of interpretation and reasoning, to the passages cited and urg'd by the apostles out of the Old Testament, he may not always have hit upon those peculiar *rules*, which the apostle had, in every citation, more particularly in view: for many of those *rules* will equally serve the same purpose; and therefore those, which he does not on some occasions make use of, may have been the *rules*, which the apostles had in view, as also those, which he does make use of, may not sometimes be the *rules*, which the apostles had immediately in view. But yet nothing can be plainer, from the reasonings of the apostles, and from the common way of reasoning used among the Jews, known

both

both by their *practice* and *rules*, as they are both explain'd with the greatest clearness by Surenhusius; than that, the apostles, who manifestly argu'd, not by scholastick rules, and interpreted not the passages they cited out of the Old Testament according to the obvious and literal sense they bore therein, did proceed by such *(t) rules* as are set forth by him.

The learned Mr. *Ockley* in a letter written to and publish'd by Dr. *Wotton*, (tt) says, *If he had an opportunity, he would certainly have gone thro' the books of the New Testament under a Jew. Whatsoever some of our gentlemen may think, this he is well assured of, that they understand it better then we do. They are throughly acquainted with all the forms of speech, and all the allusions, which (because they occur but rarely) are obscure to us, tho' in common and very familiar use among them; as has been admirably demonstrated by the learned* Surenhusius, *in his* Reconciliator.

XI.

(t) *Le Clerc.* Bibl. Choif. tom. 25. p. 413.
(tt) Wotton's *Miscell. Discourses of the Scribes and Pharisees,* &c. *at the end of the preface.*

XI.

An answer to an objection, *that the allegorical reasonings of the apostles were not design'd for absolute proofs of christianity, but for proofs* ad hominem, *to the Jews, who were accustomed to that way of reasoning.*

IT may be objected, from divers learned authors, to what I have advanc'd, "that "christianity is not grounded on the pro- "phetical or other quotations made from "the Old in the New Testament; but that "those quotations being allegorically ap- "ply'd by the authors of the New Testament, "are only arguments *ad hominem*, to con- "vince the Jews of the truth of christianity, "who allowed such a method of arguing to "be valid; and are not arguments to the rest "of mankind."

To which I answer;

1. First, that this distinction is the pure invention of those who make the objection, and has not only no foundation in the New Testament, from whence only it should be taken; but *is* utterly subverted by it. For the authors of the books of the New Testament always argue absolutely from the quotations they make out of the books of the Old Testament. MOSES and the *prophets*

are

are every where represented to be a just foundation for christianity. And PAUL expresly says, that (*u*) *the gospel which was kept secret since the world began, was now made manifest by the scriptures of the prophets* (wherein that gospel was secretly contain'd) *to all nations*, by the means of the preachers of the gospel, who gave the secret or spiritual sense of those *scriptures*. Besides, the authors of those books, being convinc'd long before the publication of them, that the gospel was to be preach'd to the Gentiles as well as Jews, must be suppos'd to design their books for the use of all men, for Gentiles as well as Jews. To both whom therefore they reason'd allegorically in those books; as particular (*w*) apostles also did in their *sermons*, therein recorded, with greater success on Gentiles than on Jews; and as PAUL did before FELIX, when he said, he took his christianity from (*x*) *the law and the prophets*, as well as before AGRIPPA. It should therefore seem strange, that *books* written to all the world by men equally concern'd to convert Gentiles as well as Jews, and *discourses* made expresly to *Gentiles* as well as to *Jews*,

should

(*u*) Rom. 16. 25, 26.
(*w*) Acts 13. 15---48. & 26. 22, 23. & 10. 37---43.
(*x*) Ib. 24. 14. Ib. 26. v. 6. & 7. 22, 23.

should be design'd to be pertinent only to Jews: much less to a very few Jews. For (*y*) from the time the Jews began to allegorize their sacred books (which was long after the captivity) there was an opposition made to that method; and the *Sadducees* in particular, who were a numerous sect, oppos'd for a considerable time before and in our Saviour's time, the new explications, and profess'd to follow the pure text of scripture, or to interpret it according to the literal sense. And tho' the *Pharisees*, who made up the body of the Jews, (as well as the *Essenes*) used the allegorical method in the times of JEsus and the Apostles; yet (*z*) they in great measure quitted that method, when christianity prevail'd, which was built on that method; and argu'd, as is well known, against the New Testament for allegorizing the *law and the prophets*. And there has been for a long time, and is at this time as little use of allegory in those respects among them, as there seems to have been during the time the books of the Old Testament

G

(*y*) *Simon.* Hist. Crit. du Vieux Test. p. 92, 97.

(*z*) Allix's *Judgment of the Jewish Church against the Unitarians*, c. 23. Simon. Ib. p. 371. Ib. Hist. Crit. du Nov. Test. p. 245. Mangey's *Remarks on* Toland's Nazarenus, p. 37. *Spencer* de Leg. Hebr. p. 185.

ment were written, which (*a*) *seem the most plain of all antient writings*; and wherein there appears not the least trace of a typical or allegorical intention in the authors, or in any other Jews of their times. All the books (*b*.) written by Jews against the christian religion,

---

(*a*) Jenkin's *Reaf.* Vol. 2. p. 153.   *Le Clerc.* Bib. Univ. tom. 10. 234.   Ib. Bib. Cho. tom. 27. p. 391, 392.   *Cuneus* Rep. des Hebr. Vol. 1. p. 377, 378, 395.

(*b*) *Scripta* Judæi in *Limborchii* Amica Collatione; & WAGENSELII *Tela Ignea Satanæ, which is a collection of Jewish Books against Christianity, wherein* Rabbi Isaac's Munimen fidei *makes the chief figure.*

Some of these are cited and answer'd by KIDDER *in his* Second *and* Third *Volumes of his* Demonstration *of the* Messias; *and others are cited by* BASNAGE *in his* Histoire de Juifs. *But the most important seem to me to be three* Spanish *Manuscripts*, 1. Fortification de la fe; *which is a translation of the aforesaid* Munimen fidei, *publish'd by* WAGENSEIL. 2. Providentia Divina de Dios con Israel, *by* SAUL LEVI MORTERA. *This* MORTERA *was the Master of the famous* SPINOZA; *and this Work of his is esteem'd by the the Jews to be the shrewdest book they have against Christianity. They are forbid, under pain of excommunication, to lend it to any christian, for fear of drawing a storm upon themselves for producing such strong objections against the christian religion. Wherefore no Copies are to be procur'd of it but by the greatest accidents.* 3. Prevenciones Divinas contra la vana Ydolatria de las gentes, *by* ISAAC OROBIO, *who was that learned Jew, that had the famous Controversy with* LIMBORCH, *concerning the truth of the christian religion mentioned above. He had been Professor of Philosophy and Physick in the Universities of* Alcala *and* Sevil, *and was a great Master in School-Divinity after the mode of the* Spanish Univer-

ligion, (some whereof are printed; and others go about *Europe* in manuscript) chiefly attack the N. Testament (*c*) for the allegorical interpretations of the Old Testament therein, and that with the greatest insolence and contempt imaginable on that account, and oppose to them a literal and single interpretation as the true sense of the Old Testament. And accordingly the (*d*) *allegorical interpretations* given by *christian expositors* of the prophecies, are now the *grand obstacle and stumbling-block in the way of the conversion of the Jews to christianity.*

2. Secondly, there will be no ground for this distinction, if we consider how much *allegory* was in use among the pagans; being cultivated by many of the philosophers themselves as well as by theologers; by some as the method of delivering doctrines; but by (*e*) most as the method of explaining away

---

Universities. The history he gave of himself, and especially of his sufferings in the Inquisition to Mr. LIMBORCH *and* LE CLERC, *is extreamly curious.* LIMBORCH *Hist. Inquis.* p. 158, 159, 223. LE CLERC, Bib. Univ. tom. 7. p. 289, &c.

(*c*) Allix's *Judgment of the Jewish Church against the Unitarians*, p. 423.

(*d*) Whiston's *Lectures*, p. 13. Mangey's *Remarks on* Toland's *Nazarenus*, p. 123.

(*e*) *Cicero* De Nat. Deor. l. 2 & 3.

Le Clerc Bibl. Chois. tom. 7. p. 80, &c. *Spencer de* legibus Hebr. p. 9.

away what, according to the letter, appear'd abſurd in the antient fables or hiſtories of their gods.

Religion itſelf was deem'd a (*f*) myſterious thing among the Pagans, and not to be publickly and plainly declar'd. Wherefore it was never ſimply repreſented to the people, but was moſt obſcurely deliver'd and vail'd under *allegories*, or *parables*, or *Hierogliphicks*; and eſpecially among the (*g*) *Egyptians, Chaldeans,* and the oriental nations. *Si quis noverit perplexè loqui, loquatur: Sin minus taceat*; was a (*h*) maxim of the Jews, but equally thought right and true by the Pagans. They allegoriz'd many things of nature, and particularly the heavenly bodies; whence came the ſaying, *tota eſt fabula cœlum*. They allegoriz'd all their (*i*) antient fables and ſtories, and pretended to diſcover in them the ſecrets of natural philoſophy, medicine, politicks, and, in a word, all arts and ſciences. The works of HOMER in particular have furniſh'd infinite materials for all ſorts of allegorical commentators to work upon;

and

(*f*) *Spencer* de legibus, p. 182, &c.
(*g*) *Simon* Hiſt. Crit. des Commentateurs, p. 4.
(*h*) Robinſon's *Natural Hiſtory of* Cumberland, &c. pt. 2. *Introd.* p. 9.
(*i*) *Clerici* Hiſt. Eccleſ. p. 23, 24.

and there is an ancient (*k*) book yet extant treating expresly of the *allegories of* HOMER, written by the famous HERACLIDES of *Pontus*.

(*l*) The *antient greek poets were reputed to involve divine, and natural, and historical notions of their gods under mystical and parabolical expressions*; and are accordingly so interpreted by the *greek scholiasts*.

The *Sybilline verses*, the *answers* given at *Oracles*, *sayings* deliver'd under *agitation*, and *dreams* (all which the antients call'd (*m*) *divinations by fury*) were seldom or ever plain, and usually receiv'd some allegorical interpretation by the skilful in divination; as did also the numerous *signs* and *prodigies*, which, in the course of things often happen'd.

The pythagorean philosophy was wholly deliver'd in mystical language; the signification whereof was intirely unknown to the world abroad, and but gradually explain'd to those of the sect, as they grew into years, or were proper to be inform'd. And in this PYTHAGORAS came up to SOLOMON's character of *wise men*, (*n*) who dealt in *dark sayings*,

---

(*k*) Apud *Gale* Opuscula Mythologica.
(*l*) Dodwell's *Letters of Advice*, &c. p. 172.
(*m*) *Cicero* de Divinatione.
(*n*) Prov. 1. 6.

sayings, and acted not much unlike the most divine teacher that ever was. Our Saviour (*o*) *spake with many parables the word unto the multitude, as they were able to hear it: but without a parable spake he not unto them: and when they were alone, he expounded all things to his disciples.*

The *stoick* philosophers are particularly famous for *allegorizing* the whole heathen theology, and all the fables of the poets. And Cicero, in the person of Balbus, (*p*) the *stoick*, gives us a curious specimen of their method in his *books* of the *nature of the gods*.

We have several (*q*) treatises of heathen philosophers on the subject of allegorical interpretation; from one of which, written by Cornutus the stoick, and from some other philosophers, *Platonists* and *Stoicks*, the famous Origen is said (*r*) to have deriv'd a great deal of his skill in allegorizing the books of the Old Testament. And Origen thought the allegorical method not only just and true in it self, but (*s*) *proper* to give *the Pagans a more exalted notion of the holy scriptures, which seem'd too low and mean*

(*o*) Mark 4. 33, 34.
(*p*) *Cicero* De Nat. Deorum, l. 2.
(*q*) *Gale* Opuscula Mythologica, &c.
(*r*) *Porphyrius* apud *Euseb.* Hist. Eccl. l. 6. c. 19.
(*s*) *Simon* Hist. Crit. du V. Test. p. 391.

mean to them, and *useful to convert the learned of his time to the christian religion.* Nor was the great St. AUSTIN less allegorical (*t*) than ORIGEN in his interpretations of scripture; in which method he greatly improv'd himself by studying platonick authors.

Many of the primitive fathers, and apologists for christianity, who for the most part wholly address themselves to Pagans, reason allegorically, not only from natural and artificial things (proving; that CHRIST was to suffer on the *cross*, from things (*u*) made after the *fashion of a cross*; that there must be (*w*) *four gospels* and no more, from the *four winds* and *four corners of the earth*; and that CHRIST was to have (*x*) *twelve apostles*, because the *gospel* was to be preach'd in the *four* parts of the world, in the name of the *Trinity*, *three* times *four* making *twelve*; and because there were (*y*) *twelve bells* which hung at the bottom of the jewish high priest's garment) but from

---

(*t*) Ib. p. 399.
(*u*) *Justin Martyr* and *Min. Felix*.
(*w*) *Irenæus*.
(*x*) St. *Austin*.
(*y*) *Justin Martyris* Opera, p. 260. *See also* MONTAGU Origines Ecclesiasticæ, *wherein there is a learned Dissertation upon the* Type TWELVE, p. 121. &c. pars posterior.

the Old Testament exactly in the same manner with the apostles; which implies, that they look'd on *allegories* to be proper topicks for Pagans: and some of them had particular reason to do so from their own experience, who while they were philosophers themselves, and before they (z) *became christians*, were accustom'd to it. It is also well known, that (a) THEOPHILUS ANTIOCHENUS, CLEMENS of *Alexandria*, (who was the disciple of PANTÆNUS) and ORIGEN, as well as the *Gnosticks*, allegoriz'd, in their explications and commentaries, the books of the New Testament; which commentaries may be justly suppos'd written for the use of Pagans as well as Jews and Christians, in order to give them all a more exalted notion of christianity, and of the New Testament.

In a word, (b) *this method of writing in matters of religion, (practis'd by apostles, companions of the apostles, and most primitive fathers) was generally used, not only among the Jews, but among the wiser and more philosophical part of the Gentiles too: and from both came to be almost universally receiv'd among the primitive christians:*
as

(z) Wake's *Prelim. to Genuine Epistles of St.* Clement, &c. p. 75.
(a) *Simon* Hist. des Comment. p. 3, 4, 5. c. 1.
(b) *Wake*, Ib. p. 71–75. *See also* Lenfant. Preface Gen. sur son Nov. Test. p. 3.

as says our most learned and judicious archbishop WAKE. And our learned (*c*) DODWELL says, that *Oneirocriticks and Hieroglyphicks, and other Pagan mystical arts of concealment*, are of *use* towards understanding the *prophetical books of the Old Testament* (the *(d) whole indulgence of God in granting the spirit of prophesy* to the Jews *being plainly accommodated to the heathen practise of divination*); and that (*e*) *the revelations of the gospel* being *made for the sake of all mankind*, its *reasonings* (which for the most part are allegorical) *were suited to the understanding of the generality of the people of that age* (and by consequence *to the people of future ages*) and in particular to that *of the philosophers*, who were the *leaders among the Gentiles*. Wherefore the arguments of the apostles were so far from being arguments *ad hominem* to the Jews, that they were then equally conclusive to great numbers among the Gentiles: and the *prophecies* cited from the Old in the New Testament, tho' (*f*) *shining in a dark place*, were a *light* both to Jews and Gentiles.

And

(*c*) Dodwell's *Letters of Advice*, &c. p. 208.
(*d*) Ib. p. 113.
(*e*) Dodwelli Prolegomena ad Stearn de Obstinatione.
(*f*) 2 Pet. 1. 19.

And I add, that almost all modern Religionists, whether Christians, Pagans, or Mahometans, are as fond of allegories, as the antients were. Which seems to make *allegorizing* the most suitable method of applying to the understanding of men. And therefore the allegorical arguments of the apostles were proper for all sorts of religious men, as well as Jews, and at present are more proper for others than Jews, (among whom there has been for a long time a direct anti-allegorical sect call'd *Caraites*) who, as they knew nothing of the allegorical method till long after the captivity, and when they became (*g*) *Hellenis'd*, so they rejected that method, as to all *prophesies* and other quotations taken from the Old Testament by the apostles, soon after the rise of christianity, and now contend for one single sense against any allegorical meaning of them, and argue against allegorical interpretations as absurd in themselves, no less than *atheists* and *deists*, and *sadducees* (who, as is before observ'd, never receiv'd (*h*) the allegorical interpretations of their Brethren-Jews) or such (rational) Christians as Mr. WHISTON: tho' herein the Jews seem to act a most inconsistent part; for

---

(*g*) *Clerici* Hist. Ecclef. p. 24.
(*h*) *Simon* Bib. Crit. Vol. 4. p. 508.

for unless they use the allegorical method, (*i*) *they will not be able to establish their own belief of a* MESSIAS *to come, which yet is one of the fundamental articles of their religion.* That article, in the judgment of the famous Rabbi (*k*) ALBO, has no other foundation than the autority of tradition. *For,* says he, *there is not any prophesy, either in the law, or the prophets, that foretels his coming by any necessary exposition of it, with respect to him, or which may not from the circumstances of the text be well explain'd otherwise.* In a word, a learned (*l*) author maintains, " that the books of " the Old Testament are of little use for " the conversion of the Jews. For almost " all which is said to be spoken in the Old " Testament of the MESSIAS must be inter" preted mystically, before it can appear to " be spoken of him, and by consequence ve" ry remotely from what the words do na" turally signify".

3. Thirdly, in answer to the objection I observe, that christianity is wholly (*m*) *reveal'd in the Old Testament*, and has its divine autority from thence; that it is not
literally,

(*i*) *Simon* Hist. Crit. du Nov. Test. p. 246, 247.
(*k*) *Albo* Oratio 1. c. 1. apud *Allix*'s Judgment of the Jewish Church against the Unitarians, p. 411.
(*l*) *Smalcius* apud Ib. p. 414.
(*m*) Dodwell's *Letters of Advice, &c.* p. 169, *&c.*

literally, but mystically or allegorically reveal'd therein; and that therefore christianity is the allegorical sense of the Old Testament, and is not improperly call'd (*n*) *mystical judaism*.

If therefore christianity is grounded on *allegory*, converted gentiles must be convinc'd by allegory, and become *allegorists* or *mystical Jews*, no less than converted Jews. For the religion itself, to which they were to be converted, was *allegory*, or christianity as taught *allegorically* in the Old Testament.

The apostle PAUL in his first *epistle to the Corinthians*, 1st and 2d chapters (*o*) (wherein it is to be observ'd, that he argues against the *greeks*, and the *philosophers*, as well as the jews) seems to disclaim all other methods of arguing besides the *allegorical*, when he says, that (*p*) *the wisdom* he *spoke* was *wisdom among them that were perfect*; that is, among them, who understood the secret, mystical, and spiritual sense of things; that his *wisdom* was the *wisdom of God, hidden* from the world, *which God had ordain'd before the world*; that is, that it was the secret, divine, and spiritual

---

(*n*) Ib. *One Altar and one Priesthood*, p. 236.
(*o*) See Whitby *on both Chapters*.
(*p*) 1 Cor. c. 1 & 2. Ib. c. 2. v. 6, 7, 8, & 10. 14, , 20, 21.

tual sense of judaism which the world that interpreted judaism literally *knew nothing of*; that this *wisdom* and method of discourse or reasoning was *reveal'd* to him and the other apostles by God, who alone *knew* his own spiritual meaning; and that the *natural man receives not* the spiritual sense of things, for they are *foolishness unto him, and cannot be known by him, because* they are not to be *discern'd* by the common rules of *wisdom* or *philosophy*, or *disputing*, but are to be *discern'd* only by a man, who has the secret, *spiritual*, or mystical meaning of things, or the rules by which to find it out, imparted (*q*) to him *by God*. In fine, is there the least ground from the literal sense in *Genesis*, to suppose (*r*) ABRAHAM's *two sons*, ISAAC and ISHMAEL, signify'd the *two covenants?* Does not St. PAUL himself call such interpretation *allegorical?* And can such a secret, spiritual, meaning of so plain a piece of history, have any other foundation than divine discernment? And what foundation is there for St. PAUL's arguing from the Old Testament, that JESUS should (*s*) *rise the third day*, but by an allegory of JONAS's being three

days

(*q*) Acts 26. 22.
(*r*) Gal. 4. 21, &c.
(*s*) 1 Cor. 15. 4.

days and three nights in the whale's belly? Which former argument could be *no argument ad hominem* to the Jews, because, as Dr. WHITBY (*t*) observes, they maintain'd their law *to be eternal*, and had not the least imagination of *two covenants*. So that I look upon all other methods of reasoning used by philosophers, except that manner of reasoning used by the apostles, and particularly by St. PAUL, to be wholly discarded, and the allegorical reasoning to be set up by them, as the true and only reasoning proper to bring all men to the *faith* of CHRIST: and the gentiles were to be wholly beat out of the literal way of arguing, and to argue as became Jews. And the event of preaching the gospel has been suited to matters consider'd in this view and light. For we know, that (*u*) *the wise* did not receive the gospel at first, and that they were the latest converts; which plainly arose from their using maxims of reasoning and disputing wholly opposite to those of christians: out of all which maxims they were indeed at length beaten by the spiritual reasoners, who have now brought the *wise* into the gospel.

4. But,

(*t*) *Whitby* in Gal. 4. v. 21.
(*u*) 1 Cor. 1. 26.

4. But, fourthly, the objection will appear to have no weight or difficulty in it, if it be consider'd, that gentiles, before they could become christians, ought to believe judaism to come from God, and to receive the jewish scriptures as of a divine autority; which, when they had once receiv'd as such, they were in an equal condition with the Jews of being converted by *type* and *allegory*. And consequently, all the *typical* and *allegorical* arguments of the apostles from the *law*, the *psalms*, the *history*, and the *prophets* of the Old Testament, were of equal force to Gentiles as to Jews; among whom they were in effect included with respect to these arguments. Nay, it seems very probable, that the allegorical arguments of the apostles from the Old Testament, as being divine and most sublime arguments, and (*w*) *infinitely better* than all human reasonings, did of themselves, or with little use of other topicks, convince the gentile-christians at the same time, both of the autority and divinity of the Old Testament, and of the truth of christianity. Which matter may not perhaps be untruly illustrated by the case of St. LUKE. He is judg'd by many learned divines to have been

a

(*w*) Bentley's *Sermon on Revelation and the Messias*, p. 30.

a *gentile convert*; and, being a great companion of St. *Paul*, was no doubt instructed by him in the *Cabala* of the Jews, and in the sublime sense of the Old Testament. Accordingly we find St. Luke, in his gospel, and *Acts*, representing the grounds of christianity, and arguing for it, in the same typical manner, from the Old Testament, with St. Paul and the other *apostles*, who were originally Jews: in which two books he may not untruly be suppos'd, to declare the grounds of his own conviction, and to design to represent those grounds to other *Gentiles*, as sufficient for their conviction also. But the (x) preaching of St. Peter to Cornelius puts the matter past dispute. He declares to him that *word which* had been *publish'd thro' all Judea*, that is, the gospel as founded on the Old Testament, and as preach'd to the Jews. He then gives a relation of the life and actions, and of the sufferings, death, and resurrection of Jesus, and of his *commands* to his disciples. And concludes with saying, *To* Jesus *give all the prophets witness, that thro' his name, whosoever believeth in him shall receive remission of sins.* Which is just the same way of arguing used throughout the New Testament to mere Jews.

PART

(x) Acts 10. 37, 38 —— 41, 42, 43.

Part II.

Containing Considerations *on the Scheme which* Mr. Whiston *sets up in Opposition to the allegorical Scheme.*

I.

Mr. Whiston's *Scheme represented; which consists chiefly in maintaining; that the Hebrew and Greek of the Old Testament agreed in the times of* Jesus *and the apostles; that the apostles cited exactly and argu'd literally from the Greek or Septuagint Translation; and that since their times both these copies of the Old Testament have been corrupted by the Jews, which makes it seem as if the apostles had not argu'd literally from the Old Testament; and in proposing, by various means to restore the Text thereof as it stood in the days of* Jesus *and his apostles.*

MR. WHISTON highly condemns the *allegorical scheme* when used in explaining the *prophesies* cited out of the Old

in the New Testament. In his *Boylean Lectures* he says, (a) *If a double sense in prophesies be allow'd by us christians, as to those predictions, which were to be fulfill'd in our Saviour* CHRIST, *and if we own that we can no otherwise shew their completion, than by applying them secondarily and typically to our Lord, after they had in their first and* primary intention been already plainly fulfill'd in the times of the Old Testament, *we lose all the real advantages of the ancient prophesies, as to the proofs of our common christianity*, and take a method which *exposes* the christian *religion to the laughter of infidels.* In the book before us, he calls the (b) *allegorical scheme weak and enthusiastical, and one of the most ill-grounded and pernicious things that ever was admitted by christians*: and he speaks of it, as *a great reproach to the gospel*, and tending to *harden the Jews in their infidelity*; tho' he confesses, that taking the present text of the Old Testament for genuine, *it is impossible to expound or apologize for the* apostle's *application* of the prophesies they cite from *the Old Testament upon any other foundation*: and he particularly calls
the

(a) Whiston's *Boylean Lectures*, p. 16, 20, 29.
(b) Whiston's *Essay, &c.* p. 92.

the *hypotheses* or allegorical scheme discover'd and explain'd by SURENHUSIUS *absurd* and *ridiculous*.

I shall therefore consider, how Mr. WHIS-TON mends the matter, and what scheme of things he would set up in the room of what he calls the *absurd* allegorical scheme; which he owns to be founded on the present text of the Old Testament.

He contends, that the (c) apostles made their quotations out of the Old Testament *rightly* and *truly*, from the *Septuagint*; which was in their times in vulgar use, and then (d) *agreed with the hebrew*; and that as they made exact quotations, so they argu'd justly and logically from the obvious and literal sense of the said quotations, as they then stood in the Old Testament: but that since their times both the Hebrew and Septuagint copies of the Old Testament have been so *greatly* (e) *corrupted*, and so many *apparent disorders* and *dislocations* introduc'd therein, so as to occasion many *remarkable differences, inconsistencies*, and *contradictions*, between the Old and New Testament, in respect to the words and sense of the quotations made from the Old in the New Testament; all which *corruptions* of

H 2 the

(c) Whiston's *Essay*, &c. p. 12; 16, 87, 176; 281; 328. (d) Ib. p. 3. (e) 182; 262; 263.

the Old Testament, and *differences* and *inconsistencies* between the Old and New Testament he accounts for in the following manner. He says, that the (*f*) Jews did in the second century *greatly corrupt* and alter both the Hebrew and Septuagint copies of the Old Testament, and especially with respect to the places cited in the New Testament, out of opposition to christianity, and with express (*g*) design to make the reasonings of the apostles from the Old Testament inconclusive and ridiculous; that the Jews did in the third century give ORIGEN one of these corrupted copies of the *Septuagint*, which ORIGEN, mistaking for genuine, put into his *Hexapla*, and thereby occasion'd the christians to receive that corrupted copy, instead of the authentick copy they had before among them; that, in the latter end of the fourth century, the Jews put into the hands of christians, who till that time had been almost universally (*h*) ignorant of the Hebrew tongue, a copy of the Old Testament in Hebrew corrupted like the *Septuagint*, which copy they greedily receiv'd as a great treasure from the Jews; and that therefore the disagreement between the Old and New Testament

---

(*f*) 220. (*g*) p. 19, 112, 254, 264, &c.
(*h*) Ib. p. 224.

ment in respect both to the exactness and sense of the said quotations, has no place between the genuine text (now not existing in any copy) of the Old Testament, but only between the present corrupted text of the Old Testament and the New Testament. And therefore, in order to justify the arguments and reasonings of the apostles, he proposes to *restore* the *text of the Old Testament* as it stood before the days of Origen, and as it stood in the days of Jesus and his apostles. From which *text*, so *restor'd*, he doubts not, but that it will appear, that the apostles cited exactly, and argued justly and logically, from the Old Testament.

The method by which he proposes to restore us the *true text* of the Old Testament, or a new and better bible, than that we have, is (not by the means of any one entire copy that has been lost, and is now found by him, but) by the help of (i) the *Samaritan Pentateuch*; the *Greek psalms*, as attested by the *Roman psalter*; the *antiquities* of Josephus; the *present Hebrew text*, the *several Greek editions and manuscripts* of the Septuagint *version*, and the *ancient translations made from it*; the *old Syriac version*, made from the *Hebrew before the copies of the Hebrew were so cor-*
rupt

(i) Ib. p. 329.

rupt as they now are; the *Chaldee Paraphrases*; the *remains of the later Greek versions*, particularly those of Aquila, Theodotion, and Symmachus; the *works* of Philo; the *remains of the old italick or vulgate version*; the *apostolick constitutions*; the *fathers* and *hereticks*, who liv'd *before, or not long after the days* of Origen; the *hebrew copies that have never come into the hands of the* Masoretes; and the *greek copies* of the Septuagint version, *read in churches in the first ages of christianity, or any parts of them*; and, above all, by the help of *criticism*, whereby he alters some passages, and changes the places of others, which he supposes (k) *dislocated*.

Upon this scheme, which consists of great variety of parts, I shall make the following observations; some of which will, in my opinion, show *it* to labour under as great difficulties as Mr. Whiston and others suppose the *allegorical scheme* attended with, and should lead them either back to the *allegorical scheme* or to some other *scheme* which may better account for all the seeming differences, and want of connection between the notions in the Old and New Testament.

II.

(k) Ib. p. 229. *and divers other places.*

II.

That it is incredible, that the Old Testament *should be so corrupted as Mr.* WHISTON *asserts.*

IT seems incredible, that ORIGEN (who was certainly a good man and good christian, as well as the most learned apologist of all the ancients for christianity) and other christians of his time; should be capable of having their (*l*) *vulgar greek Bible*, or Old Testament (of which the gentiles had copies as well as the christians) taken from them, or of letting it drop into oblivion and be lost, which inconteftably prov'd the truth of christianity by exactly recording the passages cited from thence in the New Testament by the apostles, and by manifesting to all intelligent readers, that the apostles cited, interpreted, and argu'd from, those passages justly and truly; and should receive an Old Testament, (and that with the greatest applause for its integrity, and as *a standard text*) from enemies, which subverted the truth of christianity, by making the apostles, to all appearance, cite falsely, and argue falsely from the books of the Old Testa-

---

(*l*) *Pezron* Defence de l'Antiquite des tems, p. 304.

Testament. This was being impos'd on in religion, and sacrificing christianity, which was dearer to them than their lives, in too gross a manner to be conceiv'd. The christians of old were capable of having several gross things put upon them by dishonest people among themselves; (*m*) (*lying for God and religion being deem'd by many, either no crime at all, or, however, a very pardonable one; if not perhaps meritorious*): as for example, the (*n*) story of the *Cells* at *Alexandria*, and other lyes which they receiv'd and improv'd from the Jews; who were such celebrated *lyars*, that a (*o*) *lyar* and a *Jew* signify'd the same thing: the (*p*) history of the *Phenix* to illustrate and prove the resurrection: the (*q*) account of St. JOHN's being boil'd in a cauldron of oyl, and coming out unhurt: and his constant (*r*) lifting up and stirring the earth over his grave, as a man in sleep does his bed-cloaths, to prove JOHN alive, as it was suppos'd to be foretold by JESUS in the gospel he should be

---

(*m*) Ib. p. 224.
(*n*) *Justin Martyr*, aliiq;
(*o*) *Juvenal* Satir. 6. v. 546.   *Rutil.* Itinerat. l. 1. v. 393. *See also Simon* Suppl. aux Cerem. des Juifs, p. 12.
(*p*) *Clement.* Epist. ad Corint.
(*q*) *Tertullian.* De Præscript. c. 46.
(*r*) S. *Austin* in John 21. 22, 23.

[105]

be till JESUS *came* again: (s) the transactions between PETER and SIMON MAGUS, and other sham-miracles: forg'd (t) gospels, and books under the names of the apostles: divers forg'd (u) passages put into authors and books (w) corrupted and forg'd in favour of christianity and *orthodoxy*: the (x) account of a statue erected by the Romans to SIMON MAGUS as a god, and of worship paid to him by them: and that impudent forgery of the *sybilline oracles* (wherein the history and doctrines of the gospels were taught by suppos'd ancient pagan prophetesses in as clear a manner as in the New Testament itself; and the doctrines of the christians, in that age, wherein the *sybilline oracles* were forg'd, more clearly than in the New Testament) which the ancient christians so generally receiv'd as to be call'd by the heathens in contempt (y) *Sybillists*: to which may be
added,

(s) Apostol. Const. l. 6. c. 9. *Arnobius*, l. 2. p. 64. *Le Clerc*. B. C. tom. 4. p. 203.

(t) Vid. *Fabricii* Cod. Apoc. N. T.

(u) Ap. *Josephi* Antiq. & *Luciani* Opera.

(w) Patres Antiqur. *Hermes Trismegistes, Hystaspes, Orpheus, Aristoteles* de Pomo. James's *Corruption of the Fathers*. Whiston's *Essay on the Apost. Const.* p. 158, 675, &c. Ib. *Pref. to Letter* to Earl of Nott. p. 9, &c. Ib. ATHANASIUS *convicted of forgery*. RUFINUS, JEROM, and CASSIODORE, *were remarkable forgers for the benefit of* Orthodoxy.

(x) *Justin Martyr*, aliiq; Patres.

(y) *Origen* contra *Celsum*, l. 5.

added, the fabulous and lying accounts of *numbers of martyrs*, which even the credulous and superstitious DODWELL has in some measure expos'd in his (z) *dissertation concerning the paucity of the martyrs*; being restrain'd from proceeding farther from his (a) *great veneration for the goodness and piety of several of the fathers, who*, he says, *were too easy of belief of matter of fact, not sufficiently attested.*

They might be, I say, and were capable of having such things impos'd on them in favour of christianity, but cannot be deem'd capable of having such a gross matter (b) against christianity impos'd on them, as that beforemention'd. And it seems much more reasonable to suppose, that there has been no such corruption of the *sacred text* of the Old Testament, and no such imposition of Jews on Christians, as Mr. WHISTON (and that without just proofs) pretends; but rather, that the apostles cited, interpreted, and argu'd from, the Old Testament after that allegorical manner they seem now to have done; especially, since the authors of the books of the New Testament, and all the first fathers, and ORIGEN in particular,

do

(z) Apud Dissert. Cyprianicas.

(a) *Four Letters between the Bishop of* Sarum *and Mr.* Dodwell, p. 29, 30.

(b) Lightfoot's works, Vol. 1. p. 375.

do undoubtedly often *allegorize* the books of the Old Testament (as (*c*) Mr. WHISTON himself allows both the apostles and fathers do in all other cases but that of *prophesies*); and since they all seem to look on allegorical reasoning as a method no less conclusive, than by rational proofs, nay to be a truly rational way of reasoning, and to look on reasoning from the letter to be mean and low.

This will appear yet stronger, if it be consider'd, that, as the (*d*) body of christians had the *septuagint* version, which was read in their churches, among them, from the time of JESUS, so there were many among the primitive christians who understood *hebrew*. MATTHEW is said by all the fathers to have wrote his gospel in hebrew for the use of such christians who understood hebrew: the (*e*) *nazarean* christians, who were skilful in the hebrew tongue, constantly used the hebrew books of the Old Testament, as well as the hebrew of MATTHEW's gospel: IGNATIUS, PAPIAS, HEGESIPPUS, and other Ancients, used the *gospel according to the Hebrews*, which was written in hebrew:

(*c*) Whiston's *Boylean Lect.* p. 27, 43, 51. Ib. *Essay*, &c. p. 92.
(*d*) *Petron* Defen. de l'Antiq. des Tems, p. 304. Origen Hom. 1. in Cant. Cant.
(*e*) *Epiphan.* Her. 29.

brew: the church of *Cesarea* in *Palestine* used the hebrew of Matthew's gospel, a copy whereof was, as Jerom (*f*) informs us, preserv'd to his time in the library of *Cesarea*, collected by Pamphilus the martyr: the church of *Alexandria* receiv'd a copy of Matthew's gospel in hebrew from Pantænus: and *Origen*, who was learned in the hebrew tongue, plac'd the *hebrew text*, (which he look'd on as authentick, tho' (*g*) *agreeable to the present* [suppos'd corrupt] *hebrew text*), as well as the present [suppos'd corrupt] Septuagint, and the several greek versions made from the [suppos'd corrupt] hebrew, in his famous *Hexapla*; a work receiv'd by the church in his time, with the (*h*) *greatest applause*. All which should seem to be sufficient security against the Jews making any alterations in the hebrew text to the prejudice of christianity. Besides, we are inform'd by (*i*) Tertullian, that the books of the Old Testament in hebrew, which the Jews presented to Ptolemy King of *Egypt*, were shewn in his time among the curiosities of the *Ptolomean library*; which, as well as the Septuagint version, preserv'd in the same library,

---

(*f*) *Hierom* Desc. Ecc. in Mat.
(*g*) Whiston's *Essay*, p. 297.
(*h*) Hody de Text. Origin. l. 3. pt. 1. c. 4.
(*i*) *Tertulliani* Apologeticus, c. 18.

ry, must hinder the Jews from being able to corrupt the Old Testament, as charg'd upon them by Mr. WHISTON, without being detected.

In fine, no one could well imagine that the primitive christians, and ORIGEN in parricular, should be capable of such a degree of stupidity to be so impos'd on, but Mr. WHISTON; who, notwithstanding the ancient fathers do *(k)* unanimously affirm, that St. MATTHEW's gospel was originally written, and was extant among them in hebrew, yet *(l)* maintains, they were all mistaken in that fact; which one would think, some of, if not all, those ancient fathers should know to be true. For no *real* instances of the monstrous corruptions, and impositions, and folly, and ignorance, and negligence, prevalent among christians: not even the loss of ORIGEN's *Hexapla*, a work so useful to all learned christians: nor the loss of CLEMENT's *epistle to the Corinthians* (a book esteem'd *(m) canonical* by the ancients) for many hundred years, and but lately brought to light: nor even the taking the bible out of the hands of the people both of the Greek and Latin church;

(k) Simon Hist. Crit. du Nov. Test. c. 5.
(l) Whiston's *Essay*, p. 182.
(m) Wake's *Prelim. Disc. to Genuine Epistles, &c.* p. 117.

church; which was submitted to as a piece of true religion by them, who, very naturally thought their priests better guides, than God in his word, appealing to their own understandings: I say, none of these seem equal to the imposition abovemention'd.

Besides, it is so far from being evident, that the *Septuagint*, as it was in the hands of christians before ORIGEN wrote his HEXAPLA, was uncorrupt; and that ORIGEN contributed to render it corrupt; that on the contrary, it is manifest, that *(n)* ORIGEN found the *Septuagint* in a very corrupt state, and did really restore a better text in innumerable places, and that to the satisfaction of many christians, who approv'd of and used his text as a *standard text*, without thinking in the least, that they were depriv'd of any argument for the truth of christianity, that had been urg'd from former copies of the *Septuagint.*

III. *That*

(n) See GRABE *de vitiis 70 Inter. ante Ævum* ORIGINIS, & *de Remediis ab ipso adhibitis in ejusdem Hexaplari Editione:* And *Montfaucon* Prelimin. ad Originis Hexapla. c. 4.

III.

That to suppose the Old Testament so corrupted, as Mr. WHISTON asserts, is to give up christianity to Jews and Infidels.

CAN any thing tend more to expose *christianity* to the contempt of *Jews and Infidels*, and to justify all unbelievers in rejecting it, than to suppose as Mr. *W.* does, christianity not grounded on the present Old Testament, and therefore false, if consider'd as having its dependance thereon?

Do not the Jews take it for granted on vulgar tradition among themselves, that they have a true copy of the books of the Old Testament? And do not all Infidels take it for granted, upon the vulgar tradition of Jews and Christians, that the present books of the Old Testament are the very books, upon which, not only Jews, but Christians ground their religion? And will not both Jews and Infidels think the cause of christianity sufficiently weak, if christians once allow, that the New Testament depends not on the [present] Old Testament, contrary to what christians have for many ages past asserted, and to what the primitive fathers and the apostles themselves, according to all appearance, asserted before them? It has
been

been thought by divines (*o*) to be of very ill confequence to religion, to fuppofe any alterations have been made in the Old Teftament; and PEREIRA, HOBBES, SPINOZA, SIMON, and others, have been feverely cenfur'd, as giving up or attacking the bible, for afferting, that fome few interpolations, tho' not relating to the effentials of religion, have been made therein. Of how great confequence then, muft fuch alterations be deem'd, which affect the very being and reafon of chriftianity?

Are not all unbelievers of chriftianity juftify'd for rejecting it, from the time the true copy of the Old Teftament was *loft* among chriftians, to the time Mr. *W.* publifh'd his (*p*) *Boylean Lectures* and his *Effay towards reftoring the true text of the Old Teftament*; wherein it is fuggefted to the world, that our prefent text is not the *true text of the Old Teftament* in refpect to thofe places, on which the apoftles ground the truth of chriftianity? For if the grounds and reafons for chriftianity, contain'd in the Old Teftament were *loft*, chriftianity was then *loft*.

And may not men ftill juftly reject chriftianity? For can it be the duty of men to in-

---

(*o*) *Kidderi* Epift. ad *J. Clericum* apud Bib. Choif. tom. 4. p. 379.
(*p*) Whifton's *Boyl. Lect.* p. 30. 67—72.

[113]

inquire after a *lost* book (and that impossible now to be recover'd) in order to find out, whether christianity had any solid grounds or no at first, when all the present appearances are, according to Mr. *W.* that it had no solid grounds? Or can men reasonably *suppose* without proof (for really that is all Mr. *W.* has to support his *hypothesis*, to which he seems merely driven by the conceiv'd *absurdity* of the *allegorical hypothesis*; arguing herein like (*q*) FAUSTUS the manichæan bishop, who thought MATTHEW and LUKE interpolated and corrupted on account of the difficulties in their several genealogies of JESUS, and of their contradictions to one another; and also JOHN's (*r*) gospel corrupted, wherein CHRIST says, MOSES *wrote of him*, because he could find no such passage in the books of MOSES) I say, can men reasonably suppose, without proof, that the apostles cited, interpreted, and argu'd justly from the Old Testament, when we see (as Mr. *W.* says) they did not; taking them to have cited, interpreted, and argu'd from the present Old Testament?

Lastly, may not Mr. *W.* as well hope to convert Jews and Infidels by *allegorical reasoning* from the Old Testament, how *weak* and *enthusiastical* soever that may seem to him

---

(*q*) *Faustus* apud August. contra Faust. l. 3. c. 1.
(*r*) Ib. l. 16. c. 2. *See also* l. 18. c. 3. & l. 32. c. 1.

him to be, as by a *loft* bible, now to be recover'd by *criticism*? Nay, may he not have better hopes, since that was manifestly the method of arguing used by the apostles and first fathers (by his own (s) confession in all other cases, but that of *Prophesies*) and has been deem'd (also by his own confession) to have been the method used by all christians, in all cases, from the days of JEROM, that is, from the end of the fourth century to this day: during which time christianity has greatly prevail'd over the world; tho' standing on allegorical reasons, that is, according to Mr. *W.* on (t) *weak and enthusiastical reasons*; tho' (u) *the Hebrew and Septuagint have been put upon the wrack, and even tortur'd by the criticks, to see if by any violence the citations* of the apostles from the Old Testament *can be made to accord with the texts cited*; tho' *the truly judicious and impartial know, that this has been hitherto done with little success*; and tho' the Old and New Testament *are in an irreconcilable state, to the great perplexity of good christians, and the open scandal of Jews and Infidels?*

If

(s) Whiston's *Boylean Lectures,* p. 67.   Ib. *Essay,* p. 91, 92.
(t) Ib. p. 92.
(u) Ib. p. 28s.

If therefore men have been converted to christianity by the books of the New Testament, or by the writings of christians, they have been converted by the jewish allegorical method of arguing from the Old Testament.

Typical and allegorical reasoning was deem'd so strong and useful by the most eminent of the primitive apologists for christianity, towards the conversion of Pagans, that they use this following argument to them, which I shall give you in the words of JUSTIN MARTYR, who urges it in its full strength; referring you farther to (*w*) TERTULLIAN, (*x*) MINUTIUS FELIX, and others. Says Justin to the pagans, (*xx*) *The cross is the characteristick of* CHRIST's *power and government, and is visible almost in every thing we see: for cast your eyes upon the world, and tell me, whether any thing is transacted, any commerce maintain'd without the resemblance of a cross. Without this trophy of ours, you cannot go to sea; for navigation depends upon sails, and they are made in the fashion of a cross. There is neither ploughing, nor digging, nor any handicraft work perform'd, without in-*

struments

(*w*) *Tertulliani* Apol. c. 6.
(*x*) *Reeves's* Apol. Vol. 2. p. 144, &c.
(*xx*) Ib. Vol. 1. p. 97.

struments of this figure; nay a man is distinguish'd from a beast by the uprightness of his body, and the extension of his arms, and the prominency of the nose he breathes thro', which are all representations of the cross, in allusion to which the prophet speaks, (y) the breath of our nostrils Christ the Lord. *Moreover, your banners declare the power of this figure, and the trophies you use every where in your publick processions, are symbols of power and dominion, altho' in your practice you have no regard to the reason of the figure; and the images of your departed Emperors you consecrate upon* Cross-like *engines, and inscribe them Gods. Since therefore we invite you by reason and the ceremony of the* Cross, *so much in vogue among you, we know we shall be blameless for the future, whether you embrace the christian faith or not, for we have done our best* (that is, we have argu'd typically and allegorically with you) *to make you christians.*

The fam'd Irenæus proves; that there cannot be more, nor fewer than (z) four gospels; *because there are four corners of the*

(y) Lament.
(z) *Irenæus*, l. 3. c. 11. Vide *Feuardentii* Annot. in locum.

the world, and four principal winds, and from many other such topicks. And an eminent critick (*a*) observes of all the primitive fathers, that they, *omnia gentium facta, dicta, scripta ita interpretabantur ut ea omnia proposito suo accommodarent, aliquando contra gentium mentem.*

But what seems surprizing, Mr. *W.* himself is not inferior to IRENÆUS in typical argumentation; by arguing in the same manner, and with the same strength for the *apostolical constitutions* (which is with him *the most sacred book* of the New Testament) as IRENÆUS does for the *four gospels. These* (*b*) *constitutions*, says he, *appear plainly to be genuine, and to be deriv'd by the apostles from our Saviour, because they have those distinguishing characters belonging to divine appointments, which those parallel settlements under the law of* MOSES, *that were undoubtedly divine, exhibit to us.* He mentions these following among others, *as some of the most obvious particulars.*

1. *As the jewish laws, those in particular which typify'd the christian dispensation, were given, as to place, on a mountain,* Sinai; *and as to time, in just forty*

(*a*) *Def. Heraldus in Tertullian. Apol.* p. 77.
(*b*) Whiston's *Essay on the Apostol. Constit.* p. 172.

[118]

forty days space: So were these CONSTITUTIONS *or christian laws given as to* place, *on a mountain*, Sion; (for which imaginary place of the delivery of his imaginary apostolick constitutions, he can have no (c) proof;) *and as to time, in just forty days space also,* (for which imaginary term he has equal proofs) *before our Lord's final ascension. And these circumstances are so observable under the gospel, that memorials both of the place and time continu'd many ages in the christian church* (which memorials are likewise without proof); *and by them the ancient types and prophesies were eminently fulfill'd, as 'tis easy to observe from what has been said.*

2. *As the whole body of the laws of* MOSES *seem to have been divided into two main branches, the one* secret, *but the other* open, *and publish'd to the whole world, written for their daily use, and put into every body's hands, nay part of it at least written in pillars also;* (which first branch has no foundation in the bible, and is the mere invention of modern Jews, who, a great deal above a thousand years after MOSES, publish'd an *oral Law*, which they pretended had been *secretly* given to MOSES at mount *Sinai*, at the same time that
the

(c) See his pretended *Proofs*, c. 1.

the written Law was given;) so it was more certainly as to the laws of Christ. *That part which is contain'd in the books of the New Testament being in like manner open to all, and constantly read in families and publick assemblies; but the other part, contain'd in these books, intrusted secretly with the governors of the church, as the proper rule of their publick courts, assemblies, and administrations, as we have already seen.*

He has other such typical considerations, which I omit, referring my reader to them. I shall only observe, upon these two cited, that Mr. *W.* by much out-typifies Irenæus: for Irenæus only makes things which are suppos'd to have a real existence, and have a similitude in some respect, to be *type* and *antitype*: But Mr. *W.* invents things first, and then invents *type* and *anti-type*.

If Mr. *W.* therefore will duely consider the constant practise and great success of allegorical argumentation, and the mighty force of allegorical and typical arguments upon himself; he need not have recourse to the supposition of a *lost* Old Testament to avoid the *allegorical hypothesis*; nor need he be so apprehensive of the (*d*) *insults* and re-

---

(*d*) Whiston's *Boylean Lect.* p. 16, 20, 29. Ib. *Essay, &c.* p. 92.

reproaches of *Jews* and *Infidels* on that account, who have never been able to withstand the success of that *hypothesis*; but should rather apprehend and fear their *insults* and *reproaches* upon himself, who proceeds with them on the supposition of a *lost* Old Testament.

IV.

That Mr. WHISTON *is not able to restore one prophetical quotation made out of the* Old *in the* New Testament, *so as to make that literally apply'd which now seems allegorically apply'd.*

BUT to confute Mr. *W*'s hypothesis effectually, I observe, that he is not able, either by the means of various readings drawn from the sources beforemention'd, or by critical emendations, or by taking out passages, or by placing right suppos'd dislocated passages, or by all these together, so to *restore* any *citations* of *prophesies* made from the Old Testament and said to be fulfill'd in the New, as to make them obviously, and literally, and agreeably to the context where he places them, relate to the purposes, for which they are cited by the authors of the New Testament. And if he is not, then is his *Hypothesis* a vain *Hypothesis*, and serves no purpose whatsoever; unless

[121]

unless he thinks it sufficient to *suppose*, from the mere authority of the New Testament, the *citations* pertinent in his sense, without being able to show, that it is possible for any one of them to be so; and then he need not have wrote his *Essay* to *restore the true text of the Old Testament*.

I shall go thro' those few citations of prophesies made from the Old Testament, and said to be fulfill'd in the New, which he produces in his *Essay*, and pretends so to place in the Old Testament as to make them relate, in their obvious sense, to the purposes for which they are alledg'd by the authors of the New.

1. I begin with that of St. MATTHEW, who on occasion of our Saviour's being carry'd into *Egypt*, and being brought back, says, this was done, (e) *that it might be fulfill'd which was spoken of the Lord by the prophet, saying*, " Out of Egypt have I " call'd my Son."

Upon which words Mr. *W.* (f) very justly observes, that St. MATTHEW's citation, " Out of Egypt have I call'd my Son," *no where now appears in the Old Testament as apply'd to the Son of God or* MESSIAS, *either in Hebrew or Greek; but is word for word in*

(e) Matt. 2. 15.
(f) Whiston's *Essay*, p. 88.

in HOSEA, *where it is apply'd to the people of Israel, whom God, by* MOSES, *had antiently* call'd *or* brought *out of Egypt.* Which passage is therefore suppos'd by all *christian commentators* (and perhaps by all christians but himself) to be taken from HOSEA by St. MATTHEW, and to be apply'd by him in a secondary or allegorical sense to JESUS's being *call'd out of Egypt.*

Where then does Mr. *W.* place these words in the Old Testament so as to make St. MATTHEW cite and apply them according to the obvious and literal sense, which they be arin the Old Testament, that is, according to Mr. *W.* pertinently?

He (g) *conjectures,* MATTHEW *had in his eye this noble prophesy of* ISAIAH *concerning the* MESSIAH; which I shall set down, according to the present copy of ISAIAH in one column, and according to Mr. *W*'s amendment, by the force of criticism, in the other.

Isaiah

(g) Whiston's *Essay,* p. 90.

[123]

Isaiah 41. 8, 9.	Whiston, *p.* 91.
But thou Israel art my servant, JACOB, *whom I have chosen, the seed of* ABRAHAM, *my friend. Thou whom I have taken from the ends of the earth; and* called *thee from the chief men there f, and said unto thee, Thou art my servant, I have chosen and not cast thee away.*	Thou Israel art my Son: I have chosen thee: the seed of Abraham my friend. Whom I have taken from the borders of the land, and *called thee out of Egypt,* and said, Thou art my Son, I have chosen thee, and not cast thee way.

Now let this passage of ISAIAH, wherein Mr. *W.* by conjecture puts in the words *out of Egypt,* instead of the more general words *from the chief men,* be suppos'd to be the passage referr'd to by St. MATTHEW (which yet I presume not one reader will allow); how does the literal and obvious sense thereof in ISAIAH appear to concern JESUS's coming *out of Egypt,* any more than the obvious and literal sense of the passage in HOSEA? Does not the whole chapter in ISAIAH as plainly concern the body of the Jews, spoken of in the text under the term *Son,* as the chapter of HOSEA, where the Jews are spoken of under the same term *Son*? And does

[124]

does not (*b*) *Grotius* so interpret the place; tho' he conjectures with Mr. *W.* that the prophet had *Egypt* in his view, as (*i*) others do *Chaldea*?

It is certain, that the words of Isaiah are literally and obviously applicable to the *past* calling of the Jews out of *Egypt*. And if so, it is not reasonable to make them a *prophesy*, and to relate to the future calling of Jesus out of *Egypt*, which seems very remote from the thoughts of the prophet, who has no one circumstance in the whole chapter to lead an unprejudic'd reader into such a thought. And therefore, if these words of Isaiah are referr'd to by St. Matthew, commentators will be no less oblig'd to consider them as apply'd by St. Matthew in a secondary or allegorical sense, than they do the words of Hoseah; to *which* it cannot well be doubted St. Matthew does refer, they being the express words of Hoseah, and no where else to be found in all the Old Testament.

2. The next quotation, which Mr. *W.* (*k*) endeavours to place right in the Old Testament is contain'd in these words of St. Matthew. (*l*) *Then was fulfill'd that which was*

(*b*) *Grotius* in locum.
(*i*) *White* in locum, p. 297.
(*k*) Whiston's *Essay*, p. 93.
(*l*) Matt. 27. 9.

was spoken by Jeremy *the prophet, saying,*
"And they took the thirty pieces of silver,
"the price of him, that was valu'd, whom
"they of the children of Israel did value;
"and gave them for the potter's field, as the
"Lord appointed me."

Now this quotation is not in Jeremy the prophet, but is (*m*) thought to be in Zachary; where, according to its literal and obvious sense, it bears not that meaning, which St. Matthew puts upon it; and where in Mr. *W*'s opinion, (*n*) it *hardly bears any good sense at all.*

What is it now Mr. *W*. does on this occasion?

He *believes*, (*o*) that St. Matthew *cited what was then in his copy, not out of* Zachary, *but* Jeremy: and he *believes, that not only this prediction, but several others, now inserted in* Zachary, *really belong to* Jeremy. *Belief* is a notable proof! But granting this prophesy, now to be found in Zachary, did, in St. Matthew's time, exist in Jeremy; why does he not plant this quotation in some particular place of Jeremy? For till that be done, we cannot judge of the pertinency of it. To suppose it pertinent without giving it a place in Jeremy,

---

(*m*) Whiston, Ib. p. 94. Zach. 11. 3, 12.
(*n*) Whiston, Ib. p. 95. (*o*) p. 94.

REMY, is to beg the question about the pertinency of the apostles quotations in their literal sense. He says, the quotation is (*p*) *good sense*, as it is cited in St. MATTHEW. But how does that show it to be apply'd according to the literal sense it bears in JEREMY? And yet this is all Mr. *W*. does towards placing this quotation, or *restoring* the *true text* of JEREMY, in this instance.

But to set the matter of this quotation in its due light, and effectually to confute any chimerical scheme of placing this quotation in our present book of JEREMY, or in any other authentick book of JEREMY; it appears, that it cannot be plac'd in him, but by such a method as will place any quotations, or prophesies, in him. For the quotation was made from an *Apocryphal Book*, *ascrib'd* to JEREMY, as JEROM (*q*) assures us, who *saw* and read that *Apocryphal Book*.

I add here, by the way, that the *Syriac* and *Persic* versions, and those *other copies* of St. MATTHEW, which have (*r*) *not the name* of the prophet, but barely mention *the prophet*, seem corrupted on purpose to make St. MATTHEW not guilty of citing JEREMY

(*p*) Whiston's *Essay*, p. 95.
(*q*) *Hieron*. apud *Grabe* Spicil. Sec. 1. p. 135.
(*r*) *Kidder's* Demonst. of the Messias, Vol. 2. p. 196, 197.

[127]

remy falsely; the translators or transcribers, either not knowing whence St. Matthew had this citation, or thinking that St. Matthew should not have cited a book forg'd under Jeremy's name, as a book of the *prophet* Jeremy.

3. A third prophesy, which Mr. *W.* endeavours rightly to place and regulate in the Old Testament, so as to make it pertinently apply'd, is the famous *prophesy* cited by St. Matthew, " Behod a virgin shall be with " child, *&c.*

He owns, (*s*) that the words cited by St. Matthew, " Behold a virgin shall be " with child, and shall bring forth a son, " and shall call his name Immanuel," as they stand in the *Hebrew* and *Septuagint* of Isaiah, do *include such an additional clause as seems no way applicable to the* Messiah; *and so occasions the Jews to triumph, as if the prediction were meant not of a virgin, but only of a young woman in the days of* Ahaz. *For so runs the context*, as he says, *in the Hebrew; and the present Septuagint for the main agrees to it:* (*t*) " And the Lord added to speak " unto Ahaz, saying, Ask thee a sign of " the Lord thy God. Ask it either in the
" deep,

―――――――――――――

(*s*) Whiston's *Essay, &c.* p. 229, *&c.* Matt. 1. 23.
(*u*) Isaiah 7. 10―――16.

"deep, or in the height above. But Ahaz
"said, I will not ask; neither will I tempt
"the Lord. And he said, Hear ye now,
"O house of David, is it a small thing for
"you to weary men? But will ye weary
"my God also? Therefore the Lord him-
"self shall give you a sign: Behold, a vir-
"gin shall conceive, and bear a son, and
"shall call his name Immanuel. Butter
"and honey shall he eat; that he may
"know to refuse the evil, and chuse the
"good. For before the child shall know to
"refuse the evil, and chuse the good, the
"land that thou abhorrest shall be forsaken
"of both her kings."

Upon which passage Mr. *W*. (*n*) thus argues. *What has the birth of the* Messiah, *the true* Immanuel *of a virgin, to do with the birth of another child, before whose coming to years of discretion,* Resin *king of* Syria, *and* Pekah *king of* Israel *were to leave the land of* Juda *in the days of king* Ahaz? And therefore to make this quotation of St. Matthew pertinent, Mr. *W.* strikes out, by mere force of criticism and conjecture, and without any foundation from pretended various readings, these words, which he calls an *additional clause*, and
which

(*n*) Whiston's *Essay*, &c. p. 230.

which plainly limit the prophesy to a short time to come; (*w*) *Butter and honey shall be eat; that he may know to refuse the evil and chuse the good. For before the child shall know to refuse the evil and chuse the good, the land that thou abhorrest shall be forsaken of both her kings.* I say, *by the mere force of criticism;* for as to his pretences, that, in the copies (*x*) used by JUSTIN MARTYR and TERTULLIAN, the text of ISAIAH *is not wholly in the same order wherein it now is;* and that the *apostolical constitutions* quote a part of the text of ISAIAH, *not as it is in the present copies;* I answer, 1. That whatever variations from the *Septuagint* there may be in JUSTIN's and TERTULLIAN's quotations of this chapter of ISAIAH, the *additional clause*, which destroys the literal application of the prophesy to JESUS, appears in its place, both in *(y)* JUSTIN and *(z)* TERTULLIAN: and secondly, I answer, that the *(a) apostolical constitutions* cite only one verse of ISAIAH, viz. the 14th, without a word about what precedes or follows.

(*w*) Isa. 7. v. 15, 16.
(*x*) Whiston's *Essay*, &c. p. 232.
(*y*) *Justini* Opera, p. 262, 290.
(*z*) *Tertulliani* Opera, p. 191.
(*a*) *Const.* l. 5. p. 321.

Now pursuant to this first change he reads *virgin*, according to the Septuagint, and not *young woman*; tho' the original hebrew word (*b*) signifies, as appears by its use in other places, and by the present context, as he allows, *a young woman*, who might, or might not be a *virgin*.

But what will Mr. *W.* get by these changes, except a possible application of words, taken by themselves without their context, to the event of MARY's conception of JESUS? Which will never convince a reasonable man, that the original, obvious, and literal sense of ISAIAH, was to prophesy of the conception of JESUS by the virgin MARY.

Nothing will be obtain'd, even by reading (instead of *young woman's being with child*) *virgin's being with child:* for that expression asserts no miraculous or extraordinary conception, since it does not necessarily imply, that a *virgin* shall conceive without the concurrence of a man; or, if it does, points not obviously and primarily at the *virgin* MARY. Nor will any thing be obtain'd, by supposing the *clause* beforemention'd to be *dislocated* or taken from its proper place and added to this prophesy, besides the taking away one demonstration out of several that appear in ISAIAH, that
the

(*b*) *Erasmus* in Matt. F. 30.

the prophet had the birth of a male child of a *virgin*, or *young woman* in the time of AHAZ, and not the birth of JESUS by the *virgin* MARY in his firſt thoughts. For the whole context will ſtill ſpeak againſt him, and even in his opinion, not perfectly ſerve his purpoſe. For after he has corrected ISAIAH as abovemention'd, and after he has divided ISAIAH's propheſy into ſeveral propheſies, and made thoſe propheſies independent of one another, he confeſſes, that (*c*) *the preſent order of the parts* of thoſe propheſies and their preſent coherence and context will ſtill make them look *diſorder'd*. Mr. *W.* muſt therefore, if he will go on to endeavour to make this quotation pertinent, make further alterations; for what he has done already, does not, by his own confeſſion, place it to full ſatisfaction.

V.

That *the Jews have not corrupted the Old Teſtament in reſpect to the paſſages cited from thence in the New.*

MR. *W.* endeavours to ſhow, that (*d*) *the Jews have greatly corrupted* the Old Teſtament, and more eſpecially, as to

---

(*c*) Whiſton, p. 232.
(*d*) P. 17—112. 220—281. p. 87, 88, &c. 129.

the *quotations* made from thence in the New Testament.

To prove this last point he (*e*) produces some passages cited by the apostles, which are not apply'd according to the obvious meaning which they signify in the places where they stand in the Old Testament; some passages, which seem not exactly cited by the apostles; others (*f*) wanting in the hebrew; and many (*g*) passages, such as *He shall be called a Nazarene, &c.* which, he says, are *intirely wanting in all copies of the Old Testament.* He also urges the following passage of Justin Martyr to prove his charge against the Jews.

"I would have you know, says (*h*) Justin
"to Trypho, That your Rabbins have in-
"tirely taken away many texts of scripture
"from that version which was made by
"the elders that were with Ptolomy,
"wherein it was expresly declar'd, that this
"Jesus, who was crucify'd, was God
"and man, and was to be crucify'd
"and die. Which texts, because I know,
"that all those of your nation do reject, I
"do not insist upon such inquiries; but shall
"content myself in these debates with ma-
"king use of those texts, that are still ex-
"tant

(*e*) Whiston, p. 87, &c. 103, 129, 229, 321.
(*f*) p. 63.
(*g*) p. 104——110.
(*h*) p. 140.

" tant in your allow'd bibles. For as to
" what texts I have hitherto alledg'd to you,
" you allow of them all; excepting that
" short citation, *behold a virgin shall be
" with child.*" Then TRYPHO said, " I
" desire, that you will first tell us, which are
" those texts of scripture, that you say have
" been corrupted. To which I reply'd; I
" will do as you desire me. From what
" ESDRAS explain'd concerning the law of
" the passover, they have taken away this
" part of his explication. And ESDRAS said
" to the people; *This passover is your sa-*
" *viour and your refuge: and if you will*
" *consider it, and it come into your heart,*
" *that we shall humble him for a sign,*
" *and afterward shall believe on him,*
" *then this place shall not be made deso-*
" *late for ever, says the Lord of hosts.*
" *But if you shall not believe on him,*
" *nor hearken to his preaching, you shall*
" *be rejoyced over among the nations.*
" And from the words (*i*) of JEREMIAH,
" they have cut off this: *I was an (inno-*
" *cent) lamb, that was led to be sacri-*
" *fic'd. They deviz'd devices against*
" *me, saying, Let us cast wood into his*
" *bread, and let us thrust him out of the*
" *land of the living; and let his name*
" *be remember'd no more.* Now this text,
" which

(*i*) Jer. 11. 19.

"which is taken out of the words of JERE-
"MIAH, is still found written in some copies,
"that are in the Jewish synagogues: for they
"have taken them away but a little while
"ago; and that on account of the demon-
"stration that arises from them, that the
"Jews would take council about CHRIST
"himself, to take him away by crucifying
"him; and that after such council they
"have crucify'd him. Besides, they have
"in like manner taken away what follows
"from the words of the same JEREMIAH;
"*The Lord, the God of Israel, remem-
"*bred those of his, that were dead, that
"*were asleep in the dust of the earth;
"*and he descended to them, and preach'd
"*his salvation to them.* They have also
"taken away these few short words from
"the *Psalms* of DAVID, (*k*) *from the tree.*
"For when the words were these, *say ye
"among the Gentiles, that the Lord hath
"reign'd from the tree*; they left it thus,
"*say ye among the Gentiles, that the
"Lord hath reign'd*" Mr. W. (*l*) further supports this charge against the Jews,
byproducing a passage from the same Jus-
TIN, wherein is contain'd a quotation out
of the prophet ZACHARY, which, he says,
is not now to be found in ZACHARY. JUS-
TIN'S

(*k*) Psalm 48. 10.
(*l*) Whiston p. 144.

TIN's words (*m*) are, "Now what the Jews will say and do when they see CHRIST a coming in glory, we are foretold by the prophet ZACHARY, in these words: *I will command the four winds to gather together my dispers'd children: I will command the north to bring them, and the south not to hinder them. And then there shall be a great wailing in Jerusalem; not a wailing of the mouths or lips, but a wailing of the heart: and they shall not rend their garments but their minds. One tribe shall wail another tribe: and then shall they see him whom they have pierc'd; and they shall say, why* haft thou, O Lord, made us to wander from thy way? The glory with which our fathers have bless'd us, is become a *reproach to us*.".

In fine, Mr. *W.* (*n*) says, the Jews have chang'd this clause, *they pierc'd my hands and my feet*, which he thinks evidently *foretold the piercing the hands and feet of* JESUS *of Nazareth*, and instead thereof read, *as a lion my hands and my feet*.

Before I answer to these objections, I will readily confess to Mr. *W.* that the books of the Old Testament are *greatly corrupted*,

---

(*m*) *Justini Apologia* 1. §. 67.
(*n*) Whiston, p. 78, 79. Pf. 22. *v.* 16.

that is, greatly chang'd from what they were when they proceeded from the authors of them. He has himself acknowledg'd, and in many respects prov'd, that those books are (o) *greatly corrupted*; and particularly, that they *are so frequently corrupted in the names, and numbers therein set down, especially the books written after the captivity, that it is almost endless to enter into the detail of them*; many such changes happening without any form'd design, from the nature of things. And it is now generally allow'd by the most judicious and learned (p) criticks, such as HUET, SIMON, DUPIN, LE CLERC, and particularly, of late, by our excellent PRIDEAUX; that, after the captivity, *several places were added throughout the holy scriptures:* or that there *are several interpolations, which occur in many places of the holy scriptures*; for that *there are such interpolations is undeniable,*

(o) Whiston, p. 33, 44--86. 113--129. 140, 202.
See also Simon Hist. Crit. du V. Test. l. 1. *& Capelli* Critica Sacra.
(p) *Huetii* Demonst. Evangel.
Simon, Ib.
Dupin Dissert. Prelim. sur la Bible.
Le Clerc in Vet. Testam. & sentimens des Quelques Theol. de *Hollande*.
Prideaux's *Connection*, &c. Vol. 1. p. 342, &c.
See also Episcopii instit. Theol. l. 3. c. 1. p. 217.
Limburgii Amica Collatio, &c. p. 181.

deniable, there being many passages thro' the whole sacred writ, which create difficulties, that can never be solv'd, without allowing of them.

Which *interpolations* being allow'd to be made long after the captivity, it should seem, that there are more others than are commonly thought on, and particularly, that many of the prophetical passages with their completions have been added. For if once it be allow'd, that books collected into one volume have been retriev'd from obscurity, and have had additions made throughout to them, and that without any express notice given of such *additions*, which are only to be found out by a critical examination of those books themselves; *prophesies* with their *completions* recorded in those books, or fulfill'd before those books were published with *additions*, may be justly suspected to be *interpolations* or *additions*. For plain *prophesies*, with *exact completions*, are not matters in themselves very credible without the best and most undeniable attestations, that the former existed before the latter; and it seems most natural, upon the first view of a prophesy plainly fulfilled, to suppose the prophesy made for the sake of the event, or both prophesy and event invented; as we do in the case of HOMER and VIRGIL, and other pagan authors, who make telling things by way of
prophesy,

[138]

prophesy, a method of writing; founded in all likelihood on a design to keep up *prophesy* (which made so great a part of the pagan religion) among the pagans.

The *Pentateuch*, or book of the law, *(the gross (q) whereof seems only contended for as genuine and faithfully preserv'd)* must in a particular manner have been liable to great alterations; as having been anciently much neglected by the Jews, who, both during their commonwealth and monarchy, were for the most part idolaters, and subject to some other religious law; and as having been reduc'd for a considerable time to (r) *One Copy*, which was also lost so long, that the contents of it were become unknown. And the alterations have been according to (s) SIMON, such and so many, as to *hinder us from discerning now, what truly belongs to* MOSES, *from that which has been added by those who succeeded him, or by the authors of the last collection of the books of* MOSES. Which alterations made JEROM (t) say, *It was indif-*
ferent

(q) Stanhope's *Boylean Lectures*, 1701. Sermon 2. p. 23.

(r) 2 Kings 22.
Prideaux's Connection, Vol. 1. p. 573. *See also* p. 47, 330.

(s) *Simon* Hist. Crit. du Vieux Testam. p. 50.

(t) *Hieron.* adv. Helvidium.

ferent to him, *whether you said* MOSES *was the author of the Pentateuch*, or that ESDRAS *re-establish'd it.*

Most of the books of the Old Testament were liable to great *corruptions* during the captivity, when the Jews, who went idolaters into captivity, did before the expiration of it lose their native tongue; as all the books afterwards were, when they were transcrib'd, as is usually (*u*) suppos'd out of the *Hebrew* into the *Chaldee* character; which seems to suppose the body of the Jews unable to read their own hebrew books, and consequently easy to be impos'd on in such a transcript, which in its (*w*) design and nature did in all probability produce many changes.

There seems also to be another, and that no inconsiderable source of alterations, tho' not before observ'd as I know of by any body, in the books of the Old Testament; which the reader must bear in mind were, by the confession of all, considerably alter'd by ESDRAS, or some body else after the captivity. It is to be observ'd, that the Jews, who were greatly departed from the *law of* MOSES, and especially from the doctrine of the *Unity of God*, went (*x*) *idolaters* into cap-

---

(*u*) *Simon* Ib. p. 48.
(*w*) *Whiston's* Essay, p. 266, 267, 268.
(*x*) 2 Kings. 2 Chron.

captivity; that they went into *Chaldea*, a country, where (*y*) *One God* had from remote antiquity been believ'd and worship'd; that the religious books (*y*) of that nation give a relation of matters from the creation to the time of ABRAHAM so little different from that contain'd in the *Pentateuch*, that one of the accounts must in all probability be borrow'd from the other; that particular care (*z*) was taken among the *Chaldees* to *instruct* the jewish *youths* of quality and parts in the *chaldean discipline and learning*; that the Jews came out at different times from *Chaldea* such firm believers and worshippers of *One God*, and that under the high patronage and protection of the kings of *Chaldea* ordaining such belief and worship among them, that they have continu'd in that belief and worship ever since; that it seems more natural for a body of slaves and captives to be form'd by their masters and conquerors, than that the conquerors should be form'd by them, and that the slave should rather receive histories, and antiquities, from the master, than the master

---

(*y*) *Hide* Religio Vet. Persarum.
Prideaux's Connection, Vol. 1.
Lord's Religion of the Persees.
Pocock Specimen Hist. Arabum, p. 148.
Berosus apud *Joseph*. cont. Ap. l. 1.
(*z*) Ib. Antiq. l. 10. c. 11. & Dan. 1. 4.

master from the slave; that, particularly, it seems improbable, that the Jews, who chang'd their own idolatrous notions and practices for those of the *Chaldeans*, should have so much credit with the *Chaldeans*, as to introduce new history and *antiquities* among them; and that it seems more probable, that the Jews, who became compleat converts to the notion of *one God* receiv'd among the *Chaldeans*, and were in many respects form'd and disciplin'd by them, should receive their *history* and *antiquities* from the *Chaldeans*, who were an antient, polite, and learned people, and must have some historical scheme of things going among them, which they received not only as truths, but as religious truths. From all which (as well as from many other considerations which I now omit) it should seem very probable, that the jewish books, which were new form'd, alter'd and publish'd after the chaldean, or babylonian, or persian captivity, (call it as you please) might also receive chaldean alterations, no less than those other undisputed alterations.

It may also be suppos'd, that numerous changes were introduc'd in all the books of the Old Testament, when the *Massoretes* invented points and accents, and thereby first fix'd a text, which, every one before was to find out for himself by conjecture and his own judgment.

Lastly,

Lastly, the Jews themselves (*a*) *allow of the lawfulness of making alterations or emendations of their sacred books; provided they think them for the honour of God and for religion.*

Many changes therefore in the Old Testament I readily yield to Mr. WHISTON; the nature and reason whereof I reserve for another occasion. But what I deny here, and is the question between Mr. *W.* and me, is, that the *Jews* have with design *greatly* or at all *corrupted* the Old Testament as to any of those passages cited from thence by the authors of the New Testament; and to the proofs he has offer'd to make good his charge against the Jews, I answer as follows:

1. First, I say, that the apostles might cite and apply the passages they cited out of the Old Testament after the jewish manner; as they seem to have done, and as almost all christians assert they have done. And therefore Mr. *W.* manifestly begs the question about the Jews corruption of the books of the Old Testament in all his instances; which let them seem ever so remote from the *Septuagint* or *hebrew* text of the Old Testament, may be justify'd by the known practice of citing and applying scripture used by the jewish allegorical writers.

2. Se-

(*a*) Whiston's *Essay*, p. 220.

[143]

2. Secondly, the apostles might cite the Septuagint for divers of those places, which Mr. *W.* supposes corrupted in the *hebrew.* For the *Septuagint* was not only a false translation in innumerable instances, but contain'd (*b*) *additions* to the text; some whereof were made by the *Seventy*, who were suppos'd by many to be *inspir'd* in making them, no less than in the translation itself; and others by the *hellenist Jews*, who used that translation in their synagogues; (which *additions* plainly show the reason, why (*c*) *there are not near so many texts cited in the New Testament out of the Old, either different from, or wanting in the greek version now extant*, as in the *hebrew original.*) And, I find both ancient and modern criticks defend the apostles, for citing passages out of the *Septuagint*, which either did not at all occur in the *hebrew* of the Old Testament, or were not rightly translated from the hebrew, after the following manner: *This is generally to be observed*, says (*d*) JEROM, *that whenever the apostles speak to the people, they cite*

such

(*b*) *Capelli* Critica Sacra.
Simon Hist. Crit. du V. T. p. 57, 103.
Usser de Sept. Interp. Edit. p. 8.
Simon Hist. Crit. du N. T. p. 240. Ib. H. C. du V. T. p. 294.
(*c*) Whiston's *Essay*, &c. p. 128.
(*d*) *Hieron* Quæst. Hebr. in Gen. c. 40.

such passages of scripture as were known among them; and in speaking of a passage in the (*e*) *Acts*, wherin St. LUKE follows the *Septuagint*, which says, *the family of* JACOB *were seventy five souls*, contrary to the hebrew, which says, they were but *seventy souls*, he says in justification of St. LUKE, that St. LUKE *ought not to write contrary to that scripture, which was so commonly used as the Septuagint, and which at that time had more credit, than what St.* LUKE *could say himself*. SIMON (*f*) says, *it is unjust to accuse the evangelists and apostles with being falsifyers, because they cite scripture otherwise than it is in the original, since they made use of that scripture, which was in use among the Jews*. And CAPELLUS (*g*) says, *The apostles follow'd the Septuagint, lest they should scandalize the more weak hellenists and gentile christians* (*to whom the hebrew tongue was unknown, and who therefore did, and could only use the Septuagint*); *who, if the apostles had cited genuine scripture, would have thought they had forg'd scripture to serve a purpose; and their credit would have been called in question.*

Mr.

(*e*) Acts 7. 14.
(*f*) *Simon* Hist. Crit. du V. T. p. 233.
(*g*) *Capelli* Critica Sacra, p. 54.

[145]

Mr. *W.* therefore has no reason to charge the *Jews* with *corrupting* the *Hebrew text* because it differs from the *Septuagint text* cited by the apostles.

3. Thirdly, JESUS and the apostles might cite or use a copy of the *Septuagint* very different from those copies deriv'd down to us; for the (*h*) antient copies of the Septuagint (in all which there were additions which were not in the hebrew text) differ'd much from one another; and Mr. *W.* supposes LUKE to cite a (*i*) *false copy*: or they might use and cite other translations of the Old Testament, which differ'd from the original hebrew, besides the Septuagint: for Dr. PRIDEAUX, on occasion of its being said in (*k*) LUKE, that our Saviour read in the Synagogue at *Nazareth* a passage out of ISAIAH, which passage of ISAIAH, as reported by LUKE, does *not agree exactly either with the hebrew or Septuagint*; tells (*l*) us, that *it seems most likely, that he read it out of some chaldee targum*, that is, a chaldee paraphrase or translation, *which was*

L *read*

(*h*) *Simon* Hist. Crit. du V. T. p. 235.
Montfaucon Dissert. Prelim. ad *Originis* Hexapla. c. 4.
(*i*) *See* Whiston's *Essay*, p. 115, 116, 119.
(*k*) Luke 4.
(*l*) *Prideaux*'s Connection, Vol. 2. p. 547.
See Capelli Critica Sacra, p. 58, 59.

read in the synagogue. And therefore no argument can be urged, for the *corruption* of the *hebrew* or *Septuagint by the Jews*, from the citations of the apostles out of the Old Testament, not being exactly found in either of those copies.

4. Fourthly, divers of the passages, which Mr. *W.* mentions as *corrupted,* and divers of those which he mentions as *wholly omitted* in the Old Testament, were most certainly not taken from the *Old* Testament by the authors of the *New*, notwithstanding he says the apostles took them from thence. For it is well known, that the Jews had several books deem'd sacred among them, which were forged, under the names of their prophets, and are now either lost or not rank'd among the books of the Old Testament; which forg'd books the primitive christians received as sacred in some degree from the Jews, and used them, and read them in their religious assemblies. Of this Mr. *W.* was inform'd by the late learned Bishop Lloyd, who thus wrote to him. (*m*) Vigilius *was one of those orthodox bishops, that were under the heavy persecution of those Arian kings of the Vandals about A. D.* 500, *and then did write books*

(*m*) Lloyd's *Letter to* W. apud W's *Historical Pref.* p. 34.

books against the reigning heresy; which, for concealment sake, he put out in the name of ATHANASIUS. *Thus did some of the Jews, in the times of persecution, write books against heathen idolatry. One that is call'd the* Wisdom of SOLOMON; *another call'd the* book of BARUCH; *whereof also a part is call'd the* epistle of JEREMIAH. *I cannot commend them, that to conceal themselves used such arts; but nevertheless, their books were highly approv'd; insomuch that they were read by the hellenist Jews in their synagogues, and so coming into the christians hands, they were also read in christian churches, in and next after the apostles times.* We have also an (n) account, that there were *seventy two* of this kind translated into *greek* by the *Seventy,* when they translated and finish'd the twenty two books of the Old Testament. Some of these books were intituled ENOCH; the *Patriarchs*; the *prayer of* JOSEPH; the *testament* of MOSES; the *assumption* of MOSES; ABRAHAM; ELDAD and MODAD; the *psalms* of SOLOMON; the *revelation* of ELIAS; the *vision* of ISAIAH; the *revelation* of SOPHONIAH; the *revelation* of ZACHARY; and the *re-*

(n) *See Authors cited in* Grabe's *Spicileg.* §. 1. p. 134, 135.

[148]

velation of ESDRAS; and divers others bore the names of HABBACCUC, EZEKIEL, DANIEL, and other prophets.

Now ORIGEN, TERTULLIAN, EPIPHANIUS, AUSTIN, and GEORGIUS SYNCELLUS, who saw and read many of these forg'd books of the Jews, do (*o*) assure us, that the apostles took several of these quotations, in question, from them. And ORIGEN in particular, makes the following apology for the apostles citing these forg'd books. He says, (*p*) *The apostles and evangelists, who were fill'd with the Holy Ghost, might know what was fit to be cited out of those books, and what to be rejected; but that others cannot without danger do so, who have not so great an abundance of the spirit.*

We may learn from Mr. DODWEL a threefold source of some of the quotations, whereof I am now treating.

1. First, they might be taken from certain (*pp*) *mystical paraphrases* of the Jews, on the *Old Testament*; which *mystical paraphrases* were frequently interpolated into the text of the Old Testament 2. Or, secondly, they might be the say-

---

(*o*) *Grabe*, Ib. p. 129——140.
(*p*) *Origines* Prol. duar. Homil. in Cant. Cant. Opera. Vol. 1. p. 501. Bas. 1577. & apud *Grabe*, Ib.
(*pp*) Apud *Dodwel's Life*, p. 508.

sayings, or *revelations of christian* (*q*) *prophets, who in the christian assemblies gave interpretations of things deliver'd in the Old Testament*; which being *approv'd by* those, *who had the discerning of Spirits, were preserv'd, and known* to be from God. 3. Or, thirdly, they might be cited (*r*) *from writings, which were plainly taken for those of the old prophets, tho' in truth they were not such, yet cited as theirs, because the persons who cited them knew, that the persons to whom they wrote accounted them as such.* By which Mr. Dodwel does not mean such forg'd writings of Jews as are abovemention'd by me, but books compos'd by christians under jewish names; and particularly under the name of EZRA or ESDRAS. Which practise of citing such authors continu'd, as he says, in *use* in the church, till MELITO *had settled the canon of the Old Testament.* This MELITO who liv'd late in the second century, and was esteem'd a *prophet* himself, did, it seems, in order to satisfy the curiosity of his brother ONESIMUS, (*s*) *go into the east to be certainly inform'd of the books of the Old Testament*; and did

col-

(*q*) *For an account of which* Prophets, *see the History of* Montanism, p. 87.
(*r*) Dodwel's *Life*, p. 510.
(*s*) *Eus.* Hist. Ecc. l. 4. c. 6.

collect such passages out of the law and the prophets as related to our Saviour and the several parts of the christian faith.

5. Fifthly, I proceed to consider Mr. *W*'s charge against the Jews founded on the two passages of Justin Martyr:

1. As to the first passage, I observe, that Justin objects to the Jews five places; a place in Isaiah, *Behold a virgin shall be with child*; a place *taken away* from Esdras; two places *taken away from* Jeremiah; and the words *from the tree*, taken away from the 96th *Psalm*: Of all which (except the place in Isaiah) Dr. Grabe (*t*) says, *Ne miretur* Lector, *quod mutilationes sacri textus, quas* Justinus M. Triphoni *Judæo exprobravit, haud exempli loco attulerim: siquidem pericopas objectas non a Judæis ablatas, sed potius a Primævis Christianis explicationis gratiâ ad marginem adscriptas, indeq; in ipsum textum postea illatas censeo, cujus meæ opinionis rationes dabo, ubi, deo volente Dialogum Justini edidero.*

The first place, *Behold a virgin shall be with child*, was only rejected by the Jews as a false translation of the hebrew; which, according to them, should have been render'd,

---

(*t*) *Grabe* de vitiis Septuag. Inter. p. 34. *See also* Fabricii Codex. Apoc. Vet. Test. p. 1108.

der'd, *Behold a young woman shall be with child*, and as Aquila and Theodotion render'd it: and it can by no means be said, that the Jews so much as attempted to *take away* the place either out of the *Hebrew* or *Septuagint*. The Jews had a right in the time of Justin, and have now, to argue with the christians concerning the import or use of the hebrew word *Almah* (render'd *virgin* by the *Septuagint*) without being in the least liable to the charge of corrupting the bible. And it seems to be a very proper topick for them to insist on to christians, who lay stress on the place; tho', in reality, the words, *A virgin shall be with child*, seem of themselves to signify no miraculous conception of a virgin, and especially not in their place in Isaiah, as appears by the (*w*) context, which shows the term translated *virgin* to have reference to a *young woman* in the days of Ahaz.

As to the place of Esdras, it is not cited any where by the apostles in the New Testament; and by consequence it is not an instance of the Jews corrupting passages of the Old Testament cited in the New. Besides, it is in no hebrew (*x*) copies of

Esdras,

(*w*) Whiston's *Essay*, &c. p. 229, &c.
(*x*) *Clerici* Hist. Eccles. p. 526.

ESDRAS, nor is it cited by *any ancients*, except by JUSTIN and LACTANTIUS. *Satis patet*, says (*y*) THIRLBY, *ab aliquo christiano, verba conficta esse, non a Judæis deleta.* Dr. GRABE, who discharges the Jews from *taking away* this place, would, indeed, also clear the christians from forging it, by supposing it (*z*) *a primævis christianis explicationis gratia ad marginem adscriptum; indeq; in ipsum textum postea illatum.* But to that Mr. THIRLBY (*a*) answers, *Quorsum vero quæso tam accurata imitatio styli sacræ scripturæ, & Septuaginta interpretum, si nihil suberat doli? Aut quomodo hæc* explicationis gratia ad marginem adscribi *potuerunt, cum nihil in toto* ESDRAS *sit, quod aut ab his* explicari, *aut ullis machinis huc trahi possit, imo cum neq; in* ESDRA *canonico, neq; in apocryphis, ulla extet ejus ad populum de pascha oratio, unde hæc Judæi resecare potuerint?* And the learned CROIUS (*b*) scruples not to say, *Arbitramur hanc esse piam fraudem* JUSTINI, *&* LACTANTII, *qui sequitur* JUSTINUM *ducem, qui locum hunc, ut pleraq; omnia Sybillarum Oracula, & pleraq; omnes* MERCURII *sententias,*

(*y*) *Thirlbii Justin Martyr*, p. 292.
(*z*) *Grabe* De vitiis Sept. Inter. p. 34.
(*a*) *Thirlby*, Ib.
(*b*) *Croii* Obser. in Nov. Test. p. 205.

sententias, ad doctrinæ christianæ probationem finxerint, & in lucem ediderint.

The two places of JEREMIAH, and the words *from the tree* are no where *cited* in the New Testament; and consequently they are not instances of the Jews corrupting passages of the Old Testament cited by the apostles in the New. Besides, the first place of JEREMIAH was (*c*) *quoted* both by ORIGEN and LACTANTIUS, long after JUSTIN's time, and is *still extant after a sort* (which is enough for a quotation made by the fathers) *both in the Hebrew and Septuagint.* Nay, the words were by JUSTIN's own (*d*) confession, *found written*, in his time, *in some copies that were in the Jewish Synagogues.* Mr. LE CLERC (*e*) says in vindication of the Jews with relation to those words, *Quis credat deleta in versione Græcâ, studio certè & datâ operâ, dum Hebraicè leguntur? Suntne verba adeò clara & propria Christo, nulli ut alii convenire ullo modo possint? Atqui de* JEREMIAH *sat perspicue dicuntur.*

As to the second place said to be taken from JEREMIAH, nothing seems more evident

---

(*c*) Whiston's *Essay, &c.* p. 145.
(*d*) p. 142.
(*e*) *Clerici* Hist. Eccles. p. 526.
See also *Thirlby* in Justin Martyr, p. 293.

dent than that it is a christian forgery. (*f*) *Ille quidem nusquam, neque in Hebraicis, neq; in Græcis codicibus, comparet; nec mirum, cum sit confictus a male feriato Christiano, qui descensum Christi ad Inferos in* JEREMIAH *reperiri voluit.* The place is cited several times by (*g*) IRENEUS, who sometimes ascribes it to ISAIAH, sometimes to JEREMIAH, and oftner to *a prophet*; so that he seems not to have taken it from a standing text, nor to have known to whom it belong'd.

The words *from the tree*, of which there is no footstep either in *the vulgate version*, or in ORIGEN or JEROM, or in any *Hebrew* or *Greek Copy*, are deem'd by several learned men to be (*h*) either a fraudulent or casual addition made by some christian; by which JUSTIN (to speak the best) was impos'd upon.

But however that be, they are now restor'd by JUSTIN, and may be argu'd from with the same force, as if they were extant in all copies, both of the *Hebrew* and

---

(*f*) *Clerici* Hist. Eccles. p. 526.
(*g*) *Irenæus*, l. 3. c. 23. l. 4. c. 39, 56, 66. l. 5. c. 31.
(*h*) *Grotius* in Psalm 96.
Clerici Hist. Eccles. p. 526.
Thirlby in Justin Martyr, p. 292.
Simon Bib. Crit. Tom. 3. p. 486——488.
Le Moyne not. ad Var. Sacra. p. 489.

Septuagint: and I can see no reason, why they are not restor'd to their place, but that, either the criticks think them spurious, or that they serve no christian purpose, or that they think them both *spurious*, and impertinent to any christian purpose.

2. As to the second passage (*i*) of JUSTIN, wherein a quotation is made from ZACHARY, *a great part, if not the whole, of which is,* according to Mr. (*k*) *W. now dropped both in the Hebrew and Septuagint*; I answer, that this passage is not cited any where in the New Testament; that it might be taken out of some apocryphal book attributed to ZACHARY; that JUSTIN does not say it is left out of ZACHARY; and that the citation, if taken from ZACHARY, seems to be accounted for by a learned person (*l*) in a note thereon, *viz*. that the citation *consists of various passages out of the prophet* ZACHARY, *as they occurr'd to the memory of* JUSTIN, *and the sense and not the express words set down by him*; which way of citation seems the common (*m*) method of the fathers, and makes it very absurd to pretend from thence, that the bible is corrupted,

---

(*i*) *Justin Apol.* 1. §. 67.
(*k*) Whiston's *Essay*, p. 144.
(*l*) *Reeves*'s Justin's Apology, p. 92.
See Thirlby in locum, & alibi in notis.
(*m*) *See Reeves*, Ib. p. 38.

rupted, and that it ought to be corrected by their citations.

6. Sixthly, Mr. *W.* (*n*) charges the *Jews with introducing into their copies a gross and groundless alteration into the 22d* Psalm, *which,* he says, *is one of the most eminent prophesies concerning the sufferings and passion of the* Messias, *that is in all the Old Testament.* Instead of (*o*) *they pierc'd my hands and my feet,* the Jews read, *as a Lion my hands and my feet.* But in this matter (*p*) there seems to be only a various reading of the *Hebrew,* and no manner of design to make any alteration of the text. For the Jews, tho' they have *generally put* the reading, as a Lyon *into the text* (which reading of the Masoretes (*q*) Grotius thinks defensible) yet *they have left the reading,* They pierced, *in the text of a few copies, and in the margin of many other copies*; and they have continu'd the reading They pierced in *all copies of the Septuagint,* which yet Mr. *W.*

(*n*) Whiston's *Essay,* p. 78.
(*o*) Psalm 22. 16.
(*p*) *See* Clavis Scrip. *Hottingeri,* p. 191——198.
Simon Hist. Crit. du V. Test. p. 229.
Id. Bib. Crit. tom. 3. p. 481——488.
Whiston, Ib. p. 79.
(*q*) *Grotius* in locum.

[157]

W. (r) pretends they have throughout corrupted to serve their purposes.

So that there is not the least colour of proof, that the Jews have corrupted any passages of the Old Testament, which can be apply'd to matters of christianity; much less any passages cited from thence by the apostles; but on the contrary, it seems plain by the few instances of JUSTIN MARTYR to support his charge of corruption against the Jews, that the christians had so careful an eye upon the Old Testament in respect to all passages, which could be strain'd so as to seem to allude to christianity (for of such only do the passages produc d by JUSTIN (s) consist, notwithstanding he says, that they *expresly declare, that* JESUS, *who was crucify'd, was God and man, and was to be crucify'd and dye*); that it was impossible for the Jews to make any alteration either in the *Hebrew* or *Septuagint*, without being found out and detected by the christians. Christians (t) themselves were absolute security against such corruptions of the Jews. Some others indeed of the fathers as well as JUSTIN MARTYR did charge the Jews with maliciously

---

(r) *Whiston*, Ib. p. 78.
(s) *Justin* apud Whiston's *Essay*, p. 140.
(t) *August*. De Civit. Dei. l. 15. c. 14.

liciously corrupting the scripture to the prejudice of christianity: but ORIGEN, JEROM, AUSTIN, and other fathers, vindicated (*u*) them from that charge; as have done divers learned (*w*) moderns, who contend, that those fathers who charg'd the Jews with maliciously falsifying the Old Testament were mistaken in that matter, by laying too great a stress on the *Septuagint*, which was a very faulty copy and translation, and by imagining, that the Jews produc'd corrupted Scripture, when in their controversies with christians, they produc'd either the original *Hebrew*, or the (*x*) accurate and pure version of AQUILA, in opposition to the *Septuagint*.

The Jews were so little dispos'd to corrupt the Old Testament in respect of the passages cited from thence, or capable of being

---

(*u*) *Simon* Hist. Crit. du V. Test. p. 6.
Pezron Defence de l'Antiquité des Tems, p. 133.
Capell. Critica Sacra, p. 2, &c.
(*w*) *Grabe* De Vitiis Sept. Interp. p. 84.
Clerici Hist. Eccles. p. 525———527.
Martianey Defence du Texte Hébreu.
Simon Ib. p. 102———104.
Capellus Ib. p. 2, 3.
Rivet. N. Fuller. Glassius.
Dupin, Hottenger, &c.
(*x*) ORIGEN *in Cantica*. Ib. *Epist. ad* AFRICANUM, p. 224.
HIERON. Epist. ad Marcellam, Tom. 2. Col. 507.
Ib. Epistola ad *Damasum*.

being made use of, in behalf of christianity; that AQUILA himself, tho' a Jew and a great enemy to christianity, cannot be justly charg'd with translating unfaithfully any one passage conceiv'd to have relation to christianity, as is prov'd by MONTFAUCON, (*y*) who shews the weak arguing of all those fathers, who charg'd AQUILA with such unfaithfulness, in respect to all the passages on which they grounded their charge; that (*z*) JEROM, who had ORIGEN's *Hexapla* before him, when he made his latin translation, generally preferr'd the sense of AQUILA and SYMMACHUS, as being better interpreters than the *seventy*, tho' both Jews, and translators after the rise of christianity; and that (*a*) AQUILA, THEODOTION, and SYMMACHUS, translate the famous passage of HOSEA which St. MATTHEW applies to CHRIST's coming out of *Egypt*, exactly as St. MATTHEW does, not imitating the translation of the *Septuagint*, which gives no *literal* ground for St. MATTHEW's application of it in the manner he does. And indeed I cannot imagine, why the Jews of any understanding or common sense, should have endeavour'd the alteration of any such passages

---

(*y*) *Montfaucon*, Prælim. ad *Origenis* Hexapla. c. 5.
(*z*) Ib. c. 6. & 8.
(*a*) Whiston's *Essay*, p. 90.

passages of the Old Testament; it being a matter of no manner of moment to them, but of great mischeif to them so to do. For the Old Testament, literally understood, not any where serving the purposes of christians; and the Jews rejecting all the allegorical reasonings and interpretations of christians; and likewise plainly seeing, that the whole Old Testament in any copy, or however translated, or however chang'd by them, was as capable of being allegorically apply'd to prove christianity, as their own vulgar Hebrew, or the copies of the Septuagint in the hands of christians; there was no sense nor reason in making the few changes charg'd upon them by some fathers; much less those vast changes now charg'd upon them by Mr. *W*; or indeed in making any changes at all. And besides doing what serv'd not their purpose, the Jews would therein have been certainly detected and expos'd to the just censures of christians; who, as appears, watch'd them, and charg'd them with such attempt, even without proper (*b*) materials to make good the charge. Mr. *W*. himself should allow the Jews to be under some restraints, how much soever they were dispos'd to corrupt the bible; when he can suppose, that (*c*)

(*b*) *Simon* Hist. Crit. du V. T. p. 6.
(*c*) Whiston's *Essay*, p. 220.

in the days of Josephus, *the Jews durst not make any alteration in the ſacred books,* and that (*d*) *direct corruption* was in certain caſes by *no means practicable.*

In fine, Origen himſelf, one of the moſt zealous chriſtians that ever was; and who, by the time wherein he liv'd, and by his great learning and ability, and by compiling his *Hexapla,* conſiſting of the *Hebrew* text in Hebrew and Greek characters, the verſions of Aquila, Symmachus, the *Seventy,* and Theodotion, in ſix columns; was the moſt capable of all men to know, whether the Jews had corrupted the Old Teſtament in reſpect to the citations made from thence in behalf of chriſtianity; but yet he never charg'd the Jews, as far as appears, with any ſuch corruptions, either in the numerous *notes,* which he made on his *Hexapla,* or in any of his other works; which if he had found out, he would not have fail'd to have diſcover'd. And this negative argument is the ſtronger, inaſmuch as Origen has treated of the Jewiſh corruptions of the bible in a (*e*) letter to Africanus; wherein he only charges the Jews

with

(*d*) Whiſton, Ib. p. 238.
(*e*) *Origenis* Epiſt. ad *Africanum.* Apud Whiſton's *Eſſay,* p. 133. *It is alſo printed at the end of* Westein's *Edition of* Origen's *Dialogue againſt the Marcionites.*

with corrupting such places of their holy books as seem'd to derogate from the honour of their *Rulers* in the eyes of the world. Whereby he should seem to suppose them free from all charge of corruption in respect to all passages, wherein he, as a christian, was too much concern'd to be silent, at a time when he was treating of their corruption of their holy books in other respects, and that of corruptions suppos'd by him (*f*) to be made by the Jews, since the days of the apostles. Nay, we are inform'd by two (*g*) learned authors, that ORIGEN has somewhere in his works particularly vindicated the Jews in this matter.

VI.

That *the Septuagint version was not, in the days of* JESUS *and the apostles, agreeable to the Hebrew text.*

MR. WHISTON (*h*) asserts, that *the Septuagint version was in the days of* CHRIST *and his apostles agreeable to the genuine Hebrew text of that age.*

But

(*f*) Apud *Whiston*, Ib. p. 139, 140.
(*g*) *Simon* Hist. Crit. du V. Test. p. 6. *See also Glassii* Philologia Sacra, p. 11.
(*h*) Whiston's *Essay*, p. 3——17.

But for proof of this affertion he produces nothing but mere fuppofitions, all chimerical or improbable, ridiculous commendations of partial and ignorant Jews, and forg'd tales.

He argues fuch agreement (*i*) *to be a natural confequence, from the common ftate of books tranflated out of one language into another,* and efpecially *in the cafe of facred books, own'd for fuch both by tranflators and copyers.* Whereas it is as probable, that books fhould be *ill* as *well* tranflated; and it is more probable, that books deem'd *facred* fhould be *ill* than *well* tranflated; for the directors in fuch tranflations, tho' real believers of the *facrednefs* of the books, are very capable of finifter views, and being govern'd by them, as having ufually departed in many refpects from the original fenfe of their facred books, and having divers ill-grounded things receiv'd among them to fupport and maintain; to fay nothing of their ignorance. And accordingly, if we may be govern'd in this cafe by feeming fact, the *Septuagint* feems the work both of *ignorant* and *unfaitbful* tranflators, as will particularly appear in the fequel of this article.

(*i*) Ib. p. 41.

He argues that agreement from the *Septuagint*'s reception (*k*) among *Jews* and *Christians*, as *a faithful* version; insomuch, that it *was made use of* in their *publick worship*, where it would be *impossible to introduce a version, unless it were known to be a just and accurate version*; and he argues, from its reception among the former as an (*l*) *inspir'd version*. In which last he might also have join'd the (*m*) christians, who for many ages after the rise of christianity, receiv'd the *Septuagint*, as an *inspir'd version*; but that such junction would have spoil'd his argument: for Mr. *W.* dates the corruption of the *Septuagint* in the hands of christians long before the christians quitted their original notion and constant tradition of the divine inspiration of the *Septuagint version*; and consequently must have suppos'd them to have look'd on what he deems, *a greatly corrupted book*, as divinely *inspir'd*. But nothing seems more easy, than to get *ill* versions of books to be receiv'd as *faithful* or *divine*, and to be read as such in places of publick worship, where

---

(*k*) Ib. p. 5.
(*l*) Ib. p. 9.
(*m*) *Simon* Hist. Crit. du V. T. l. 1. c. 18, & 19. l. 2. c. 2.
Fenardentii Annot. in *Irenæum*, p. 137. Edit. *Massuet*.

where (if we will reflect on the practise of the popish church, to say nothing of other churches, where people seem little to understand what is *read* and *sung*) we may judge, that nothing is too absurd and too gross to be in use. And I am surpriz'd that Mr. *W.* who charges both Jews and Christians with receiving into their canon of scripture a most *obscene song*, (*n*) which they both so grosly mistake as to take not only for a moral but divinely inspir'd *song*; who charges the Jews with wilful and great corruption of the Old Testament, part of which is read in synagogues, and almost all read in christian churches; who has so abject an opinion of the primitive christians, as to think them capable of having their *bible* taken from them, and of receiving a false *bible* in its stead; who takes all the ancient christians to be (*o*) deceiv'd in believing MATTHEW's gospel to be written originally, and extant among them, in *Hebrew*; who thinks the christians reject the *most sacred book* of the New Testament, viz. The *Apostolical Constitutions* from their *Canon* as well as other *canonical books*; who thinks the primitive christians for many centuries almost wholly (*p*) ignorant of the

hebrew

(*n*) *Suppl. to Essay.*
(*o*) Whiston's *Essay*, p. 182.
(*p*) Whiston's *Essay, &c.* p. 224.

hebrew tongue, from which language the *Septuagint* was translated, and in which only the grounds of christianity could be authentickly contain'd; who is so deeply sensible of the anti-christianism of popery, and of the numerous and gross impositions in most churches; and who thinks the *Athanasian creed*, not only to be a modern, forg'd work, but to be contrary to the most express and plain meaning of the gospel, to all primitive antiquity, and to the clearest dictates of reason, tho' it be receiv'd by almost all christians as the *faith once deliver'd to the saints*, and *repeated* in churches with the utmost devotion by the people, and contended for with the greatest zeal by the clergy; I am surpriz'd, I say, Mr. *W.* should not think the Jews and ancient christians capable of receiving the *Septuagint*, and reading it in their religious assemblies, on supposition, that the Septuagint was not an accurate version of the hebrew, and that there was so great a discordance then between the *Septuagint* and *hebrew* as now appears to be! This will yet seem more surprizing, when it is consider'd; that the copies *(q)* of the *Septuagint* in the apostles times differ'd greatly from one another;

(q) Simon H. C. du V. T. p. 235.
Montfaucon Prelim. ad Origenis Hex. c. 4.

ther; that LUKE himself cited (*r*) *a false copy* of the *Septuagint*; that *the whole* christian *world fought* (*s*) *one against another about three different editions* of the *Septuagint*, as says JEROM; that the *Septuagint* (*t*) had been corrupted by the Jews, and by them deliver'd to ORIGEN, upon whose credit their corrupt copy became in time to be generally receiv'd; and yet, that during these first ages the christians look'd on the *Septuagint* as *divinely inspir'd,* and as such read it in their churches.

He (*u*) argues the same agreement from the extravagant *applauses* given to the *Septuagint translation* by the ancient Jews. But these applauses plainly proceeding from their ignorance and partiality, are of no more weight, than the excess of disparagement they afterwards run into; for, notwithstanding those excessive applauses, when they found the christians used the *Septuagint* in their controversies with them, they readily took hold of all advantages they could; and not contenting themselves with showing, that the christians did not argue literally and logically from the Old Testament,

---

(*r*) Whiston's *Essay*, p. 119.
(*s*) Ib. p. 115, 116.
(*t*) Whiston, *as cited above by me.*
(*u*) Ib. p. 6, 7, 8.

they charg'd them with arguing from paſſages of the Old Teſtament falſely tranſlated in the *Septuagint*; about which paſſages they were little or not at all concern'd, till the chriſtians, by citing and applying them, made them review the *Septuagint* Tranſlation, and gave them this advantage over them.

He argues (w) it from *the miraculous ſtory of* the *ſeveral interpreters being ſhut up in cells* apart; each whereof *tranſlated* the whole by *inſpiration*, and *concurred word for word* with one another. Which ſtory he himſelf allows *cannot be juſtify'd*; and tho' it ſhows a *great approbation* of the work, yet it ſhows the approvers to be weak men, and their approbation to be of no weight, to ſay nothing worſe of this matter.

He argues, (x) from the *ſilence* of authors *before the ſecond century*, and eſpecially of *the enemies of the goſpel*, as to any *differences* between the *Hebrew* and *Septuagint*; as alſo (y) from *the converſions* wrought by the apoſtles, in virtue of *citations*, or proofs brought from the *Septuagint*, among the Jews; who, in conſequence of their
con-

(w) Whiſton, Ib. p. 10.
(x) Ib. p. 11.
(y) Ib. p. 14.

conversions, must, according to him, have *own'd those citations for genuine and agreeable to the then known bible among them*; it being (z) *impossible*, as he says, for them to have been converted, *if the citations had been as different from what they found in their bibles, as the like citations frequently are now from what we find in ours.*

But both these considerations will seem of little weight, if it be consider'd:

That we have no jewish authors of that time extant who treat of these matters:

That perhaps no jewish authors did at that time treat of these matters:

That the Jews did, in general, approve of the allegorical way of reasoning used by the apostles, tho' they might dislike the application of it to JESUS CHRIST:

That PHILO the Jew, who wrote in the apostolical age voluminous works, wherein there is not the least notice taken of christianity (which seems surprizing) cites, and reasons from, the Old Testament in the same allegorical manner with the apostles; wherein it may be suppos'd that he follow'd the method of his nation, and especially of the prevailing sect of Pharisees, who first introduc'd it:

That

(z) Ib. p. 15.

That men might be satisfy'd then, as divines and others are now, notwithstanding *the citations* made by the apostles out of the Old Testament are so *different from what we now find* therein:

That it appears from almost every part of the New Testament, that the Jews and the apostles were perpetually disputing about the mystical sense of the Old Testament; which, as it was the sole foundation of christianity, so it was the sole subject of dispute; tho' we know not how the Jews, who were not converted, answer'd the apostles:

That St. PAUL argues against some Jews, as much concern'd for the *letter* of their law, in opposition to the *spirit* of the law, which he contended for; and that his enemies and accusers (a) among the Jews were the *Sadducees*, who contended for the literal interpretation of the Old Testament; the *Pharisees*, who contended for *allegorical* interpretations of the Old Testament, *finding no evil in* him:

That the first converts among the Jews to christianity were *Pharisees*, it not appearing that any (b) one *Sadducee was ever converted to the faith in the whole new Testament*:

That

(a) Acts 23. 8.
(b) Wotton's *Mis. Discourse*, Vol. 1. p. 95.

That the body of the Jews did reject JESUS, whom they *knew not* to be the CHRIST, and whom they rejected as pretending to be the CHRIST, in virtue of their interpretations (whether literal or allegorical) of the Old Testament, which they took to be perverted and misapply'd in behalf of him:

That it would have been no wonder, if the Jews had not at first made objections to the apostles for their not citing, and reasoning from, the *letter* of the Old Testament, when they had for a considerable time before the days of JESUS and the apostles, (c) *neglected the literal sense of, and used to allegorize the bible*:

That when the Jews did attack christianity by writings and books, they did censure the apostles and christians (d) for citing falsely, and for arguing falsely, because not literally from the Old Testament; and to expose them more effectually they caus'd other and more literal and faithful translations to be made, than the *Septuagint*, which was much used by the christians, and greatly receeded from the hebrew text by its additions, omissions, and false translations:

†

That

(c) *Simon* Hist. Crit. du V. Test. p. 97.
(d) *See* Justin Martyr, Origen *and* Jerom, *as cited in* PEZRON Defense de l' Antiquite des tems, p. 136, 137, 174, 337, 398, 400.

That *(e)* Festus, the Heathen, did, upon hearing St. Paul declare his manner of arguing from the Old Testament, and proving from thence, *that Christ should suffer and rise from the dead,* tell Paul that he *was beside himself, and that much* (Jewish) *learning had made him mad;* wherein Festus has the same thoughts of the manner of arguing of Paul, which Mr. Whiston has of the present, apparent, reasoning of the apostles from the Old Testament: *(f)* and that Agrippa, who was *expert in all customs and questions among the Jews,* and *believ'd in the prophets,* was *almost perswaded to be a christian* by that very way of reasoning whereby Festus concluded St. Paul *mad*:

That Celsus, who seems the oldest heathen author, that has attack'd christianity, whereof we have any remains, did not only attack *(g)* christians for their *allegorical interpretations* of the Old Testament, *who,* he said, *by a most astonishing folly, and a stupidity without example, endeavour'd to find out relations between things, for which there was not the least foundation;* but for their

---

(e) Acts 26. 6, 7, 22, 23, 24.
Le Clerc sur cet endroit.
(f) Acts, Ib. v. 3, 27, 28.
(g) Origen contra Celf. p. 187, 196—198.

[173]

their application of the prophesies in the Old Testament to JESUS, *which, he (b) said, agreed to a thousand other persons with equal or more probability than to him, and were apply'd by forc'd interpretations;* several of which prophesies ORIGEN (*i*) yields to CELSUS to be *enigmatical* and *allegorical,* and to be so apply'd by the christians: and that CELSUS, speaking of some of the prophesies cited by the apostles, says, (*k*) most satyrically, that they *are unintelligible, enthusiastical, and perfectly obscure sayings, which no wise man can understand a tittle of, but only occasion fools and jugglers to apply to their purposes:*

That PORPHYRY, a most acute pagan philosopher, wrote a voluminous work (now lost) against christianity, to which EUSEBIUS of *Cesarea* wrote an answer (now lost); wherein the said PORPHYRY thus charg'd the christians in general, and ORIGEN in particular (*l*) with allegorizing the Old Testament. *Some being resolv'd,* says he, *to find out solutions for the difficulties which occur in the writings of the Jews, rather than reject them, have recourse to incon-*

fistent

(*b*) Ib. p. 39, 44, 78.
(*i*) P. 39.
(*k*) *Origen* contra *Celf.* as cited and translated by *Nicholls* in his Conference with a Theist, Vol. 3. p. 10.
(*l*) Apud *Eusebii* Hist. Ecclef. l. 6. c. 19.

sistent interpretations, nothing relating to what is written, and which are not so much in defence of those strange doctrines, as in confirmation and praise of their own. For vaunting in great words, that what MOSES *spoke with all imaginable plainness, are dark riddles, they enthusiastically give them out as so many divine oracles pregnant with hidden mysteries; and after confounding the judgment with this sublime language, they deliver their own explications. For an example of this folly, let us take* ORIGEN, *a person, with whom I had some acquaintance, when I was very young. He was then and still remains in great esteem with the teachers of this doctrine, who loudly spread his fame for the volumes he left behind him. As for his opinions concerning the divinity and other things, he was a disciple of the greek philosophers, and endeavour'd by their principles to support the exotick fables of the Jews. Moreover the writings of* PLATO *were never out of his hands; nor those of* NUMENIUS, CRONIUS, APOLLOPHANES, LONGINUS, MODERATUS; *nor those of* NICHOMACHUS, *and the most celebrated pythagoreans. He read likewise the books of* CHEREMON, *the stoick; and of* CORNUTUS; *of whom having learnt the allegorical method of explaining the gre-*

cian

[175]
cian mysteries, he did accommodate it to the writings of the Jews:

That JULIAN did attack *(m)* the apostles for misapplying passages of the prophets, and applying them to JESUS:

That FAUSTUS, the Manichæan, not only speaks *(n)* of divers particular quotations from the Old Testament, as unfaithfully made and urg'd in the New Testament, because not literally made and urg'd, and therefore charges the New Testament *(o)* with corruption, as Mr. WHISTON does the Old:

And that St. AUSTIN, who was not inferior in allegorical interpretations to ORIGEN himself, and who had the same Old Testament we now have (which Mr. *W.* supposes *corrupted*) and who contended that the Jews never *(p)* corrupted the *Old Testament*, tells us, how effectual *that* was for the conviction both of Jews and Pagans in these *(q)* words. *Propterea Judæi adhuc sunt, ut libros nostros portent in confusionem suam. Quando enim volumus ostendere, Christum esse prophetatum,*
pro-

(m) *Julian* apud Cyril, l. 8. p. 253, 261, 262.
Grotius *in* Matt. 1. 22.
(n) *Faustus* apud *August.* contra *Faustum*, l. 3. c. 1. l. 16. c. 2. l. 18. c. 3. l. 32. c. 1.
(o) Ib. l. 12. c. 1.
(p) *Augustin.* de civ. dei, l. 15. c. 13.
(q) *Augustin.* in Psalm 56.

proferimus Ethnicis istas literas: & ne fortè illi duri ad fidem ducant, nos Christianos illos composuisse libros, & una cum Evangelio confinxisse, hinc illos convincimus, quod omnes illæ literæ, quibus CHRISTUS *prophetatus est apud Judæos sunt. Proferimus ergo codices ab inimicis Judæis; ut confundamus inimicos infideles. Codicem portat Judæus, unde credat christianus:*

And that therefore the truth seems to be what a very learned man (r) asserts, *that the apostles in their writings, as well as* JESUS CHRIST *in his discourses, cited the texts of the Old Testament according to the commonly receiv'd sense of the synagogue; and that the autority of these proofs in that receiv'd sense, did not a little contribute to the conversion both of Jews and Gentiles.* Which thought Mr. *W.* (s) himself seems to fear may be true, when he says, He *assuredly* HOPES *the difficulties themselves* (that is, the incoherency of the New on the Old Testament) *were not* GENERALLY *in being in* the first century.

Lastly, Mr. *W.* (t) argues from *the apostolick citations of the first century out of the Pentateuch*

(r) Allix's *Judgment of the Jewish Church against the Unit.* p. 40.
(s) Whiston's *Essay*, p. 264, &c.
(t) Whiston's *Essay*, p. 16.

[177]

Pentateuch *and* Pfalms; out of the firſt, as agreeing to the *Samaritan Pentateuch*, which he calls *the original hebrew*; out of the latter, as agreeing *almoſt exactly to the Septuagint verſion* of the Pſalms, as *atteſted by the Roman pſalter*. From whence he infers, that ſince the *Samaritan Pentateuch* and *Greek pſalms do ſo nicely anſwer the citations of the firſt century, it is next to demonſtration, that*, the vulgar Hebrew and Septuagint *did then anſwer the one to the other*. But granting, that *the apoſtolical citations* agreeing to the *Samaritan Pentateuch* and *Greek Pſalms* demonſtrate an agreement ſo far between the *Hebrew* and *Septuagint*; how is it demonſtrated from thence, that there was an agreement between the *Hebrew* and *Septuagint* in reſpect to paſſages not cited by the apoſtles, or to the books of the prophets, which are the books of the Old Teſtament, whoſe agreement in both copies we are chiefly concern'd to know in the preſent argument? Beſides, the criticks pretend; that (*u*) the *Pentateuch* (of the Septuagint verſion) was tranſlated long before the other books of the Old Teſtament, and by different hands; and that the latter

N books

(*u*) Whiſton, Ib. p. 113.

books were not near so well translated as the *Pentateuch*. And it is now (*w*) known, that *long before the days of* Origen *the Septuagint versions of* Ezekiel *and* Daniel *were laid aside and lost*, and other versions substituted in their stead; and that the version of Ezekiel in particular was so much better done than the Septuagint versions of the other books, that Jerom, who took that version to be done by the *Seventy*, was *surpriz'd, how it came to pass, that it agreed so much better with the Hebrew than most of the other books* of the Old Testament.

As these general topicks of Mr. *W.* seem of very little force, so they ought to be deem'd of no force, when it is consider'd that the Jews themselves had (*x*) a tradition, that *thirteen passages of* Moses *were with design falsely translated by the Seventy*; that many ancient Jews, and especially the (*y*) *Jerusalem Jews*, seem to have been far from concurring with the (*z*) *Alexandrian Jews*, who as they were the translators, so they seem the chief applauders of the Septuagint translation; that the

ancients

(*w*) Whiston, Ib. p. 113.
(*x*) *Usserii* De Edit. Sept. Int. p. 11.
(*y*) Lightfoot's *Works*, Vol. 1. p. 488.
(*z*) *Hody* De Text. l. 3.

[179]

ancients give an account of great (*a*) *omissions* and *additions*, which were all noted in ORIGEN's *Hexapla*; that there is now in fact *a great disagreement* between the present *Hebrew* and *Septuagint*; and that to assert an ancient agreement is (*b*) *new and contrary to the general belief of the learned, both in the present and past ages*: but especially when such agreement seems so contrary to undeniable matter of fact: for by the meer comparing of the *Hebrew* and *Septuagint* together, notwithstanding the changes either or both of them may be suppos'd to have receiv'd, it will appear to be (*c*) *an ill version of a very hard book, and must be allow'd by those who can judge of it, to be far from being exact and true; and should any body now adays make a version so imperfect, instead of admiration and esteem, his work would be much despis'd by the modern criticks.* Let any one compare (*d*) the citations out of the

N 2 *Sep-*

(*a*) *Simon* Hist. Crit. du Vieux Testam. p. 103.
Montfaucon Dissert. Prelim. ad *Origenis* Hexapla, c. 1, & 4.
See Origen. Hom. 12. in Jerem.
Hieron. in c. 17. Jerem.
(*b*) Whiston, Ib. p. 3.
(*c*) Hare's *Difficulties and Discouragements*, p. 6.
See also Capelli Quæstio de Parallel. §. 7.
(*d*) *See Le Clerc* Bib. Univ. Tom. 22. p. 418.

Septuagint, to be met with in PHILO and JOSEPHUS, with the hebrew text (I say, those citations, that it may not be pretended, that the passages which the *Seventy* have ill translated, have been corrupted); and he will find these interpreters to have had but a very moderate knowledge of the hebrew tongue, and to have proceeded by no certain rules in their translation.

But by the account given of the Septuagint translation in our learned divine and hebrician LIGHTFOOT, no translation was ever more unfaithful, or more remote from its original, than the *Septuagint* was from the hebrew.

He says, (*e*) " That the Seventy did that
" work unwillingly, and for fear: for the
" scripture was the treasure of the Jews,
" which made them more glorious, than
" any nation under heaven. Therefore, to
" communicate this their riches to the hea-
" then, whom they abominated and de-
" tested, was as much against their heart,
" as what was most. So that had not the
" fear (*f*) of the power of PTOLEMY
" brought them to the work of the transla-
" tion, more than their own good will,
" there

(*e*) Lightfoot's *Works*, Vol. 1. p. 488, &c.
(*f*) See *Usserii* De Editione Sept. Inter. p. 114, 115.

" there had been no such thing done. Pto-
" lemy Lagus, the father of Ptolemy
" Philadelphus, for whom they translated,
" had carry'd away an hundred thousand
" Jews captive into *Egypt*, as saith Ariste-
" as, so the fear and dread of that house lay
" upon them, that they durst deny it nothing,
" which otherwise they would most vehe-
" mently have done such a thing as this,
" to have communicated their scriptures to
" the heathen in a vulgar tongue.

" Secondly, the translation being then un-
" dertaken for fear, and with so ill a will,
" and that they kept a mournful fast every
" year, sorrowing for the work of that tran-
" slation; it cannot be expected, that the
" translation will be done without any more
" fidelity, than barely what will keep the
" translators out of danger.

" Thirdly, therefore they strive as much
" as they can, to conceal the truth and
" treasure of the scripture from the heathen,
" and as much as they dare to delude
" them. Their chief means for this is to
" use an unprick'd bible, in which the
" words written without vowels, might be
" bended divers ways, and into divers sen-
" ses, and different from the meaning of the
" original, and yet if the translation were
" question'd, they might prick or vowel
" the

" the word, so as to agree to their transla-
" tion. How they have dealt in this kind,
" there is none that ever laid the hebrew bi-
" ble and the Septuagint together, but hath
" observ'd.

" Fourthly, their differences from the ori-
" ginal, which were innumerable, were part-
" ly of ignorance, they themselves not being
" able to read the text always true in a copy
" unvowell'd. But this ignorance was also
" voluntary in them, they not caring to mi-
" stake, so they might do it to their own
" security.

" Their general care was, that since of
" necessity they must translate the bible, as lit-
" tle of it might be imparted and reveal'd by
" the translation as was possible.

" Their particular and special heed was
" also, that those places of the text, which
" translated literally, or according to their
" true meaning, might prove dangerous any
" ways to the nation of the Jews, or bring
" them into distaste with the potent king,
" for whom they were translated, should be
" so temper'd and qualify'd that no hazard
" might arise, nor any such matter might be
" seen."

In

In fine, there is *so great disagreement* between the present copies of the *Septuagint* and the *hebrew*, (tho' the former (g) *has been corrected* to the latter) and that to all appearance between the ancient ones; that many learned men, and particularly our great (h) USHER, have been mistakenly induc'd to believe, that there were two greek versions of the hebrew before CHRIST; and that the first, which was an accurate version of the books of MOSES only, and was the work of the Seventy under the reign of PTOLEMY PHILADELPHUS, and was conformable to the hebrew, is now lost; but that the second, falsely call'd the *Septuagint*, and now receiv'd as the *true Septuagint*, was a subsequent and unfaithful translation made in the fourth year of PTOLEMY PHYSCON.

So that nothing can seem more remote from all appearance of truth, than to suppose, that so *ill a version* as the present *Septuagint version* seems to *all learned men* to be, should ever have agreed with the original hebrew.

VII.

(g) Whiston's *Essay*, p. 48, 49.
(h) *Usserii* De Edit. Sept. Interp.

VII.

That *the Samaritan Pentateuch is not an uncorrupt copy of the books of* MOSES, *and originally deriv'd from the first separation of the ten tribes themselves in the days of* JEROBOAM.

MR. WHISTON (*i*) deems the *Samaritan Pentateuch* (which is one of the means, whereby he proposes to *restore the true text of the books of the Old Testament*) *an uncorrupted copy of the books of* MOSES, and to be *originally deriv'd from the first separation of the ten tribes themselves in the days of* JEROBOAM.

1. Whereas, if the ten tribes, that under the conduct of JEROBOAM set up a worship at (*k*) *Dan* and *Bethel*, had a Pentateuch among them (which may justly be suspected and cannot be prov'd): yet that proves nothing in relation to the present *Samaritans* and those from whom they are deriv'd. For the ten tribes were all carry'd (*l*) captive by SHALMANESSER into *Assyria*, where they

---

(*i*) *Whiston's* Essay, p. 2, 16, 48, 49, 164, 175, 183, 242.
(*k*) 1 Kings 12. 28.
(*l*) 2 Kings 17. 6———18.

they were (*m*) difpers'd and loft: and thofe who were fent to inhabit *Samaria* in their ftead, and had foon the name of *Samaritans*, appear (*n*) not for a long while to have had the Pentateuch among them. For they were all (*o*) *Heathens*, and *continu'd* fo for many ages, as the bible informs us; which reprefents them as idolaters at firft, and as being like what they were in the beginning, at *the time* when the *fecond book* of *Kings* was publifh'd: and the *Jerufalem* Jews conftantly gave them the name of *Cutheans*, as coming from *Cuthah* in *Affyria*; thereby fignifying them to be idolaters and heathens, as well as originally heathens. *Had the Samaritans*, fays (*p*) PRIDEAUX, *receiv'd the law of* MOSES *from the firft* (that is, from the time of the ifraelitifh prieft being fent (*q*) by ESERHADDON among them, as is fuppos'd by many) *and made that the rule of worfhip, which they paid the God of Ifrael, they could not have continu'd in that grofs idolatry, which on all hands it is agreed they did, till the building the tem-*

(*m*) *Simon* Hift. Crit. du V. T. p. 66.
(*n*) Ib. p. 65.
(*o*) 2 Kings 24. 29———41.
See Prideaux's Connection, Vol. I. p. 416, 417.
(*p*) *Prideaux*, Ib.
(*q*) 2 Kings 17. 28.

temple on mount Gerizim in the time of ALEXANDER *the great*.

2. There is a *corrupted* passage of great importance in the *Samaritan Pentateuch*; which enjoins, an *altar to be built*, and *sacrifices* to be offer'd, (not at (*r*) *mount Ebal*, as all our hebrew and greek copies have it, but) *at mount Gerizim*; where (*s*) SANBALLAT, above a thousand years after the times of MOSES, did, at the instigation and with the assistance of MANASSEH, son of JOIADA the high priest of the Jews, and other disoblig'd Refugee-Jews, first, build a temple in opposition to the temple at *Jerusalem*; where Refugee-Jews, from the time the temple was built, continu'd frequently to resort; and where, for the most part from the same time a jewish-temple-worship has been kept up by persons, who have been call'd *Samaritains*, from *Samaria*, the name of the district, wherein mount *Gerizim* lyes. And this corruption affects the autority of the *Samaritan Pentateuch* the more, in that, it was a *design'd* corruption, in order to justify and autorize their new place of worship at mount *Gerizim*. The Samaritans have also added a large passage to the same effect in their *Pentateuch*; which has no (*t*)

foot-

(*r*) Deut. 27. 4.
(*s*) *Joseph*. Antiq. l. 11. c. 8.
(*t*) Exod. 20. 17.

foot-steps in our hebrew and greek copies. In both these cases, indeed, Mr *W.* (*u*) declares, he sees *no reason to accuse the Samaritans, but the Jews of corruption.* And he endeavours to support the *Samaritan* readings by several (*w*) *reasons* in his book, and by (*x*) *one* added since, which he thinks *determines the point* in favour of the *Samaritans*; which therefore, tho' equally precarious with the rest, I shall here examine.

There was, it seems, a contest (*y*) between the *Jews* and *Samaritans* at *Alexandria* in *Egypt*, " Whether the temple at " mount *Gerizim*, or that at *Jerusalem*, was " warranted and autorized by the Mosaick " law ?" The cause was, by way of appeal, brought before PTOLEMY PHILOMETOR, king of *Egypt*; who, upon hearing the pleas on both sides, (of which JOSEPHUS seems to give but a very general and imperfect account) gave judgment in favour of the Jews against the Samaritans. But yet Mr. *W.* thinks it appears from JOSEPHUS's relation, that the Jews copies had those passages then in them, and did not disagree from the *Samaritan*; and, by consequence, that the Jews have since corrupted their copies.

But

(*u*) Whiston's *Essay, &c.* p. 169.
(*w*) Ib. p. 169——172.
(*x*) Ad finem Errat.
(*y*) *Joseph.* Antiq. l. 13. c. 6.

But the consideration of Josephus's relation (which the reader is desir'd to have before him) will, in my opinion, produce a very different conclusion, and *induce* the reader to believe, that the Samaritan readings were corruptions, and that the jewish copies stood then as they do now in that respect; as the pleas which the king heard *induced* him to determine for the Jews.

It does seem possible from Josephus's relation, that the two *Samaritan advocates* did insist before king Ptolemy on those passages before-mention'd of their Pentateuch, for the autority of their temple at *Gerizim*, tho' it is not any where said so, or that their *Pentateuch* had then any such passages in it. For there seems no other foundation in the *Mosaick law*, from whence they are suppos'd to argue, for making mount *Gerizim* the place appointed for a temple in opposition to *Jerusalem*, and for the great confidence they had of being able to prove their point: all traditional pretences in favour of the antiquity of the temple at *Gerizim* before the temple at *Jerusalem*, being not only undoubtedly false, but capable of being easily prov'd so, as they could not but know themselves; for their temple had been built but 150 years, whereas the temple at *Jerusalem* had been built long before, in the days of Solomon.

It

It may also be suppos'd possible, that the jewish advocate might argue against the Samaritans from his *Pentateuch*, as not having the Samaritan readings: for nothing appears, from whence it can be concluded he did not. Nay, if the Samaritan advocates urg'd their two present readings, we have reason to believe he did so; since those readings were certainly wanting in his copies. For both the *Hebrew* and *Septuagint* copies had been, before this contest, in the hands of the heathens, and particularly in the library of PTOLEMY, who would never have given judgment against the *Samaritans*, and condemn'd their *advocates* to *dye*, if the jewish copies had favour'd the autority of their temple at *Gerizim*.

All therefore that can be *suppos'd* in favour of the *Samaritan Pentateuch* from JOSEPHUS is, that it, alone, perhaps, then had the two passages mention'd; there being no ground in JOSEPHUS (or else where) to suppose, that the Jews *Pentateuch* then had them. But this supposition in favour of the Samaritan Pentateuch, will not prove the two readings genuine.

But there are two considerations, which seem to me to determine the corruption to be on the part of the *Samaritans*.

1. First, there have been three different sorts of people, who at different times have inhabited *Samaria*, and been call'd *Samaritans*, and were different religious Sects.

1. Those

1. Those of the ten (z) tribes, who, under the conduct of JEROBOAM, revolted from the tribes of *Judah* and *Benjamin*, and set up a worship at *Dan* and *Bethel*, in opposition to the worship establish'd at *Jerusalem*. 2. The heathens, who were sent to inhabit *Samaria* in the room of the ten tribes that were carry'd into captivity and never return'd, were call'd *Samaritans*. 3. The apostate Jews, who with SANBALLAT, first, built a temple at mount *Gerizim* in opposition to the temple at *Jerusalem*, and their successors, were also so call'd; among whom perhaps, some of the Samaritans last mention'd, at length became embody'd.

Now, neither the *Jews*, before the separation of the tribes into the kingdoms of *Israel* and *Judah*, nor the first sort of *Samaritans*, seem ever to have had the least thought of worshipping at *mount Gerizim*; and the contest between the *Jews* and *Samaritans*, after the separation, was, whether worship was to be perform'd at *Jerusalem*, or at *Dan* and *Bethel*; for the sacredness of which two (zz) last places, there was some pretence in antiquity. It should seem therefore, that there was no pretence at that time in the Pentateuch for making mount *Gerizim*

(z) 2 Kings 12. 27—29.
(zz) *Patrick* on 1 Kings 12. 29.

Gerizim a place of worship. And therefore it seems most probable, that those Samaritans, who consisted chiefly of apostate Jews, and first built a temple at *Gerizim* in opposition to the temple at *Jerusalem*, and would be glad of an autority for so doing, or their successors, corrupted the Pentateuch; and not the Jews, who, at a time when they had no interest nor malicious purpose to serve, acted as if there had been no such passages in the Pentateuch as the *Samaritans* produc'd.

2. Secondly, Our Saviour may not improbably be suppos'd to determine against the *Samaritan* readings in his conversation with the woman of *Samaria*. That conversation, which is but briefly represented, seems to admit and require the following interpretation:

(xzz) " Since you are a Jew, says the wo-
" man of *Samaria* to our Saviour, tell me,
" why the Jews contend, that God is to be
" worship'd at *Jerusalem*, since our fore-
" fathers worship'd in this mountain of *Ge-*
" *rizim*. To which Jesus answer'd, there
" is little reason to trouble your self about
" this question, inasmuch as the occasion
" will soon be remov'd: for the worship of
" God will not much longer be confin'd to
" any place; and so the privilege about
" which you contend, will come to nothing.
" Never-

(xzz) John 4.

"Neverthelefs, to fatisfy your prefent que-
"ftion, I tell you, you *Samaritans*, who
"are moderns, and can know nothing but
"from us, *worſhip God without knowing*
"*his precepts:* but we Jews, who are
"from all antiquity, know all his laws;
"and that *Jeruſalem* is the place of wor-
"ſhip appointed by God, and that the
"true worſhip is only among the Jews,
"who worſhip at the true place appointed
"by God.

To confirm this interpretation and para-
phraſe I will offer three particulars:

1. Firſt, If Jesus be ſuppos'd to affirm,
according to the vulgar tranſlation, that the
Samaritans *worſhip'd they knew not what*,
(meaning thereby, that they worſhip'd not
the God of the Jews) it is to make him aſſert
what was falſe in fact: for the Samaritans of
that time had the ſame ſole object of worſhip
with the Jews, whom they *knew*, or underſtood as well as the Jews: and they do not
then appear to have oppos'd the Jewiſh law
in any other reſpect, than about the place
of worſhip (which was indeed a matter en-
join'd, and was ſo (*a*) judg'd by Jesus);
for in differing from the Jews about traditions, they adher'd more ſtrictly to the
Jewiſh law, than the Jews themſelves; and
our

(*a*) v. 22.

our Saviour himself concurr'd with the *Samaritans* in rejecting those traditions. Besides, Jesus, in this very conversation, supposes *(b)* them to *know what they worshiped*, when he supposes them equally with the *Jews*, to *worship the Father*. And this very *Samaritan woman* and other *Samaritans* (*c*) do by their speedy conviction, that Jesus *was the* Messias *they expected*, manifestly show themselves to be better prepar'd by their sentiments to receive christianity, than the *Jerusalem* Jews.

2. Secondly, to tell the woman, *Ye worship ye know not what*, relates not to the woman's inquiry about the place of worship, but to a matter wholly foreign. And the answer of Jesus seems only pertinent by being understood to the effect I have abovemention'd, that is, as relating wholly to the ignorance of the *Samaritans* about the place of worship, which was the sole matter in question.

3. Thirdly, the words, *for salvation is of the Jews*, imply a foregoing resolution in general of the question concerning the place of worship. For the sole reason, why *salvation was of the Jews*, and *not of the Samaritans*, was only, that the *Jews* did, and the

Sama-

(*b*) v. 21.
(*c*) v. 25, 29, 39, 41.

Samaritans did not worship at the place appointed by God.

But setting aside this interpretation, I contend, that our Saviour has determin'd for *Jerusalem*, by saying, *salvation is of the Jews*, and by what he adds in relation to the *times coming*, when men might worship any where, and when nothing would be requisite but to worship *God* or the *Father*, in *spirit and truth*. For if the time was to come, when men might worship any where, then they might not worship any where when Jesus spake; and either mount *Gerizim* or *Jerusalem* was then the sole true place of worship and *salvation*. But one only of those places being then the true place of worship and *salvation*; Jesus plainly declares which of the two was that place, by saying, *salvation was of the Jews*.

(*d*) [Tho' the nature of the privilege and advantage imply'd in the term *salvation*, used by our Saviour, be not the matter here in question; and it does not import me to settle its signification: yet I beg leave to interpose so far here as to observe,'

First, that I do by no means think it signifies, as it may be vulgarly suppos'd, *the eternal reward of heavenly happiness*; and that I cannot without horror suppose the
blessed

(*d*) *Digression.*

blessed and charitable Saviour imply'd thereby, that the *Samaritans* and all other men, besides the *Jerusalem* Jews, were to be *eternally damn'd*; and especially for such a matter, of no consequence in it self, as the mere place of worship, whether on this or that mountain. Such a notion, so manifestly absurd and uncharitable, can only be grounded on the spirit of *Sectarianism*, and can only proceed from the most weak and self-interested men.

God in dealing with the ten tribes, after their revolt from the tribes of JUDAH and BENJAMIN, and setting up a worship in *Samaria*, throughout the Old Testament always acts with such of them as his *people*, who fell not into idolatry: and in a very general defection of those tribes to the worship of BAAL, God owns *seven thousand* of them to be his *people*; when he (e) says; *yet I have left me seven thousand in Israel, all the knees which have not bow'd to* BAAL, *and every mouth which hath not kissed him.*

Most of the prophets (f) themselves, whose works make a part of the books of the Old Testament, were of the *Samaritan schism*. HOSEA was of the tribe of ISSACHAR;

JOEL

(e) 1 Kings 19. 18.
(f) *Basnage* Hist. des Juifs, l. 2. c. 12. p. 277—288.

JOEL was of the tribe of RUBEN; JONAH was of the tribe of ZABULON; and OBEDIAH was born at BETHACAD in the neighbourhood of the city of *Samaria*. And yet I presume no one will say, these prophets are *damn'd*.

ELIJAH and ELISHA, two renown'd prophets and workers of many miracles, always liv'd in the schism; the first whereof had a miraculous passage to heaven, going thither in his life time in a fiery chariot; which is a more evident proof of his not being *damned*, than can be had of any man of the most *orthodox* church.

Nor do we ever hear of any of these prophets going to *Jerusalem* to worship, or exhorting the people of *Samaria* to do so; tho' it was the known practise of other Jews to come annually from very remote places to worship at *Jerusalem*: and they seem concern'd only to keep up the worship of God, according to the institution of MOSES, in *Samaria*, and to prevent and root out idolatry.

From all which it should seem, that the *Samaritan* separation, or worship set up at *Samaria*, in opposition to the worship establish'd at *Jerusalem*, did not *damn* all those who were engag'd in it, but was a way to heaven no less certain than the same worship at *Jerusalem*.

Besides,

Besides, our blessed Saviour (*g*) by his parable of the *good Samaritan* seems to suppose the *Samaritans* in a better way to heaven, than even the Jewish Levites: and it (*h*) seems, that he should not condemn the *Samaritan* woman with whom he convers'd, and other *Samaritans* whom she brought to him; who all believ'd him to be the Messias, and that with more readiness than the *Jerusalem Jews*.

Secondly, that *salvation is of the Jews* seems to me (*i*) to signify only, that the Messias, or *Saviour*, or *Redeemer of Israel*, should arise out of those Jews who worship'd at *Jerusalem*, and not from among those Jews who worship'd at *Samaria*, or mount *Gerizim*]

3. But in relation to the *Samaritan Pentateuch*, I would ask Mr. *W.* whether that has not the same account of Moses's death, and burial, and comparison between him and the succeeding prophets in *Israel*, together with the other allow'd interpolated passages, which are to be found in the vulgar *Hebrew* and *Septuagint* Pentateuchs; which interpolated passages are usually (upon tradition or conjecture) attributed to Esdras, who, on his return from the Babylonish captivity

---

(*g*) Luke 10. (*h*) John 4.
(*i*) Luke 1. 69———77. Ib. 2, 30.

tivity is suppos'd to have publish'd the Old Testament, or a great part of it, corrected and enlarg'd? And if it has them; how can that *Pentateuch* be deriv'd from a copy extant several hundred years before the time of Esdras? Must it not be from a copy made long *after the separation of the ten tribes*, even long after the first return from the Babylonish captivity? *All the passages*, says Simon, (k) *which I have produc'd to prove, that* Moses *was not wholly the author of the Pentateuch, as we now have it, are exactly the same in the* Samaritan *Pentateuch; and therefore we cannot say, that the* Samaritans *have kept a copy of the original as it was before the captivity of the Jews.*

4. I observe, also, that there is a great agreement in *chronology* after the deluge, between the *Samaritan* and *Septuagint Pentateuchs*, wherein they both differ from the original hebrew about 700 years; which *chronology* (l) may be justly deem'd invented and forg'd, and inserted into the *Septuagint*, in order to render the books of the Jews more credible to the heathens, and from thence, like other particulars, *added*

to

(k) *Simon* Hist. Crit. du V. Test. p. 66.
(l) Ib. p. 68, 207.
Lightfoot's *Works*, Vol. 2. p. 701.

to the *Samaritan Pentateuch*. And this the Jews of *Jerusalem*, *Alexandria*, and other places, and the *Samaritans*, might all tacitly concur to practise as a *pious fraud*, like the Missionaries of our days to CHINA; who, tho' they may think the Septuagint chronology *false*, yet use that chronology in (opposition to their bible) the better to prepare the *Chinese* for the reception of the gospel: for which *wise conduct* the Missionaries are much (*m*) commended. *Il sera toujours permis aux Missionaires de la Chine de se servir de la Chronologie des 70 toute fausse qu'elle est, dans les Entretiens qu'ils ont avec les Chinois. Cette sage Oeconomie, dont les Jesuites qui prêchent l'Evangile en ce païs la scavent si bien se servir, & avec tant de fruit, n'a jamais eté defendue. Les Peres & mesme les Apostres (n) l'ont mise en pratique, sans nuire a la verité de la Religion Chrètienne, comme le Pere* PETAU *l'a demontré par plusieurs exemples, dans la judicieuse preface qu'il a mise a la tête du second tome de ses Dogmes Theologiques.* Mr. *W.* in a former (*o*) work makes it one of his *Postulata* or *Axioms*, that the *Hebrew text of the Old Testament, being the origi-*

(*m*) *Simon* Bibl. Crit. Vol 2. p. 472.
(*n*) *See Erasmus* in Acta Apost. c. 17. v. 23.
(*o*) *Whiston's short View of the Chron.* p. 2, 3.

original it self, is reasonably to be allow'd our most authentick guide in the CHRONOLOGY *of the Old Testament, and not the Septuagint Translation*; and by consequence not the *Samaritan Pentateuch*. Which passage I urge to Mr. *W.* no further than the *reason* imply'd in it will bear. For I am sensible Mr. *W.* has much (*p*) chang'd his thoughts in respect to the chronology of the *Hebrew* and *Samaritan* texts; the first whereof he now thinks *false*, notwithstanding he formerly thought it so evidently *true* as to lay it down for an *axiom* to be granted him without contest, and the latter *true*. Nor do I in the least blame him for so doing; who has a right to follow his judgment, in all matters where-ever it leads him: but, perhaps, he may need to be told, that it very much becomes him, to bear with the differences of others from him; who by his own great change of opinion, and by the difficulties wherewith he sees himself encompass'd, should naturally think most of the *theological subjects* he treats of to be of the utmost uncertainty, and, bating their curiosity, to be in themselves of no manner of importance to the world.

5. To

(*p*) Whiston's *Essay, to restore,* &c. p. 214.

5. To derogate yet further from the autority of the *Samaritan Pentateuch*, I observe with the learned Prideaux, that tho' that *Pentateuch* be said to be written in the *old Hebrew* (or *Phænician*, or *Canaanitish*) *character*, and so may seem to have some advantage over the vulgar hebrew Pentateuch, which is written in the Chaldee character, yet is that *Pentateuch*, according to him, but *a transcript* from the *vulgar Hebrew* out of the *Chaldean* into the old hebrew character. *For,* (*q*) says he, *first, it has all the interpolations, that* Esdras's *copy* (that is, the vulgar Hebrew) *hath; whereas had it been ancienter than* Esdras's *copy, it must have been without them. Secondly, there are a great many variations in that copy, which are manifestly caus'd by the mistake of the similar letters in the hebrew alphabet; which letters having no similitude in the Samaritan character, this evidently proves those variations in the Samaritan copy were made in transcribing that from the vulgar Hebrew, and not in transcribing the vulgar Hebrew from the Samaritan.* From whence it seems past doubt, that the *Samaritan Pentateuch*, such as it now is, was not in being among the

---

(*q*) Prideaux's *Connection*, Vol. 1. p. 416.
See also Simon. H. C. du V. T. p. 66, 67.

the *Samaritans* till after the compilation of the vulgar hebrew Pentateuch by Esdras, and transcript of it into Chaldean characters. How long after I pretend not to determine. Dr. Prideaux (r) supposes, or conjectures, that Manasseh, *when he fled to the Samaritans with other apostate Jews, and settled in Samaria, first brought the law of* Moses *among them*; which was not long after the suppos'd compilation of Esdras, and was about 400 years before Christ. I should suppose they had their present *Pentateuch*, first, among them, much later. For about 160 years before Christ, they seem to me to have had as little occasion for the *law* of Moses, as the mere *Cuthean-Samaritans* (s) had from the time of their establishment till long after the return of the *Jerusalem* Jews from the Babylonish captivity; during all which time they (t) serv'd *their own* heathen *gods*. For so lately, as 160 years before Christ, they (u) *petition'd* Antiochus king of *Syria*, to whom then all *Judæa* was tributary, *that their temple on Gerizim, which had been dedicated to no especial deity, might thenceforth be made.*

(r) *Prideaux*, Ib. p. 416, 417.
(s) 2 Kings 17.
(t) v. 33, 34, 41.
(u) *Prideaux*, Ib. Vol. 2. p. 177, 178.

made the temple of the GRECIAN JUPITER, *and be so called for the future.* And ANTIOCHUS gratify'd their *request*; and caus'd their *temple* to be *consecrated to the* GRECIAN JUPITER, by the name of JUPITER THE PROTECTOR OF STRANGERS; *which additional title,* they themselves also *desir'd, that it might thereby be express'd, that they were strangers in that land, and not of the race of Israel.*

Mr. *W.* labours (*w*) to prove, that ESDRAS was not the transcriber of the Old Testament out of the Old Hebrew into the Chaldee character; as is asserted by PRIDEAUX and others, in virtue of some conjectures: and he (*x*) guesses, that it was a work done *about the end of the first, or beginning of the second century of the gospel.* Now, if the *Samaritan Pentateuch* was transcrib'd from the vulgar hebrew bible, after that was transcrib'd into the *Chaldee character;* and if the vulgar hebrew bible was not transcrib'd into the *Chaldee character,* till the time Mr. *W.* mentions; then is the present *Samaritan Pentateuch* not only not *deriv'd originally from the first separation of the ten tribes in the days of* JEROBOAM; but very modern, and not
even

(*w*) Whiston's *Essay*, p. 149.
(*x*) Ib. p. 159.

even of autority and antiquity enough to *settle* the hebrew text, as it stood in the times of JESUS and his apostles; to *settle* which was the end for which Mr. *W.* lays so much stress on the *Samaritan Pentateuch*.

But after all, supposing with (*y*) SIMON and many other learned men; that the present *Jewish* (which is, the *Chaldean* or *Assyrian*) *character*, was the *character* always in use among the Jews; and that the *Samaritan* (that is, the *Phœnician*, or *Canaanitish*, or, as it is also call'd, the *old Hebrew*) *character* was never used by the Jews before the captivity, in any manner, either in books or medals: it will then follow, that the *Samaritan Pentateuch*, as written in the *Samaritan character*, could not be the *Pentateuch* in its *original character*, but must have been transcrib'd into that *character*, either to give it a pretence to antiquity, or to distinguish it from the Jews *Pentateuch*, or to render it legible to the inhabitants of *Samaria*, who, upon the *Pentateuch*'s being first introduc'd among them,

---

(*y*) *Simon* Bibl. Crit. Vol. 2. p. 389——435.
Toinard apud *Le Clerc* Bibl. Univ. Tom. 21. p. 131.
Allix apud *Spanhemii* De Numismi. Vol. 1. p. 69, &c.
Rhenferd Opera Philolog. p. 225—253.
See *Basnage* Hist. des Juifs, l. 6. c. 24.

them, might be vers'd in no other character but the *Samaritan character*. And therefore the *Samaritan Pentateuch* is of less autority and antiquity *for being written in the Samaritan character*; and must for that very reason have been transcribed from the Pentateuch of the Jews written in the *Chaldean* or *Assyrian character*; to say nothing more here of the other reasons to prove it was so tranfcrib'd.

6. Dositheus, a Samaritan, who (z) liv'd after the times of Jesus, is said by (a) Photius to have *adulterated* the *Pentateuch* (by mistake (b) call'd the *Octateuch*) of Moses *with many corruptions*. This *adulterated Pentateuch* our learned Usher takes to be the present *Samaritan Pentateuch*: and he supposes, that Dositheus compil'd this *new hebrew book out of the hebrew copies of Palestine and Babylon, and the greek version receiv'd by the hellenist Jews; adding and taking away some passages, and changing others, according to his pleasure*. And he particularly supposes him to have corrupted that *Pentateuch* by inserting therein some of the *Septuagint chronology*; which also was a corruption
first

(z) *Origen* contra *Celf.* l. 1. & in Matt. 27. Tract.
(a) *Photii* Bibl. p. 883, 886.
(b) *Usserii* De Edit. Sept. Int. p. 216.

first introduc'd in the *Septuagint*. (By which the reader may easily see, why the *Septuagint* is more conformable to the *Samaritan* than to the *hebrew text*; and also how (*c*) *improper* it is to settle the true reading of the *Pentateuch*, even as it was in our Saviour's time, by the *Samaritan Pentateuch*.) But whether or no, Dositheus, the Samaritan, was the compiler of the *Samaritan Pentateuch*; it is not improbable, according to (*d*) Dupin, to suppose, that some modern *Samaritan* compil'd it chiefly out of the different copies of the *Palestinian* and *Babylonian* Jews, and the *Septuagint* (the sources, from whence Usher supposes Dositheus compil'd it); because it sometimes agrees with the hebrew copies of *Palestine*, sometimes with those of *Babylon*, and sometimes with the *Septuagint*.

I would not be thought in this matter of Dositheus, &c. which I borrow from the great Usher, and from Dupin, to espouse either of their *hypotheses*; to which they seem driven by their judgment on the state of things, and by their inclination to solve difficulties pursuant to their religious notions.

But

(*c*) Ib. p. 218, 219.
(*d*) *Dupin* Dissert. Prelim. &c. p. 533, 534.

But I use those *hypotheses* here, as I do the *hypotheses* of other learned divines in relation to many parts of the dispute between Mr. *W.* and my self, merely to oppose Mr. WHISTON; who every where proceeds on the most precarious *hypotheses*; because seemingly proper to solve difficulties, in his way. And the sole inferences I would make from such topicks, against Mr. *W.* are; that there is no end of *hypotheses*; that they are so uncertain, that nothing serving to establish an opinion can be justly inferr'd from them; and that by their number and uncertainty, they seem the effects of not understanding rightly the christian religion it self, and the true grounds and reasons of it.

7. Lastly I observe, that ORIGEN; who understood *hebrew* well, and liv'd and convers'd much with the Jews in *Palestine*; who was greatly skill'd in the literature of the Old Testament; and who compleated three most laborious and useful works towards understanding the Old Testament, *viz.* his *Tetrapla*, *Hexapla*, and *Octapla* (in the two last whereof he inserted the vulgar hebrew text); wholly omitted the *Samaritan Pentateuch*, and gave the hebrew text in the *vulgar jewish*, and not (*e*) in the *Samaritan*

(*e*) *Montfaucon*, Prælim. ad *Origenis* Hexapla, p. 21.

ritan character; tho' he thought fit to give the *hebrew text* over again in *greek characters*. Nor does he appear to have used the *Samaritan Pentateuch* in his *notes* on the *Hexapla*, towards settling the text in any respect. And consequently ORIGEN must have judg'd the *Samaritan Pentateuch* of no importance towards *settling* the reading and sense of that part of the Old Testament.

8. So that I think I may venture to conclude, that Mr. *W*. has not the least ground to date the *Samaritan Pentateuch* so high as the times of JEROBOAM, against which three have appear'd several demonstrative arguments; and for which he has as little colour, as the *Samaritans* themselves have for a manuscript copy of their *Pentateuch* (*f*) pretended to be deriv'd to them from the times of PHINEAS, contemporary with MOSES; whereby they are equally absurd with the *Jerusalem* Jews, and others, who make MOSES author of the account of his own death and burial, and of the comparison between himself and the prophets in *Israel*, who succeeded him; to say nothing of the absurdity in pretending to have a *manuscript* of a (*g*) book, whereof it will be *diffi-*

†

(*f*) *Simon* Hist. Crit. du V. Test. p. 136.
(*g*) Ib. p. 512.

difficult to find one of above 600 or 700 years old.

VIII.

That the apostles did not always quote the Septuagint version.

IT has been (*h*) *long disputed* among the *learned*, whether the citations made from the Old in the New Testament were taken from the *Hebrew* or *Greek bible.* Which seems a strange dispute: for it should seem easy to know from whence a man who makes several hundred quotations from the Old Testament, should take them. But several of those *quotations* being made after the jewish manner of quoting authors, wherein great liberty was taken in varying, both as to words and sense, from the authors quoted; the learned are at a loss how to account for many quotations, which neither agree to the *Hebrew* or *Septuagint*, and also how to account with certainty even for such as agree either with the *Hebrew* or *Septuagint*.

Mr. *W.* (*i*) contends, that the apostles always quoted the *Septuagint*. But, if we
may

(*h*) Whiston's *Essay*, p. 87.
(*i*) p. 176, &c.

[210]

may be govern'd in this case by the agreement of quotations with their originals, nothing seems more true, than what is imply'd in these words of *St.* Austin. (*k*) *For my part,* says he, *being desirous to follow the example of the apostles, who made use both of the Hebrew text and Septuagint version in citing the prophets, I thought, that I ought to make use of both, as being both the same, and having both the same divine autority.*

What can be more evident, than that the apostles sometimes cited the hebrew? For if there be a citation made by the apostles from the Old Testament, which, word for word, agrees with the hebrew text, and differs from the *Septuagint*, must not the said citation be suppos'd taken from the hebrew text, to which it agrees, and not from the *Septuagint*, to which it does not agree? Now this is the case (*l*) of the famous passage cited by Matthew out of Hoseah, "Out of Egypt have I called my *Son*;" which is read word for word in the hebrew bible; but in the Septuagint is, "Out of Egypt have I called my *Sons*." And this citation

---

(*k*) *August.* De Civitate Dei, l. 18. c. 44.
(*l*) *See Hieron.* in Os. l. 3. c. 11. & in Matt. l. 1. c. 2. *Capelli* Critica Sacra, p. 55.
Dupin Dissert. Prelim. sur la Bible, l. 1. c. 4. p. 87. Le note.

citation seems also to discover to us the reason, why the apostles do sometimes cite the *Hebrew*, as at other times they do the *Septuagint*, when these two texts differ, *viz.* because the hebrew reading seems sometimes more applicable to their purpose than the Septuagint reading. For in the case before us, the term *Son*, as the *Hebrew* reads it, seems more to favour the application of the passage to JESUS, than the *Septuagint* reading *Sons*, which, beyond all dispute, determines the citation to relate primarily to the children of *Israel*.

Again, does not MATTHEW (*m*) manifestly cite the hebrew text for these words, " (*n*) Behold my servant whom I have " chosen, my beloved, in whom my soul is " well pleased; " which agree to the *Hebrew*, and not to the *Septuagint*, that differs (*o*) greatly from the *Hebrew*, and makes express mention of JACOB and ISRAEL therein?

St. JEROM (*p*) says, *It is evident, that the apostles and evangelists made use of the hebrew scriptures. Our Lord and Redeemer,*

(*m*) Matt. 12. 18.
(*n*) Isaiah 42. 1.
(*o*) *See Kidder's* Demonstrat. of the Messias, Vol. 2. p. 207, 208.
(*p*) *Hieron.* l. 2. Apol. contra Ruffinum.

deemer, says he, *whenever he cites passages out of the Old Testament takes them from the Hebrew: As for example,* " He that belie-
" veth on me, *as the scriptures have said,*
" out of his belly shall flow rivers of living
" water;" *and upon the cross,* " Eli, Eli,
" Lamazabackthani," *that is to say,* " My
" God, my God, why hast thou forsaken me;"
and not as the Septuagint has render'd it, and divers other places. I say not this, says JEROM, *to discredit the Septuagint, but because I believe, that the autority of the apostles and* JESUS CHRIST *is preferable to theirs.*

I confess the apostles do seem (*q*) much more frequently to cite the Septuagint, than the *Hebrew* (tho' herein it may be easy to mistake, if it be true, what SIMON and Mr. *W.* affirm, that the Septuagint version has (*r*) *been accommodated* to the citations of the apostles; or what Mr. *W.* (*s*) himself also says, who not only *finds plain indications of the frequent accommodation of the Septuagint version to the latter Hebrew,* but the *alike* FREQUENT ACCOMMODATIONS OF

THE

(*q*) *See* Earl of Nottingham's *Answer to Mr.* Whiston's *Letter,* &c. p. 105.

Capelli Critica Sacra, l. 2.

(*r*) *Simon* Hist. Crit. du N. Test. p. 234. *and* Whiston's *Essay,* p. 199.

(*s*) p. 48, 49, 298, 299.

THE READINGS IN THE NEW TESTAMENT, *as also in* JOSEPHUS, *and others*, TO THOSE OF THE SEPTUAGINT, *whence they were commonly suppos'd to have been taken)*; and it is particularly manifest, that, in the famous (*t*) speech before the *Sanedrim*, attributed to St. STEPHEN, the *Septuagint*, and not the *Hebrew*, is cited in respect to the *number of souls*, that went down into *Egypt*; the *Septuagint* reckoning *seventy five souls*, and the Hebrew but *seventy*. But I must own my concurrence with father (*u*) SIMON in his conjecture, that it is not credible, that St. STEPHEN in the original *speech deliver'd by him to the Jews of Jerusalem recited the words otherwise than they were in the hebrew bible*; but that St. LUKE writing to those who either understood no Hebrew, or who chiefly or wholly used the *Septuagint version, was the author of that change*; which is so different from what is contain'd in the original of the Old Testament. For it seems very unaccountable, that St. STEPHEN should in his defence before the *Sanedrim* argue from an antient jewish fact, which that assembly by their knowledge in the hebrew tongue were undoubtedly able

P 3 to

(*t*) Acts 7. 14, 15.
(*u*) *Simon* Hist. Crit. du V. T. p. 186, 187. l. 2. c. 2.
See also Dupin Dissert. Prelim. l. 1. c. 4. *Note.* p. 486.

to detect as a misrepresentation of the jewish story, and would not fail to do so to the confusion of St. STEPHEN.

For further satisfaction in this point of the apostle's citing the hebrew text (and that even in places, where they seem to depart from the *Hebrew*) I refer him to the (*w*) *truly learned* Dr. (*x*) HODY; and to (*y*) SURENHUSIUS, who shows, how all the *apostolick quotations*, by being consider'd as *quotations*, made after the manner of the jewish doctors, were (or might be) taken from the *Hebrew*. It is evident; that, in many instances, the apostles cite passages, from the Old Testament, not only in a different literal sense from what they bear in their places both in the *Hebrew* and *Septuagint*, but whose words are to be found in neither of them; and, in particular, that many parts of the *genealogies* in the New Testament, which should seem to be taken from the Old Testament, are very different from the same genealogies recorded both in the *Hebrew* and *Septuagint*. So that, the citations of the apostles, whether consider'd as taken from either the *Hebrew* or *Septuagint*, must be accounted for from the jewish man-

---

(*w*) Whiston's *Essay*, p. 11.
(*x*) *Hody* De Text. Bibl. p. 243——271.
(*y*) *Surenbusii* Tract. &c. See p. 177, &c.

manner of making citations so as to serve the purposes for which they were produc'd. And therefore with as great reason, many of the apostolical citations may be suppos'd taken from the *Hebrew*, as from the *Septuagint*.

IX.

That the means whereby Mr. WHISTON *proposes to restore the true text of the Old Testament in respect to citations made from thence in the New, will not reach that end.*

THE design of Mr. WHISTON is to *vindicate the citations made from the Old in the New Testament*; and particularly such, as now seem either wholly wanting in the Old Testament, or seem unaccurately cited, or seem not justly apply'd by the authors of the New Testament; of all which sort of citations he gives us divers (z) examples.

This discordance between the Old and New Testament, he attributes to the Jews, whom he charges with corrupting the Old Testament in respect to those citations, with
ex-

(z) p. 281, 282. p. 88——109, 301——317, 321, 326, 329.

express design to make the reasonings of the apostles appear groundless and impertinent.

To *vindicate these citations* he proposes to *restore* a *true text* of the Old Testament, as it stood in the days of Jesus and his *apostles* (not the original text, which may have been (*a*) very different from that cited by the apostles); which *true text* is to manifest the truth and justness of the apostles citations and reasonings.

The (*b*) means, by which he proposes to *restore* this *true text*, are, The *Samaritan Pentateuch*; *the Greek psalms, as attested by the Roman psalter*; the *present Hebrew text*; the *several Greek editions* and *manuscripts of the Septuagint version, with other translations anciently made from it*; the old *Syriac version* made from the *Hebrew, before the copies of the Hebrew were so corrupt as they now are*; the *Chaldee paraphrases*; the *remains of the later Greek versions, particularly those of* Aquila, Theodotion, *and* Symmachus; the *antiquities of* Josephus; the *works of* Philo; the *Apostolick Constitutions*; the *fathers* and *hereticks, who liv'd before, or not long after the days of* Origen; the *Remains of the old italick or vulgar ver-*

(*a*.) *Simon* Hist. Crit. du V. T. p. 494.
(*b*) Whiston, p. 329, &c.

version; *Hebrew copies, which have never come into the hands of the* MASORETES, and *Greek copies of the vulgar Septuagint version* read in churches *all the first ages of christianity, or any parts of them*; and, above all *criticism* (tho' he places it not among his means) whereby he proposes to alter some passages, and to change the places of others, which he supposes *dislocated*. Upon all which means I shall make the following observations.

1. As to all the present known *Hebrew* and *Septuagint* copies; they being themselves *greatly corrupted*, and particularly, as he says, *corrupted* by the Jews with express design to confound the applications of the *apostolick citations* from the Old Testament; and their *true text*, with respect to those *corruptions* being the thing propos'd to be *restor'd*; the *true text* cannot be *restor'd* by any of, or all, those copies.

2. The *Chaldee Paraphrases were*, according to him, all (*c*) *made* for the support of the *new hebrew* (or *corrupted*) *text*, and for *securing its reception over all the world*. And the *later* (*d*) Greek *versions* plainly *follow that Hebrew text*, and *were made*, (*e*) *as it were, on purpose*
to

(*c*) p. 241, 242, 249.
(*d*) p. 267, 268.
(*e*) p. 233.

[218]

to establish and spread the new corrected or corrupted Hebrew *copies;* and some of them with (*f*) express design to oppose the *Septuagint*, which the apostles and first christians cited as favourable to christianity. So that these can no more restore a *true text*, than the *Hebrew* or *Septuagint* themselves.

3. As to the Syriac version, the copies of it are *less* (*g*) *exact, than the Hebrew text of the Jews, and the Greek version of the Septuagint:* And as to the *remains of the old italick, or vulgate version;* that was cited in a very (*h*) *inexact* manner by the Fathers, and was a verbal, barbarous, and unintelligible translation from the Septuagint, by an author, who understood no Hebrew; was *very different in different countries;* and was corrected by JEROM chiefly from the (corrupt) *Hebrew:* from whence it should seem, that the *remains* of it, which have been collected, are not much to be depended on. But to invalidate both the beforemention'd and all other *ancient translations;* it is sufficient to observe, that Mr. *W.* does not pretend from thence to render pertinent any citations made from the Old Testament, which
seem

(*f*) p. 241, 246, 247, 249.
(*g*) *Simon* Hist. Crit. du Vieux Testam. p. 277.
(*h*) p. 243, 244.

seem at present not pertinent, as they stand in the Old Testament.

4. As to the *Samaritan Pentateuch* (whose autority we have already particularly consider'd) and the Greek *psalms*, as *attested by the Roman psalter*; they can affect very few important citations, and particularly but few of the prophetical citations. And as to the citations they do affect, it is sufficient to observe, that the differences (*i*) *between the Hebrew original or the Greek version* of the Septuagint, *and the New Testament-citations, are but few, excepting in points of chronology, through the whole Pentateuch; and still fewer in the psalms of* DAVID, *as they now stand in the Greek. So that in the* Pentateuch *we have commonly the* Hebrew, *the* Samaritan, *and the* Septuagint; *and in the* Psalms, *the* Septuagint, *and the* Roman Psalter, *agreeing in their readings.* Wherefore, the *Samaritan Pentateuch*, and Greek *psalms*, *as attested by the Roman psalter*, cannot *restore* to us *the true text*, which Mr. *W.* contends for, in any important apostolick citations, whereon the truth of christianity is grounded.

5. As

(*i*) Whiston, p. 300.

5. As to the *antiquities of* Josephus; the (*k*) greatest liberty is taken therein to recede from the manifest sense of the Old Testament according to all copies thereof; the Old Testament is cited in such manner, as makes learned men dispute, whether he used the *Hebrew* or *Septuagint* text, or sometimes one and sometimes the other, or a different translation from the *Septuagint*; they have been (*l*) *accommodated* to the *Septuagint*, as the *Septuagint* has been accommodated to him; and (*m*) the *chronology* has been greatly *chang'd and alter'd*: so that it would be difficult to settle any certain readings of the Old Testament in virtue of his (*n*) *antiquities*. And as to the *works of* Philo, there are but *few citations* therein out of the Old Testament; and those only out of the *Septuagint Pentateuch*, whereof he had a very (*o*) *incorrect copy*. So that neither Josephus nor Philo concern the important citations in que-

---

(*k*) *Simon* Hist. Crit. du V. T. l. 1. c. 17.
Gregory *Disco. of the 70 Interpr.* p. 32, &c.
Wotton's *Preface to Misc. Disc.* p. 33, &c.
Whiston's *Essay*, p. 197, 216, 218, 299.
(*l*) p. 299.
(*m*) p. 21, 28, 195, 196, 197, 299.
(*n*) *For the State of* Josephus's *Antiq. see* Fabricii Bibliotheca Græca & Hueriana, p. 94.
Ib. p. 332.
(*o*) *Simon* Hist. Crit. du V. Test. p. 98.

question: nor does Mr. *W.* (*p*) pretend to *restore* a *true text* of the Old Testament from these two authors, in respect to any important citations made from the Old in the New Testament.

6. As to the *Hebrew copies, that have never come into the hands of the* MASORETES, and the Greek *copies* of the *vulgar Septuagint version, read in churches all the first ages of christianity, or any parts of them*; they no where appearing, and being themselves (*q*) to be *recover'd*, cannot, till *recover'd*, be of any use *towards restoring a true text*. They are themselves to be *restor'd*, in order to *restore a true text*.

7. As to the *apostolical constitutions*, the *fathers*; and the *hereticks*; it is sufficient to observe of them, as I have done of several of his former means (without taking notice, after what manner they cite the Old Testament) that Mr. *W.* is not able to settle by their help any apostolick quotations in the Old Testament, so as to make them pertinently apply'd, which now seem, according to him, to be impertinently apply'd. And I add, that these and all the foregoing *means*, will be so far from effecting what he proposes, that they will on the contrary show

that

(*p*) Whiston, p. 330, 391, 292, 289.
(*q*) p. 333.

that the apostles cited, and reason'd from, the Old Testament, just as they now appear, from our present view of the Old and New Testament, to have done. All which must be unaccountable on Mr. *W*'s *hypothesis*: for it cannot be suppos'd, that if the Jews have so *greatly corrupted* the Old Testament as Mr. *W.* pretends, but it would appear in some one instance at least, in some *one copy* or *author* exhibiting to us what would justify the pertinency of the application of what now seems impertinent.

8. The last *means* are, *making alterations* by the force of *criticisms*; which, tho' he has omitted among his *means*, is by the use he makes of it, and by the necessity he has of it, his principal, and, indeed, only means, and will, if any can, serve his purpose. For that extends to every quotation made from the Old in the New Testament; and gives him liberty and scope to chop and change the whole Old Testament as he pleases. Besides, the books of the Old Testament seem to give a just occasion for making many alterations, and especially to him, as will appear, if we consider the original condition of those books, (of whose method and order the *Rabbins* (r) had *this common maxim,*

(r) Lightfoot*'s Works*, Vol. 1. p. 666.

im, that *there is no first and last in the Holy Scripture*); if we consider the great changes and alterations which from time to time they have receiv'd; if we consider his opinion (*s*) of the corrupt state of those books, and especially of the books of the prophets; which were not only corrupted, according to him, in common with the other books of the Old Testament, before the coming of CHRIST, but have since the coming of CHRIST been corrupted by the Jews with express design to render the quotations made by the apostles from thence, seem impertinent; and lastly, if we consider his rejecting the (*t*) *Song of Songs* from the *Canon*, as an impious, loose, and obscene book, which *pious* (*u*) Christians *in all ages have esteem'd an allegorical dialogue between God and his church*. And it is not to be doubted but that his own inclination to admit the most precarious hypothesis, which he thinks necessary to support religion, will carry him to great extreams in alterations with the respect to the whole, as it has done already with respect to some parts of the Old Testament. For can there be, for example, a greater liberty taken in making alterations than by the mere force of *criticism*, to strike

out

(*s*) Whiston's *Boyl. Lect.* p. 67, and *Essay*, &c.
(*t*) *Suppl. to Essay.*
(*u*) Nichols's *Conf.* Vol. 3. p. 57.

[224]

out passages, which evidently determine the sense of *prophesies* to persons living in or near the suppos'd times of the prophets, and the applying those prophesies to Jesus as the Messias, or to very remote events from the times when the prophesies were deliver'd; as Mr. *W.* does in several (*w*) instances? For herein Mr. *W.* makes *prophesies*; which being *miracles*, and not things naturally to be suppos'd and credited, are at all times liable to *suspicion*, without the best proofs, that they were really made at the time they were said to be made. A man may fairly, with many christian divines, strike out the last chapter in *Deuteronomy*, and suppose, that Moses did not write historically of his own *death*, and *burial*, and of *matters* which came to pass long *after his death*; but to strike (*x*) out a passage in Samuel, which limits a *prophesy* to Solomon, and to strike out a passage in Isaiah, which limits a prophesy to a year or two from the time Isaiah deliver'd it, in order to make a prophesy of the Messias in the first case, and a prophesy about the birth of Jesus of the virgin Mary in the latter, is directly to make *prophesies* relate to persons, not only
not

(*w*) Boyl. Lect. p. 256. Essay, p. 229, &c.
(*x*) Boyl. Lect. p. 247, &c. 2 Sam. 7. 14. Essay, p. 229. Isaiah 7. 15, 16.

[225]

not thought of, but excluded, according to the literal sense of the prophets, by the prophets themselves; which is enthusiastical and absurd to the highest degree, and criticising and mending authors by *rules* the most improbable, and inconsistent with all true rules of *criticism*, which should lead a man frequently to lessen, but never to multiply, *miracles*. Mr. *W.* (y) is himself of opinion, that the *miracles themselves* reported by St. ATHANASIUS in the *Life* of St. ANTHONY do both denote their own falshood, and create a *suspicion* of the *integrity* of St. ATHANASIUS; tho' he relates them partly from St. ANTHONY himself, partly from the attestation of witnesses, and partly from his own knowledge.

So that I will venture to say, that a *bible restor'd*, according to Mr. *W*'s *Theory*, will be a mere WHISTONIAN BIBLE; a BIBLE confounding, and not containing *the true text of the Old Testament*.

In fine, Mr. *W.* (z) tells us himself, that he *finds plain indications of the frequent accommodation of the readings in the New Testament to those of the Septuagint*. Which, if true, seems to render an *Essay towards restoring the true text of the Old Testament*,

Q in

(y) Whiston's *Hist. Pref.* p. 120, 121.
(z) Whiston's *Essay*, p. 298, 299.

in order to *vindicate the apostolick citations*, a most unaccountable work. For by this account, the true or original apostolick citations are not themselves all known; and if all the present *citations* are plac'd according to Mr. *W*'s mind in the Old Testament, we shall not have *a true text restor'd*, but *a text frequently accommodated* to the corrupted text of the Septuagint, introduc'd into the Old Testament. And the work of restoring *a true* or genuine *text* of the Old Testament with respect to the apostolick citations from thence, seems a most impracticable work; when all the copies of the Old Testament are corrupted with express design to make those citations seem impertinent; and when the citations themselves, as standing in the New Testament, have receiv'd changes and alterations there.

X. *Typical*

[227]

X.

Typical or Allegorical reasoning defended against Mr. WHISTON; wherein is a digression that compares together the allegorical scheme, and Mr. WHISTON's literal scheme, and that proves his literal scheme false and absurd.

MR. WHISTON (*a*) condemns so highly the typical or allegorical interpretations of the *prophesies* cited from the Old in the New Testament, which yet the present state of the Old Testament makes necessary; that rather than come into that *weak and enthusiastical* method, as he calls it, he runs to the supposition of a *lost text*, of the Old Testament.

1. But yet he (*b*) justifies *typical* arguing *from the ritual laws of* MOSES, *and from passages of History in the Old Testament*, by the example of St. PAUL; who (being bred up (*c*) at the feet of GAMALIEL, the great

Rabbi,

(*a*) Whiston's *Essay*, p. 92.
(*b*) Whiston's *Boyl. Lect.* p. 27, 43.
(*c*) Jenkin's *Reasonab. of Christ. Relig.* Vol. 1. p. 321, 322.
 CUNEUS Rep. des Hebr. Vol. 1. l. 3. c. 8. p 373—376.
Simon Hist. Crit. du V. Test. p. 96.

Rabbi, by whom he was instructed in hebrew literature, and by consequence in all *the mysteries of the Jewish Cabala*) appears by his writings to be a great proficient in *types* and *allegories*, and is esteem'd by some Jews themselves as a *great Mekubal*, and profoundly skill'd in *the sublime sense of the bible*. Indeed, he pretends, (*d*) *this* last to be *quite another thing from the odd* (typical) *application of prophesies*. *For*, says he, *the ancient ceremonial institutions were, as to their principal branches at least, in their own nature* (*e*) Types *and* Shadows of future good things *under the christian dispensation. And several remarkable events and histories of old time, seem to have been particularly recorded for the sake of some future truths and discoveries, which were to be drawn from them. But the case of the ancient prophesies, to be alledg'd from the old scriptures for the* CONFIRMATION *of christianity, is quite of another nature, and of a more nice and exact consideration.*

But how are these things different? For are not *the ritual laws of* MOSES, *by being in their own nature* types and shadows of future good things, *prophesies*? And are not
the

(*d*) Whiston, Ib. p. 27.
(*e*) Heb. 16. 1.

the events and histories of old time, by being *recorded for the sake of some future truths and discoveries, which were to be drawn from them*, (f) *prophesies* also? And does not our Saviour himself say so, when he affirms, that the (g) *Law prophesies*, and that he came to *fulfil* the *Law*, as well as the *Prophets*? And do not Mr. *W's prophetical types confirm* christianity? And may not *typical prophesies confirm* it in the same manner?

Mr. *W.* therefore ought to own, either that our *Saviour* and St. PAUL talk'd *weakly* and *enthusiastically*, when they interpreted *the ritual laws of* MOSES, and the *passages of history* contain'd in the Old Testament (which they look'd on as *prophesies*) typically; or else to allow the typical and allegorical method of interpreting the *passages* cited in the New Testament from the prophets, which he now calls *weak* and *enthusiastical*, to be excellent and divine. Besides, as to strength of argument; what is the difference between an allegorical interpretation of a prophesy, and an allegorical interpretation of a *law* or *passage of history*? Is not there as much force in the allegorical interpretation of any prophesy, as

---

(f) *See* Justini Martyris Opera, p. 261.
(g) Mat. 11. 13.

as there is in the two following typical arguments in the *Apostolick Constitutions*, which Mr. *W.* deems *the most sacred of the canonical books of the New Testament?* (*h*) *Tythes belong to those who minister to* CHRIST, *because tenths of salvation are the first letter of the name of* JESUS, i. e. I, IOTA.—— *Hear, O thou holy catholick Church, who hast receiv'd the* TEN *Commandments, and hast escap'd the* TEN *Plagues.* Ergo, pay tythes to the Priest.——(*i*) *Let a widow who is the altar of God sit at home: for the altar of God never runs about, but is fix'd in one place.*

Why cannot Mr. *W.* as well allow of the force of typical interpretations of prophesies as of the typical arguments of St. BARNABAS, who is one of his canonical authors? BARNABAS's *epistle* is wholly made up of typical reasoning; of which take this one Specimen. " (*k*) The Scripture says, that ABRAHAM
" *circumcis'd three hundred and eighteen*
" *men of his house.* But what therefore
" was the mystery that was made known
" unto him? Mark first the EIGHTEEN, and
" next the THREE HUNDRED. For the nu-
" meral letters of *Ten* and *Eight*, are I. H.
" And

(*h*) *Apostol. Constit.* l. 2. c. 25.
(*i*) Ib. l. 3. c. 6.
(*k*) Wake's *Genuine Epistles, &c.* p. 175, 176.

"And those denote JESUS. And because the
"cross was that by which we were to find
"grace; therefore he adds, *three hundred*;
"the note of which is T (*the figure of his
"Cross*). Wherefore by two letters he signi-
"fy'd JESUS, and by the third his Cross. He
"who has put the engrafted gift of his doctrine
"within us, knows that I never taught to
"any one a more certain truth." And accordingly this argument was deem'd of so
much weight, that our learned Archbishop
tells us, in a note, that (*l*) *many others of
the ancient fathers concurr'd with* BARNABAS
in this, and he refers us to authors for proof
thereof.

In fine, is there not as much force in typical prophesies as in the typical arguments
of St. CLEMENT, another of Mr. *W*'s canonical authors? To say nothing here of
St. CLEMENT's *history of the* PHENIX, which
he (*m*) makes *a type of the Resurrection*, I
desire Mr. *W.* attentively to consider the following passage.

"(*n*) The spies gave RAHAB moreover
"a Sign; that she should hang out of her
"house a (*o*) *Scarlet Robe*: shewing there-
"by, that by the blood of our Lord there
"should

(*l*) p. 175.
(*m*) Ib. p. 21.
(*n*) Ib. p. 10, 11.
(*o*) Josh. 2. 18.

" should be redemption to all that believe
" and hope in God. Ye see, beloved, how
" there was not only faith, but Prophesy
" too in this woman." Which words contain not only a typical argument for christianity, (which was deem'd so strong as to be (*p*) *apply'd by many of the fathers to the same purpose*), but assert Rahab to make a *prophesy* in hanging out the *Scarlet Rope*. From whence it appears, that *types* are *prophesies*, and that the distinction Mr. *W.* would make between them, is groundless and false.

2. Mr. *W.* (*q*) says, Jerom *was one of the first christian writers now extant, that ever gave such strange interpretations of these ancient prophesies.*

I find (*r*) indeed Jerom represented as *thinking*, that the passages of the Old Testament were quoted, *susq; deq;* in the New Testament. Upon which account he was necessarily driven into the *allegorical hypotheses*. But yet, he seems to me, to have acted liked all others before him, and not to have been *one of the first christian writers, now extant*, who *gave allegorical interpre-*

(*p*) Wake, Ib. p. 11.
(*q*) Whiston's *Essay*, p. 91, 92.
(*r*) *Surenhusii* Prefat. ad Concil. p. 4.
Ib. Concil. p. 177.

pretations of the prophesies cited in the New Testament.

[1.] First, it is notorious, and has been made *(s)* appear by others, and is confessed by Mr. *W.* himself, that the *apostles* and primitive *fathers* interpreted the *ritual ceremonies of the law*, and the *historical passages* of the Old Testament, *typically:* which, as appear'd just now, is interpreting *prophesies* in that manner. As to the commentaries of the fathers on, and their interpretations of, the Old Testament, they are so wholly allegorical, that it would be difficult to find many passages, not so interpreted, if interpreted at all by them. They were no criticks, and despis'd the literal sense of the Old Testament as low and mean, and imploy'd their invention to find out sublime senses thereof.

[2.] Secondly, Mr. *W.* *(t)* says, that the Apostles themselves do *so* seem to have cited and *apply'd* the *prophesies* they take from the Old Testament, that if you consider them as taken from the present Old Testament, it is *in a manner impossible to expound or apologize for those applications of the Old prophesies*

(s) Platonisme Devoilé, p. 162——197.
Simon Hist. Crit. du V. T. p. 97.
Whiston's *Lect.* p. 27.
Wake's prelim. to genuine Epist. p. 71——75.
(t) Whiston's *Essay*, p. 92.

phesies upon any other foundation, than by the said typical, mystical, secundary, or allegorical way of application; and that *(u) the ancient predictions concerning the* Messias *and his character, tho' of so great importance to be easily understood, are* (originally) *some of them so obscure and doubtful in their designation of persons, or in their expressions, and others of them so hidden in unsuitable places, and introduc'd upon very remote occasions,* in a word, *(w) fram'd on purpose to be long conceal'd, as to have given a handle* to the introduction of the *allegorical hypothesis*. Which two considerations make it seem a very difficult matter to lay aside the *allegorical scheme*, and not to admit it as the *scheme* by which the apostles themselves proceeded. For, if the present state of the Old and New Testament, in respect to the quotations made from the former in the latter, does admit of no other *scheme* to justify their application but the *allegorical scheme*; and, if the original state of the ancient predictions was such, that they were *obscure and doubtful in their designation of persons* (that is, that they seem'd as applicable or more applicable to others, than to the Messias,) *or hidden in*

un–

(*u*) Ib. Boyl. *Lect.* p. 58.
(*w*) Ib. p. 15.

unsuitable places, and introduc'd upon remote occasions (that is, that by their context they seem'd not to bear the sense put upon them by the apostles) and thereby *gave* a *handle* for the *allegorical scheme:* what is so natural, as to suppose, from the said present and original state, the *allegorical scheme* to be the *scheme* by which the apostles made application of the prophesies they cited from the Old Testament?

But Mr. *W.* himself seems to me by many particulars, which he advances, to give up his own *literal* or *rational scheme*, and to lay a just foundation for us to suppose, that the apostles proceeded on the *allegorical scheme*.

He says (x) SCARCE *any of the quotations in the evangelists are taken out of those prophesies, which by evident circumstances belong to any other person, but the Messias.* Whereby he owns, or, at least distrusts, that some of the *quotations in the Evangelists are taken out of prophesies, which by evident circumstances belong to* some *other persons, than the* MESSIAS. And consequently, he must suppose those *quotations out of the prophesies* to be typically apply'd; the very nature of typical application lying, in applying passages, which in their literal and

---

(x) Ib. p. 45.

and obvious sense, belong to one person, to another

Again he says, (*y*) MUCH *the greatest part of those prophesies, which are alledg'd by the evangelists, are plainly and certainly meant of the* MESSIAS. Which implies, that *some* of the *quotations alledg'd by the evangelists* are not *plainly and certainly* meant of the MESSIAS; and, by consequence, that they are, or may be, typically apply'd by the evangelists.

He says, that several (*z*) of the quotations taken out of the Old Testament by the evangelists, *do better and more literally agree to the* MESSIAS *than to those of whom they are ordinarily expounded, and have* COMMONLY *some one or more characters, which will agree to no others but him.* Which is a confession against himself, and in favour of the *allegorical scheme.* For if the prophesies cited *agree* to others, tho' not so *well* nor so *literally*, as to the MESSIAS, and have not ALWAYS some character, which will *agree* to none but him; then those prophesies do agree to others, and can, with certainty, be only urg'd *typically*.

He says, there are (*a*) quotations *which do seem by the coherence of their places* in the

---

(*y*) Ib. p. 48.
(*z*) Ib. p. 49.
(*a*) Ib. p. 51—54.

the Old Testament *to belong to others than the* Messias; nay, are *contrary to the coherence, wherein they appear* there. Which should make those quotations *seem* allegorically apply'd, as being apply'd in a sense not only seemingly different from, but *contrary* to that sense they bear in the Old Testament. For, as the apostles could be guilty of no mistakes, and could not intend to apply those quotations *literally*, and yet apply them in a sense *contrary* to their literal meaning, that is, could not mistake their literal meaning in the application of them, so, by not applying them in their true literal sense, but in a sense *contrary* to that, they must, by consequence, intend to apply them in an allegorical sense.

He seems to allow St. Paul argu'd typically from the *scripture-prophesies* in these words; (b) *I do not*, says he, *undertake to account for all the quotations of St.* Paul, *out of the Old Testament in his epistles,* (that is, he does not undertake to show that they are literally apply'd); *not only because his style is peculiar, and he together with his fellow-worker St.* Barnabas *did, more than all the rest of the apostles, make use of allegorical notions and interpretations, then own'd among the Jews;*
but

(b) p. 43.

[238]

but also because FEW *or none of his quotations of this nature are taken from the* scripture-prophesies, but GENERALLY *either from the* histories *or* ceremonies *contain'd* in the Old Testament. For if some FEW of his quotations are taken from scripture-prophesies, and if his quotations are, but *generally*, or for the most part, taken from the *histories* and *ceremonies* recorded in the Old Testament, the point is yielded with respect to St. PAUL.

Mr. *W.* is reduc'd to great (*c*) shifts by his *literal* or *rational scheme*. Not being able to reconcile the (*d*) application made by St. MATTHEW, of a quotation out of JEREMY (*e*) in relation to the slaughter of the *children* in *Bethlehem*, by his scheme; he denies that quotation to be a *prophesy* (tho' St. MATTHEW cites the words of JEREMY as *fulfill'd*; which is the very term he uses in relation to all the prophesies cited by him) alledging, that it is a *poetick description or lamentation fulfill'd or verify'd*. Which is, at the bottom actually running into the allegorical or typical hypothesis, that he pretends to avoid and to dread. For what is a *poetick description fulfill'd*, but a typical

---

(*c*) Ib. p. 55, 56.
(*d*) Matt. 2. 17, 18.
(*e*) Jer. 31. 15.

pical prophefy *fulfill'd?* And why does he call the quotation in queſtion *a poetick deſcription;* but becauſe it is a moſt manifeſt deſcription of another fact, and not of that fact, for which it was cited; wherein conſiſts the very nature of an allegorical quotation? The quotations made from the *Old* Teſtament, and ſaid to be *fulfill'd* in the New, had ſome of them, perhaps, no meaning in the minds of the prophets, who ſometimes (*f*) *underſtood not* what they *meant themſelves:* and all the quotations, as far as we can underſtand them, ſeem to have as remote a *ſenſe* given them from the prophets words, as the quotation in queſtion; which *ſenſe* would have had no foundation, had not the inſpir'd apoſtles put that ſenſe upon them; nay, many of thoſe quotations would ſeem not to be *propheſies*, did not the apoſtles ſay, they were *fulfill'd*, or *propheſies fulfill'd.* This being the Caſe of the quotations made by the apoſtles, they are ſaid by the learned to be typically or allegorically apply'd by them: Now this is alſo the caſe of the quotation, which Mr. *W.* calls a *poetick deſcription fulfill'd.* It conſiſts of words, which as they ſtand in JEREMY, bear a different literal ſenſe from that

---

(*f*) Ib. p. 78.
Nichols's *Conf. with a Theiſt*, Vol. 3. p. 69.

that for which they are cited, and are there apply'd to another matter, and would not be deem'd to lignify that for which they are cited, nor even deem'd a prophefy, did not the apoftle fay, they were *fulfill'd*. Mr. *W.* therefore plainly has recourfe to the *allegorical hypothefis* in this one cafe; and fince he admits it in one cafe, he may as well admit it in all cafes. For if it be a *weak* and *enthufiaftick* hypothefis, as he affirms, it is an equal imputation on the apoftles to make them once argue *weakly* and *enthufiaftically*, as to make them always argue fo. And if it be a good method of arguing, as he muft allow it to be in this inftance, it is a good one in all cafes.

He is reduc'd to the *(g) fhift* of denying a quotation made by our Saviour himfelf to be taken from a place, whence it is manifeftly taken. To which he is merely driven, by the faid quotation's manifeftly belonging to another matter in its literal fenfe, in the place where it ftands in the Old Teftament, than that for which it is cited. Our Saviour's quotation *(h)* in thefe words (*I fpeak not of you all; I know whom I have chofen: but that the fcripture may be fulfill'd*, "He "that eateth bread with me hath lift up "his

---

(g) Ib. p. 56.
(h) John 13. 18.

"his heel againſt me") is plainly taken from *Pſalm* 41. 9. where the words are, *The man of my peace, which eateth my bread, hath lift up his heel againſt me.* (*i*) But Mr. *W.* ſenſible that that pſalm does not in its literal ſenſe *belong to the* Messias, does, to ſave his *hypotheſis*, and for fear of having recourſe to the *allegorical hypotheſis* for a ſolution of our Saviour's application of the paſſage cited by him, believe it taken from another place; which place no one ever found out before him, and plainly cannot be intended by Jesus, and only ſerves to furniſh matter for wrangling.

But Mr. *W.* himſelf ſeems to me directly to ſet up the *allegorical hypotheſis*, and to make it uſed univerſally by the apoſtles. He contends (*k*) *the propheſies of ſcripture, which relate to chriſtianity, are cover'd, myſtical and enigmatical.* Thus in the prophefy of Hoseah (*l*) referr'd to and cited by Matthew, " When Iſrael was a child, " I loved him, and called my ſon out of " Egypt," he underſtands without any grounds from language, Israel to be *a prophetick name of* Christ (tho' that language is with him ſo uncertain, that he has

ſince

(*i*) Whiſton's *Lect.* p. 57, 58.
(*k*) Ib. p. 7, 9, 11, 12.
(*l*) Hoſea 11. 1.

since chang'd his mind, and by (*m*) *Israel* in this place does not now understand CHRIST, but the *Israelites*) and *literally* (that is, as he owns himself, *covertly*, *mystically*, and *enigmatically*) to signify him. What then is the difference between him, and his *weak and enthusiastical* adversaries? They say, that ISRAEL signifies, first, literally in HOSEAH the children of *Israel*, and then typically signifies CHRIST, grounding this last on MATTHEW, who puts that typical, mystical, or secondary meaning upon it. And Mr. *W.* says, the prophet meant by ISRAEL, CHRIST only: which is exactly equal *mysticism* with, and just as remote from the real literal sense of HOSEAH as the mysticism of the *allegorists*, and is altogether as obscure to the understanding. And I do not see, why Mr. *W.* may not as well suppose two meanings, the one *literal* and the other *allegorical* or *mystical*; as to lay aside the *true literal meaning*, and yet contend for the same (mystical) meaning with his adversaries, under the notion of that *mystical meaning* being the *literal meaning*. Certainly he would be less absurd, if he contended at the same time for the true literal meaning together with his mystical-literal meaning.

Thus

(*m*) Whiston's *Essay*, &c. p. 88, &c.

Thus again Mr. *W.* understands the famous passage (*n*) in *Genesis*, (*The Lord God said unto the serpent, because thou hast done this thou art cursed above all cattle, and above every beast of the field; upon thy belly shalt thou go, and dust shalt thou eat all the days of thy life: and I will put enmity between thy seed and her seed; he shall bruise thy head, and thou shalt bruise his heel*) to be all (*o*) *prophetick dialect*, and that the *serpent* in that *dialect* signifies the *Devil*, and the *seed of the woman*, CHRIST; tho' no words can more plainly express, nor any context more evidently prove, that *serpent*, signifies a real serpent, *a beast of the field*, and that the *seed of the woman* signifies the descendants of EVE; and some Theologues (*p*) themselves confess, they *would not chuse this* prophesy *to convert an Infidel*.

So that it is plain Mr. *W.* is as great a typist, mystist, or allegorist, as his adversaries; and he must make the apostles such as himself.

R 2 And

(*n*) Gen. 3. 14, 15.
(*o*) Whiston's *Lect.* p. 35, 82 —— 93.
See Grotius & Clericus in Locum.
Blackmore's *Redemption*, p. 62.
Spencer De leg. Heb. p. 181.
(*p*) Nichols's *Conference with a Theist*, Vol. 3. p. 34.

(*q*) And I add, that if the *allegorists scheme* be *weak and enthusiastical*, his scheme is yet more so, by receiving the *weak and enthusiastical* part of their scheme, and rejecting the *rational* part.

The *allegorists* do in the first place, endeavour to find out the true literal sense of the prophets, in the same manner that good criticks do with respect to all other authors; which certainly is a method highly rational in it self. When they have done this, if they find quotations of the prophets apply'd by the apostles in another sense, or not according to the literal sense which they bear in the prophets themselves, they put that sense also upon them, in which the apostles apply'd them. Thus they act the part of good interpreters with respect to the Old prophets themselves, and with respect to the apostles, and to the Holy Ghost, whose sense of the prophets the apostles declar'd. This is the method of the great GROTIUS; whose commentaries on the bible will ever be esteem'd by all those who desire truly to understand it; notwithstanding the imputation of some upon him, that he could *neither find the* MESSIAS *in the Old Testament, nor the pope in the New*. But the anti-allegorists rejecting the method of GROTIUS;

of

(*q*) *A Digression against Mr.* W's *Literal Scheme.*

of a critical examination of the writings of the prophets by the common use of language, and supposing the prophets to use common words in a peculiar and enigmatical sense, and most remote from vulgar acceptation, and making that remote-enigmatical sense to be the literal sense, are guilty of the highest absurdity imaginable. For they not only put a sense upon the prophet's words, which is remote from the literal sense (wherein they so far concur with the allegorists); but proceeding by rules contrary to all use of language and to common sense, they put a sense upon the words subversive of the true literal sense; whereby properly speaking they are no interpreters at all, or rather worse than none, being mere indulgers of fancy. And there has never been a typist, mystist, or allegorist (no, not BURMAN or ALTING, or ALLIX, or the great COCCEIUS himself, all celebrated for putting remote allegorical senses on the Old Testament) that have exceeded Mr. *W.* in extravagancy: who, for example, finds (*r*) the *destruction of Jerusalem by the Romans* in the four first verses of the 29th of ISAIAH; the (*s*) *destruction of the Turks* at *Armageddon* in the

---

(*r*) *Whiston*'s Essay on the Revelations, p. 303, 312.
(*s*) Ib. p. 361, 363.

four next verses; the same (*t*) *destruction of Jerusalem by the Romans*, in the first 20 verses of the 24th chapter; the (*u*) *restoration of the Jews to their own country*, in the 23d verse of that chapter; and, what is still more extravagant, the (*w*) *destruction of the Turks, &c.* in verses 17———23 of the same chapter, whereby the same verses have, according to him, at the same time several remote-absurd-pretended-literal meanings: tho' ISAIAH's view and intention in all these places have no obscurity or difficulty in them, and do most plainly relate to the great ravage the Assyrian army should make in *Judea*, and of the destruction of that army. And Mr. *W*. to support this hypothesis of such remote-literal meaning, is forc'd to represent the prophets, as the most incoherent and (*x*) *abrupt* writers imaginable, and to break their several books, whose parts are connected and depend on each other, into independent prophesies; for did he consider them as authors having the least connection in their writings, that connection would limit their sense to some very obvious mat-

---

(*t*) Ib. p. 303, 310.
(*u*) p. 322, 325.
(*w*) p. 361, 362.
(*x*) Whiston's *Lect.* p. 67. *See also his Collection of Scripture-Prophesies at the end of his Essay on the Revelation.*

matters, and take away all colour for such increase of prophesies, and for the chimerical meaning he puts upon those his fictitious prophesies.

He endeavours (*y*) to support his hypothesis by saying, *If the prophesies are allow'd to have more than one event in view at the same time, we can never be satisfy'd, but they have as many as any visionary pleases; and so instead of being capable of a direct and plain exposition to the satisfaction of the judicious, will be liable to the foolish application of fanciful and enthusiastick men.* As if his method which, as has appear'd, subjects the prophesies to the very same kind of chimerical meanings, and often to the very same meanings with the allegorists, was less absurd, because every single visionary can have but one such chimerical meaning at a time, or exercise but one (*z*) *extravagant liberty of fancy or of interpretation.* As to his saying, (*a*) *that if this double intention in prophesies be allow'd by us christians, we lose all the real advantages as to the proof of our common christianity; and, besides, expose ourselves to the insults of Jews and Infi-*

(*y*) Whiston's *Lect.* p. 15.
(*z*) Ib. *Essay on the Revelation*, p. 24.
(*a*) Ib. *Lectures*, p. 16.

Infidels in our discourses with them: I answer, how can he hope less to expose himself to *Jews* and *Infidels* than the *allegorists*, by putting the same remote meaning on the prophesies with them under the notion of that remote meaning being the literal meaning? Will not, nay must not the *Jews and Infidels* see each of their meanings to be equally remote from the true literal meaning, by what ever names their meaning is call'd? And by consequence, must they not reject with equal contempt the enigmatical-literal meaning of Mr. *W.* as well as the allegorical meaning of others? And will not they in a particular manner insult, when they find him (*b*) changing and altering the *holy bible*, according to his pleasure, in order to avoid the scheme of a *double sense of prophesies*, and to introduce his own *cover'd, mystical, enigmatical-literal* scheme.

I know he pretends in behalf of his *scheme*; that there is a peculiar (*c*) *prophetick language*; and that the words of the prophets, tho' not understood according to their common sense, or in the same sense as in any other discourses, have yet a single, fix'd, and determinate signification. And he and others sup-

---

(*b*) *Allix's* Rem. on Whiston's Papers, p. 7.
(*c*) Whiston's Boyl. Lect. and Essay on the Revelation of St. John.

suppose, that they have in divers respects found out the certain *rules* of that language; in virtue of which they pretend to be no less positive in their interpretations of certain prophesies, than if they were historical passages, wherein words are used in their common sense. And it must be confess'd, that many prophesies explain'd and apply'd, according to those *rules*, to certain past events, have such an *agreement* to those events, as to occasion many to think those prophesies rightly explain'd, and even to (*d*) excuse some disagreement between the *prophesies* and the *events*, as a defect only in the explainers.

But such *agreement* ought to carry no real conviction along with it. For the reason of such *agreement* is plainly this, that the explainers have had both the *prophesies* and *events* lying for a long time before them, with a view to make them accord. In consequence whereof, they have by mending and piecing of systems, and varying and changing ideas to words, found out the most plausible meanings possible for certain words in the prophesies, in order to apply those prophesies to the events they would have to be intended in them. For nothing is easier than for artful and learned men to make accommodations,

---

(*d*) Nichols's *Conf. with a Theist*, Vol. 3. p. 107.

tions, in this case, between things, to a certain degree. But perfect accommodations seem impossible: and accordingly, no explications grounded on the before-mention'd pretended *rules*, of any prophesies existing before the events, and referr'd to past events, will perfectly agree to those events (tho' the pretended *peculiarity* of the language gives the explainers the utmost latitude to assign what ideas they please to words); as (for an example) may be seen by the several explications invented in relation to DANIEL's *weeks*, or any other such prophesies. For as to DANIEL's *weeks*; let them understand by *weeks*, *weeks of years* (tho' there be no (*e*) foundation in the Old Testament for such use of the word) or what other portion of time they think fit; let them understand by *a year*, the Jewish or Chaldean, a lunar or solar year, or a mystical year, which, it seems, consists (*f*) of 343 *days*; let them begin the *weeks* in the reign of CYRUS, or DARIUS, or XERXES, or in the seventh or twentieth of ARTAXERXES LONGIMANUS, or when DANIEL had his vision (for the (*g*) *going forth of the commandment to build and restore Jerusalem*, which is suppos'd to

fix

(*e*) *Le Clerc* Bibl. Choif. tom. 15. p. 201.
(*f*) *Crenii* Fascic. primus, p. 406.
(*g*) Dan 9. 25.

fix the time when the *weeks* begin, is thus variously understood); let them fix the time of Jesus's birth, or beginning to preach, or death, when they please (for very different years are assign'd for each of these); and let them assign the time of the expiration of the 70 *weeks*, which is very variously fix'd, when they please: yet cannot this prophesy be made to square to the event they would refer it, and it will after all be subject to great (*b*) *difficulties.* Bishop MOUNTAGUE, after having finish'd his explication of this prophesy, (*i*) says, that *Prophesies are accompany'd with extensions, not ever precisely at, or upon, but about such a time, to be accomplish'd; and therefore they are not to be streighten'd to an hour, a day, a month, or certain set period, punctually, but left unto a latitude or extent.* The learned (*k*) ISAAC VOSSIUS says, *Nulla Chronologiæ pars vexatior est, ac illa, quæ agit de* 70 *hebdomadibus* DANIELIS. *Ab Apostolicis temporibus ad nostram usq; ætatem laboravere in hoc argumento complures, Viri sancti & eruditi. Sed si usquam, certè hic vanus & irritus fuit ipsorum labor. Peccavere tam in principio quam fi-*
ne

(*b*) Prideaux's *Connection*, Vol. 1. p. 306.
(*i*) Mountague's *Acts and Monuments*, p. 149.
(*k*) *Vossii* de Sept. Interp. &c. p. 183.

ne hebdomadibus istis adsignando, adeoq; a se invicem longe abivere, ut si quis discrepantes eorum evolvat sententias, facile intelligat, ubi tanta est contentio, ibi vel nullam vel incertam esse veritatem. Dr. NICHOLS, in his (*l*) elaborate work against the *deists*, says in relation to this prophesy of DANIEL, *The wise providence of God hath suffer'd these matters to lye in some manner of confusion, that our faith might be founded on a nobler principle than that of chronological niceties.* And the ingenious and learned Sir JOHN FLOYER, one of the latest explainers of this prophesy, says, (*m*) *That the Holy Spirit seems always to design a variety of computation in* MOST *prophesies, that the completion might not be exactly known; and the design of the computations is only to point out the age when the great events are to happen, and begin or end.*

But the *agreements* beforemention'd, between *explications* and *events*, being often such as greatly affect men, who are willing and forward to believe certain prophecies rightly explain'd, I will make a further observation; which will in my opinion confound this scheme of *literal-mystical prophesy*

(*l*) Nichols's *Conf. with a Theist*, Vol. 3. p. 107.
(*m*) Floyer's *Prophesies of Esdras, &c.* p. 139.

phefy founded on the pretended intelligibility of *prophetick language* as a *peculiar language*; and that is as follows. If Mr. Whiston, and others, have, as they pretend, found out the *rules* of the *prophetick language* of the *bible*, they muſt be as able to explain, in virtue of thoſe *rules*, the prophefies therein contain'd, which relate to events to come, as thoſe which relate to events that are paſt. For if the language be fix'd and certain, there can be no more difficulty in underſtanding the former than the latter. But there have been no explainers of the *Revelation* of St. John (for example) but are at endleſs and at the greateſt contradictions with each other about the *trumpets*, the *ſeals*, the *vials*, and the *white horſe*, &c. and time has and daily does diſcover their egregious miſtakes (not excepting the miſtakes of Mr. Whiston himſelf, who has liv'd long enough to ſee himſelf miſtaken in ſome of the *prophetick language* of the *Revelation*) in explaining the ſaid book, which has been apply'd to all ages of the church, as having a view to the ſeveral hereſies, ſchiſms, battles, and revolutions which have happen'd.

This ſcheme of a *prophetick language*, therefore, being not yet underſtood by any mortal, ſhould be wholly laid aſide; and by conſequence a *literal propheſy* in Mr. Whis-

WHISTON's sense is a mere *chimera*, that never existed, but in the explainer's brain.

[3.] Thirdly, the allegorical method of explaining and applying prophesies should seem very proper for the apostles; who were Jews; and who were used not only to the *parabolical* and *mystical* discourses of our Saviour (many of which are suppos'd to have been common (*n*) among the Jews, and are now to be found in their *Talmud*), but to his *mystical prophesies*.

He often spoke only to those who (*o*) *had ears to hear*, and sometimes so as (*p*) *not to be understood* by any body at the time he spoke. He spoke of *bread*, and of *water*, and of the *temple*, and of *being born again*, but meant contrary to the judgment of his hearers (some of whom he knew, as he intended they should, would understand him according to the letter) *spiritual bread, mystical water*, the *temple of his body*, and *spiritual birth*. He prophesy'd of his own death and resurrection in so *typical* a manner (saying for example, (*q*) *destroy this temple, and in three*

(*n*) *Fabricii* Cod. Apoc. Nov. Test. pars 3. p. 431. *Ockley's* Letter before Wotton's Misc. Disc.
(*o*) Luke 14. 35.
(*p*) Ib 9. 45. John 16. 17, 18.
(*q*) John 2. 19.

three days I will raise it up---(r) *As* Moses *lifted up the serpent in the wilderness,
so must the son of man be lifted up*---(s) *As*
Jonas *was a sign to the Ninevites, so shall the
son of man be to this generation)* that his disciples expected no such thing as his resurrection, and when they were first told of it by
very unexceptionable witnesses, *women* of their
acquaintance, look'd on it as an (t) *idle tale.*
Which ignorance of theirs in this case seems, I
must confess, surprizing; because the Jews
themselves understood our Saviour to have
plainly declar'd, *while (u)* he was alive, that
after three days he would *rise again*, and therefore watch'd his grave, lest his disciples should
take away his body.

His *prophesy* about his (w) coming again,
which he expresly limits to the lives of some
of his auditors, and to the present *generation,*
is wholly *mystical*: for it is manifest, that
the apostles, who understood him literally
(at first) and expected his speedy reign upon
earth, were all (x) mistaken, and should
have understood him *mystically*, as they did

(r) John 3. 14.
(s) Luke 11. 30.
(t) Ib. 24. 11.
(u) Matt. 27. 63----66.
(w) John 1. 51. Matt. 16. 28. Luke 21. 27—36.
Whiston's *Essay on the Revel.* p. 129----135.
(x) *Millii* Proleg. ad Nov. Testam. p. 146. col. 2.

at length, when they came to understand that *(y) a thousand years were with the Lord as one day, and one day as a thousand years.* Our Lord himself no less mystically declar'd the time of his coming to reign, when he said to those who ask'd him about it, *that his reign would begin* (z) *cum duo erunt unum, & quod foris, ut quod intus est, & masculum cum fœminâ, neq; mas, neque fœminâ.* In like myftical manner our Saviour CHRIST deſcrib'd, or propheſy'd of, the *ſtate* of his *kingdom*, which was ſoon to come. *I will,* ſays he (a) to his diſciples, *appoint you a kingdom, that ye may eat and drink at my table in my kingdom, and ſit on thrones, judging the twelve tribes of Iſrael.* But this, he ſeems to have done in the ampleſt manner in a paſſage recorded by IRENÆUS, upon the autority of PAPIAS and ſome *old men,* who had it from St. JOHN, that our Lord (b) ſhould ſay, *The days ſhall come, in which there ſhall be vines, which ſhall ſeverally have ten thouſand branches, and every of thoſe branches ſhall have ten thouſand leſſer branches, and every of theſe branches ſhall have*

(y) 2 Pet. 7. 4, 8.
(z) *Clemens* apud *Grabe,* Spicil. Vol. 1. p. 35.
(a) Luke 22. 29, 30.
(b) *Irenæus,* l. 5. c. 33.

have ten thousand twigs, and every one of these twigs shall have ten thousand clusters of grapes, and in every one of these clusters there shall be ten thousand grapes, and every one of these grapes being press'd shall yield 275 gallons of wine; and when one shall take hold of one of these sacred bunches, another bunch shall cry out, I am a better bunch, take me, and bless the Lord by me. I omit what our Lord adds of *every grain of wheat,* and of *apples, seeds,* and *herbs.*

The few denyers, of a *kingdom, immediately to come,* among the primitive christians, attempted (c) to allegorize the places produc'd for it, and upon that account were call'd *allegorists*; as on the contrary Papias, Justin Martyr, Irenæus, Origen, Eusebius, Epiphanius, and others, who believ'd it soon to come, were call'd *disciples of the letter.* And all christians may now be justly styl'd *allegorists*; since (d) none of them *agree* with the primitive christians in the literal interpretation of these matters.

But the *Revelation* of St. John is certainly a master-piece of *mystical-prophesy,* being

---

(c) See Whitby's *Treatise of the Millennium.*
(d) Ib. p. 254.

being (*e*) written, as 'tis said, in the *cabalystick style*: and no doubt but it will appear so; when things, the most remote from the literal sense of the words used, appear intended to be foretold; and shall come to pass, and by coming to pass shall show the sense of the prophesies contain'd therein, perhaps to the disappointment of every interpreter that it has hitherto had.

[4.] Fourthly, the primitive fathers or authors before JEROM do apply passages of the PROPHETS in the same typical manner with the apostles, who were *models* to them in that respect; tho' they may not (any more than the apostles) directly say, they apply those passages typically; which they might think needless to observe to the reader, who could not fail to observe it himself.

Among other instances that might be given out of the *catholick epistle* of BARNABAS (whom Mr. *W.* seems to give up (*f*) as an allegorical interpreter of *prophesies* of the Old Testament, and whose *epistle* he deems *canonical scripture*) take that which follows. He cites these words of ISAIAH, as containing (*g*)

a

(*e*) Rhenford Opera Philolog. Diff. 1.
Vitringæ Obser. Sacr. l. 1. c. 10.
(*f*) Whiston's *Lect.* p. 43. Ib. *Essay on Apostol. Constit.* p. 33, 34, 67.
(*g*) Wake's *Apostol. Fathers*, p. 179, 186.
See Irenæus, l. 4. c. 66.

a prophesie *both of the cross and of him that was crucify'd upon it,* " I have stretch'd
" out my hands all the day long to a peo-
" ple disobedient, and speaking against
" my righteous way." Which passage, as it lies in Isaiah, has not, in its literal and obvious sense, the least relation to Jesus *stretching out his hands on the cross,* but with its context seems to bear this sense. " (h) Tho'
" the Jews deserve it not, yet I will redeem
" them *from captivity,* and would never have
" suffer'd them to fall into such misfortunes,
" had they had any regard to my commands;
" but *I spread out my hands every day to a*
" *rebellious people,* who were obstinately re-
" solv'd to follow the conduct of their cor-
" rupt imaginations; I call'd upon them by
" the voice of my prophets, and earnestly
" intreated them to be guided by me, and so
" he goes on drawing such a character of the
" Jews, as cannot be apply'd to them at
" any time after their return into their own
" country."

Justin Martyr (i) cites the before mention'd passage of Isaiah to the same purpose with Barnabas: as also the follow-

---

(h) *White* in locum.

(i) *Reeves*'s Justin, Apol. p. 68.

ing (*k*) passage of the same prophet, " Unto us a child is born, and a young man given, and the government shall be upon his shoulders;" *which*, he says, is *a prophetick description of the power of the cross, to which* Jesus *apply'd his shoulder at his crucifixion;* tho' the passage as it stands in Isaiah, relates in its obvious and primary sense to Hezechiah, and that part of it, whereon Justin lays stress, most manifestly relates to the bearing the office of a civil magistrate, and not to *carrying of a cross.*

Justin (*l*) also makes Moses to (*m*) prophesy of Christ in these words, *Binding his foal unto the vine, and washing his garments in the blood of the grapes.* Which are, according to him, *a significative symbol of what* Christ *was to do and suffer: for there stood the foal of an ass ty'd to a vine at the entrance of a certain village, which he order'd his disciples to go and bring him, upon which he got and rode into Jerusalem, where the stately temple of the Jews then was. And to fulfil the*

(*k*) Isaiah 9. 6. *See also* Origen in John, p. 42. Basil. Tom. 2. p. 212. Aliiq; Patres.
See Grotius *and* White in loc. & Clerici Hist. Eccles. p. 623.
(*l*) *Reeves*, Ib. p. 64.
(*m*) Gen. 45. 11.
See other explications of the Fathers, of this place cited by Whitby, *in* Stricturæ Patrum, p. 13, &c.

the sequel of the Prophesy *he was afterwards crucify'd.* For washing his garments in the blood of the grapes, *prefigur'd the passion he was to undergo, purifying by his blood such as should believe in him; for what, by the* Prophet, *the divine spirit calls his* garments, *are the faithful, in whom the* Logos, *the seed of God, dwells. The blood of the grapes typifies, that he who was to come should have blood, but not of human, but of divine generation*——*And as man had no hand in making the blood of the grape, but God only, so this is an emblem, that the blood of the Logos was of no human extraction, but descended from the power of the most High.* Upon this passage, as it again occurs and is urg'd by Justin in his *dialogue* with *Trypho*, the ingenious and learned Mr. Thirlby makes the following remark, very pertinent to the question of the fathers, applying the prophesies of the Old Testament allegorically, whereof I am now treating. (*n*) *Eandem interpretationem ad Gentiles quoq; convertendos adhibuit Apol. 1. p. 52. satis eam quidem ridiculam hâc ætate plerisq; visuram, at iis autem temporibus tolerabilem. Judæi certè non habebant quod aut reprehenderent aut riderent, id quod norunt omnes qui ingenium & doctrinam Judæorum non penitus ignorant.*

(*n*) *Thirlby* in *Justin Martyr.* p. 246.

rant. Sed neq; Ethnicis, sive doctis sive indoctis, Allegorica veterum scriptorum, præsertim sacrorum & VATICINORUM, explanatio, mirum aut novum videri poterat.

The same JUSTIN (*o*) affords many more instances of the like kind in his *first apology*; to which I refer the reader. His *dialogue with Trypho* also abounds with such; of which work BASNAGE, the learned author of the late *history of the Jews*, gives (*p*) us this account, *Je remarquerai*, says he, *seulement que comme* JUSTIN *avoit lu fort exactement les ecrits des Prophêtes, il a fait son fort de les entasser les uns sur les autres sans beaucoup d'art, & peut-être sans beaucoup des choix; & le Juif auroit eu raison de lui dire plus souvent qu'il n'a fait, que ces citations ne prouvent pas ce qu'il veut prouver.*

Thus also do IRENÆUS, TERTULLIAN, ORIGEN, LACTANTIUS, EUSEBIUS, BASIL, and all the other *(q)* fathers, both before as well as after JEROM, who cite the books of the prophets, as fulfill'd in the gospel, make application of the passages they cite from those prophets; whose words are only per-

---

(*o*) *Reeves*, Ib. p. 68—94.
(*p*) *Basnage* Hist. des Juifs, l. 8. c. 1. 6. 13.
(*q*) *See Whitby* Stricturæ Patrum apud Disser. de Scrip. Interp.

pertinent to the purpose for which they produce them in an allegorical sense. This the learned well know. And SIMON, in particular, speaking of EUSEBIUS's EVANGELICAL PREPARATION, (r) says, *that if you will examine with any care many of the* PROPHESIES *which* EUSEBIUS *understands of* JESUS CHRIST, *his reasonings are not always conclusive, because these* PROPHESIES *seem to have another literal sense:* but *therein he follow'd the method, which was* (s) *received before him in the church.* How could JUSTIN MARTYR (t) pretend to prove *from the* BOOKS *of the* PROPHETS; *that* JESUS *who was to come into the world, was to be born of a virgin, should cure every disease and malady in nature, and raise the dead, and be treated with spite and ignominy, and at length should be fastned to a cross, and dye, and rise again, and ascend up into heaven; and that he was truly the son of God, and should be worship'd under that title; and that he should send out some to preach these tydings to every nation; and that the gentiles should come over to the faith in greater numbers than the Jews; and that these very prophesies*

(r) *Simon* Bib. Choiſ. Vol. 1. p. 40.
(s) *See Grabe* apud *Thirlbii, J. Martyr,* p. 82, &c.
(t) Juſtin Martyr's *Apology, by* Reeves, p. 62, 63.

phefies went of him, thousands and hundreds of years, before his coming; but by arguing from the allegorical sense of those prophesies, which, literally understood, have no manner of relation to these matters, and so visibly relate to other matters, that it is hard to conceive JUSTIN could be so ignorant as not to know he argu'd allegorically, and not from the literal sense of them?

[5.] But several christian authors before JEROM not contenting themselves with arguing (and that knowingly as it ought to be judged) from the prophesies of the Old Testament, in the same allegorical manner with the apostles, do directly assert (contrary to what Mr. WHISTON affirms of them) a twofold sense of those prophesies, a literal and a mystical, and make them applicable in a mystical sense only to our Saviour.

Thus JUSTIN MARTYR (*u*) asserts a double sense of some prophesies. He gives us an account, how *the devils* introduc'd into the pagan religions several things in imitation of what they found *prophesy'd* of CHRIST, in the Old Testament; but says, they did not cause (*w*) *one of* JOVE'*s sons to be crucify'd*, because that *being* SYMBOLICALLY *represented in the Old Testament, they could not spell out the meaning of the* SYMBOL; *tho' the cross,*

(*u*) Justin Martyr's *Apol.* by Reeves, §. 75.
(*w*) Sect. 72.

cross, according to the prophet; was the great characteristick of his power and government.

Thus *Origen* (x) directly advances such a distinction, and defends the *mystical sense* of the prophesies of the Old Testament against CELSUS, who attack'd the christians for their mystical and forc'd interpretations of the Old Testament.

Thus EUSEBIUS (y) of *Cesarea*, in interpreting the celebrated prophesy of ISAIAH of a *virgin's conceiving and bringing forth a son*, said to be fulfill'd in JESUS by St. MATTHEW, refers it primarily to the prophet ISAIAH's own son, whom he expresly makes a type of CHRIST; as does also (z) St. BASIL. And EUSEBIUS (a) affirms in general, that there *are many allegorical explications of the* PROPHETS *in the gospels and epistles of the apostles, and especially in the epistle to the Hebrews*; and that *such was the method of explaining scripture used by* the *doctors* of the christian church.

The *gospel according to the Egyptians,*
which

(x) *Origen* contra *Celf.* p. 39, 343.
See Simon Hist. Crit. du Nov. Testam. p. 261.
(y) *Eusebii* Demon. Evang. l. 7. p. 328——335.
(z) *Basil* apud *Huetii* Dem. Evang. p. 355.
(a) *Eusebii* Hist. Eccles. l. 2. c. 17.

which was extant before any of the four gospels, and suppos'd to be one of those gospels referr'd to by LUKE; was, as (b) appears *by the remaining fragments*, a gospel *sufficiently* MYSTICAL *and* ALLEGORICAL, *according to the genius of the Egyptian nation*. And tho' among those few *fragments* which remain of it, there appear no allegorical interpretations of prophesies, yet it may be justly suppos'd, to have as much or more abounded with them than St. MATTHEW's *gospel* it self; which being written chiefly for the use of the Jews, has in it more allegorical application of prophesies than the other gospels, according to the genius of the Jewish nation at that time. Nor can this be much doubted, if it be consider'd, that the (c) *Therapeutæ* (who are suppos'd to be those christians of *Egypt* that receiv'd the *gospel according to the Egyptians*) *explain'd all the scriptures of the Old Testament in an allegorical and mystical manner*; and took *the gospels and epistles of the New Testament to be mystical books, and proper to guide* them in their *mystical explications of the Old Testament*.

We

(b) Whiston's *Essay on the Apostol. Constit.* p. 74, &c.
Grabe Spicil. Vol. 1. p. 51.
(c) Whiston, Ib. p. 74.
Euseb. Hist. Ecclef. l. 2. c. 17.

We may also fairly judge (*d*) the *gospel according to the Hebrews*, which was also publish'd before our four gospels for the use of the *Nazarenes*, (as the first christians were call'd) was written in the spirit of *allegory:* since their successors allegoriz'd the bible in the same manner with the pharisees, who began the method of allegorizing among the Jews, which was afterwards follow'd in the christian church. But however that be; the *Nazarenes* before JEROM's time were undoubtedly *allegorists*, as appears by the proofs SIMON brings out of JEROM.

In fine, Mr. *W.* (*e*) himself says; He *will not affirm, that what* predictions *the fathers alledge* out of the Old Testament *do always bear that sense they ascribe to them, yet he thinks they* GENERALLY, *if not wholly, believ'd them to do so.* So that he hereby allows; that the fathers did argue after a typical and allegorical manner from the predictions of the prophets; and that they might *sometimes*, 'tho' not *generally*, believe they interpreted those predictions, not in a literal, but allegorical sense.

[6.] The system therefore or scheme of things set up by Mr. *W.* seems to me to com-

---

(*d*) *Simon* Hist. des Comment. p. 1——3.
(*e*) *Lectures*, p. 28.

combat the christian scheme receiv'd in all ages and times, and asserts what is contrary to the most notorious fact, and to the most universal practise of all christians before, as well as after, JEROM. For if any one christian fact be true, it is, that christians in all ages and times, and more especially in the primitive times, have both understood the apostles to have argu'd allegorically from the prophesies cited by them out of the Old Testament, or have themselves argu'd allegorically from the prophesies they themselves cited out of the Old Testament; which last seems sufficient to prove the apostles to have been allegorical interpreters of the Old Testament, according to the common topick of divines, who contend that the earliest fathers best teach us the sense and doctrine of the apostles. And Mr. *W.* is the first Theorist-divine, who, to assert the autority of the New Testament, has pretended, that the Old Testament (in really genuine passages) is *corrupted*; all other christians asserting the integrity of the Old (and some even with respect to corrupted passages) to prove the autority of the New: And I believe he is the first christian author, who ever asserted, either that all the prophesies cited by the authors of the New Testament from the Old, were fulfill'd in their literal sense; or that to consider the apostles as applying any of them in an allegorical manner,

was

was *a weak and enthusiastical* scheme: all others, as far as I can learn, contending at most for the literal sense of some prophesies only: and some (f) making it the glory *of christianity* to be founded on *allegory*, and not in *criticism*, which, they say, would have render'd the *writings* of the apostles *ten times more liable to exceptions than now they are*; and also to be *a wonderful confirmation of christianity*, that *the apostles*, who were *men of no literature and education*, and *never spent their time in the schools of the Rabbi's*, should *be such eminent masters* in allegory or *Rabbinical learning*, and *should be so excellently vers'd in their traditionary explications of prophesies*.

It seems therefore most destructive of christianity to suppose; that *typical* or *allegorical arguing* is in any respect *weak and enthusiastical*; and that the apostles always argu'd in the matter of *prophesies* according to the literal sense of the *prophesies*, and the way of reasoning used in the schools: since it is most apparent; that the whole gospel is in every respect founded on *type* and *allegory*; that the apostles in most, if not in all cases, reason'd *typically* and *allegorically*; and that, if the apostles be suppos'd to (g) reason always after the

rules

(f) Nichols's *Conf. with a Theist*, Vol. 3. p. 64, 65.
(g) *Simon* Hist. Crit. du N. Test. c. 21 & 22.
Cuneus Rep. des Heb. Vol. 1. p. 376, 377.

rules used in the schools, and if their writings be brought to the test of those *rules*, the books of the Old and New Testament will be an in *irreconcileable state*, and the *difficulties* against christianity will be incapable of being solv'd. *Any that call themselves christians,* says, (h) Dr. ALLIX, *should take heed how they deny the force and autority of that way of traditional interpretation, which has been anciently received in the jewish church.*

XI.

That *Mr.* WHISTON's *first proposition is subverted by his book.*

MR. *W*'s first proposition, (i) That *the present text of the Old Testament is, generally speaking, both in the history, the laws, the prophesies, and the divine hymns; or as to the main tenor and current of the whole, the very same now that it ever has been from the utmost antiquity*; is subverted by and inconsistent with the whole scheme, and most of the following parts of his *book, which* chiefly consists in asserting and proving, that the text of the Old Testament is (k) *considerably*

(h) Allix's *Judgment of the Jewish Church against the Unitarians,* p. 51.
(i) Whiston's *Essay,* p. 1.
(k) Ib. p. 15, 18, 33, 40, 88, 115——116. 128, 182, 185, 220, 262, 263, 281——289.

rably and greatly different from what it was in the second century, and not a little corrupted; and that the New and Old Testament are in so *irreconcileable a state*, by means of *diflocations* in the Old Testament, and of the introduction of such other changes therein, which make *the most apparent inconsistencies and contradictions between the Old and New Testament*, as to overthrow the proofs of the truth of christianity cited by the apostles from the Old Testament; which *great corruptions* are the foundation and reasons of Mr. WHISTON's *Essay towards restoring the true text of the Old Testament.*

The

The Conclusion:

Containing an account of Mr. Whiston *himself.*

Having made an end of my remarks on Mr. *W*'s *Essay*, I proceed to give you some account of the gentleman himself; who for some time past has made no small noise, not only in *England*, but in divers parts of *Europe*, by his numerous writings.

He is a person of extraordinary natural parts, and of great acquir'd learning, particularly in *philosophy* and *mathematicks*; but, above all, in *theology*, which he has study'd with the greatest application and integrity in the *scriptures*, and in the writings of the *ancients*; despising the *catechisms*, *confessions*, or *articles* of *faith* and *traditions* of all modern churches, and the *commentaries* on scripture and *systemical books* of all modern theologues.

He knows how to make the best of every argument he takes in hand. By his sagacity and quickness, by the compass of his reading, and by his great memory, he omits nothing,

thing, that can be urg'd or wiredrawn to support any sentiments he espouses; as is manifest from many of his theological works.

He is an upright and very religious man, and a most zealous christian: leading a moral life, as is common to most who are styl'd *hereticks: cultivating* (a) in himself and *promoting in others such virtue and learning, as he thinks would conduce most to the honour of God, by manifesting the greatness and wisdom of his works*: renouncing glory, riches, and ease (which he might have had with the applause of all, and envy of none) and willingly and courageously undergoing obloquy, poverty, and persecution (all three whereof have been His lot, and the two former will be always) for the sake of a good conscience: deeming *prudence to be the worldly wisdom condemn'd by* CHRIST *and his apostles*, and *concealment* of religious sentiments to be a great crime; and unmov'd by the example of several (b) learned divines, who, as is well known, have great *prudence*, and, thro' fear of the *ignorant*, the *bigots*, and the crafty,

---

(a) Hare's Diff. and Disc. p. 16, &c.
(b) *Erasmi* Epistolæ, p. 501, 507, 583, 672. See also Whiston's *Reflections on a Discourse of Free thinking*, p. 53.
Id. Prim. Chrift. Vol. 1. Hist. Pref. p. 27.

crafty, (who govern the two former) do, most of all men, conceal their religious *sentiments* from the world; *which*, if they happen in confidence to discover to him, he without scruple publishes (c) in print: sacrificing his understanding to the obedience of faith, and believing *mysteries*; and not rejecting even the *Athanasian creed* it self (tho' in his opinion contradictory in it self, and to reason) but only as not grounded on *scripture* and *antiquity*: following some practises how rigid and seemingly ridiculous soever, and how remote soever from the practises of the age and country, wherein he lives, which he thinks requir'd by CHRIST and his apostles (which has made some people wonder, that he continues, as in the time of his darkness, to *shave his beard*, contrary to the express declaration of the (d) *Apostolick constitutions*) finding out and seeing clearly the revolutions of all the following ages, both past and to come, in the writings of the *prophets*, and in the *Revelation of St.* JOHN: taking up with all manner of false proofs in behalf of christianity, such as forg'd books, forg'd passages, precarious suppositions, tales, and sham-miracles, as well as with the most substantial proofs:

en-

(c) *See his Histor. Pref.* and Allix's *Remarks on* Whiston's *Papers.*

(d) *Apostol. Constit.* l. 1. c. 3.

endeavouring (*e*) to explain *scripture difficulties*; wherein, tho' he, *like others, who have meddled with the same subject, has not succeeded*, as Dr. Hare says, yet he has shown his zeal: holding (*f*) a society in his own house of *honest and inquisitive men of all parties and notions among christians*, in order to search after, and find out, *genuine and original christianity*; and in fine, as much in earnest, as some others seem to be in jest.

He is the very reverse of many most eminent divines. He thinks himself oblig'd in conscience to be dutiful, submissive, and loyal to his Majesty, to whom he has sworn allegiance; and it is not a *church point* with him to *act* one way and *pray* and *swear* another, or not to be in earnest in those two most serious and solemn actions. He speaks what he thinks, and is not guilty of the contradiction of making the christian religion a matter of great importance, and yet concealing his thoughts about the particulars of that religion; any more than he is of professing a religion which he does not believe. He pays no regard to fashionable doctrines; nor to fashionable divines, who, in obedience

---

(*e*) Hare's *Diffic. and Discourage*. p. 7. *See* Whiston's *Dedication to his Chron*. p. 4.

(*f*) Whiston's *Pref. to Letter to the* Earl of Nottingham, p. 7.

to one another and in harmony, vary, change, and regulate the faith of the vulgar. He will not be bound by *articles* which he has subscrib'd, but renounce them, when he judges them erroneous; nor will he subscribe articles, which he does not believe true, or subscribe them in senses contrary to those design'd by the imposers. He renounces all preferments, and will not so much as receive money from (*g*) *infidel* hands. And he thinks himself oblig'd to imitate the apostles in their low estate; and he believes it no less inconsistent with christianity, to aim at and contend for, and to possess that worldly greatness and wealth, which their pretended successors of the *Romish* church enjoy and contend for as due to them by the gospel, than to contradict the apostles in other respects.

He is a zealous member (*h*) of the church of *England*, as by law establish'd: keeping to that church; tho' several parts of the worship therein perform'd be, in his opinion, blasphemy and contradiction; tho' he knows he hears daily the most absurd, sophistical, declamatory, and factious discourses from the pulpit; tho' he be attack'd and abus'd on most sundays from that *high place* to the understanding of the auditory, who on such

occa-

(*g*) *Second Append. to Hist. Pref.* p. 58.
(*h*) *Papers relating to Mr.* Whiston's *Cause*, p. 168—171.

occasions turn their eyes upon him; tho' he be refus'd to partake of the blessed sacrament, which (*i*) *goes near his heart*; and tho' he be forbid coming to church by the rector of his parish, who has endeavour'd to set the mob upon him.

But his judgment does not seem to be equal to his sagacity, learning, zeal, and integrity. For, either thro' the prejudices of education, which he still retains, or thro' some superstition, which, notwithstanding his examination, sticks by him, he seems still qualify'd to admit the most precarious suppositions, and to receive many things without the least foundation. The warmth of his temper disposes him to receive any sudden thoughts, any thing that strikes his imagination, when favourable to his preconceiv'd scheme of things, or to any new schemes of things, that serve, in his opinion, a religious purpose. And his imagination is so strong and lively on these occasions, that he sometimes even supposes facts, and builds upon those facts. Thus, for example, he acted in the (*k*) case of an *Arabick manuscript* (whereof he understood not one word) which he *hoped* was or took to have been a translation of an ancient book (*l*) of scripture, belonging to the New Testament,

---

(*i*) *Postscript to his Hist. Pref.* p. 72. *Papers relating to his Cause*, p. 156; &c.
(*k*) *Advertif. before Prim. Christ.* Vol. 1. p. 1.
(*l*) *Reply to Allix*, p. 33.

ſtament, and written by the *apoſtles*, ſtyl'd, the *doctrine of the apoſtles*, and propos'd to publiſh it as ſuch. But when it came to be read by men skilful in the *Arabick tongue*, it prov'd a tranſlation of another book before extant in print in its original language. And thus, tho' he be a lover of truth, yet by his warmth of temper, he is drawn in and engag'd ſo far in the belief and defence of many things, as gives a turn to his underſtanding, and thereby makes his conviction of miſtakes in ſome caſes difficult, and in others, perhaps, impoſſible.

He did, ſoon after his conviction of the errors of his education, in a proper manner, both by diſcourſes and writings, declare openly his religious ſentiments, which as an honeſt man he could not conceal. And he moſt ſubmiſſively addreſs'd (*m*) himſelf, in particular, to both the archbiſhops, and to ſeveral of the biſhops, and other learned divines, and to the convocation, and to both the univerſities, offering to lay before them *papers* for their examination, which have been ſince publiſh'd; *wherein* he pretended to diſcover the true, old, original chriſtianity, from which all chriſtians had for many ages before the reformation departed, when, according to him, a part only of primitive chriſtianity was reviv'd. But this free,

---

(*m*) *See his* Hiſtorical Preface.

free, open, christian proceeding, had no other publick effect, than to draw upon him, an arbitrary and illegal expulsion *(n)* from the *university* of *Cambridge*, and from his *mathematick-professor-ship* there, by the *heads of houses*, and that *without conferring* with him in relation to his notions, they urging, that it was *(o) not usual to argue with hereticks*; an *address* of the *convocation* to the *queen* against him, wherein they desire to be put into a method how to punish him; a *representation* of him, by the said convocation to the *queen* and the *nation*, as a person carrying on the cause of irreligion; the convocation's *secret censure (p)* of divers of his positions, which *censure* has since stole out into print; and their *open refusal (q)* to examine his *papers*, and to hear him in his own defence, tho' he demanded it of them, as a matter of right; and lastly, a prosecution commenc'd against him by Dr. PELLING, which upon the death of her late majesty dropp'd.

He lives for the most part in *London*, the place of the greatest resort of men of understanding, birth, fortune, and learning in the universe. There he visits persons of *both sexes*,

---

(n) Appendix to Hist. Pref. p. 160.
(o) Account of his Banishment, &c. p. 38—42.
(p) Supplement to Hist. Pref. p. 63.
(q) Second Append. to Hist. Pref.

[281]

sexes, and of the highest rank, who are delighted with his plainness, integrity, sense, and learning; and to whom he discourses with the greatest freedom about many important points, and especially about *Athanasianism*, which seems his most peculiar concern. He frequents the most publick coffeehouses, where most are prone to show him respect, and none dare show him any disrespect: the clergy, either flying before him, or making a feeble opposition to him. By all which he has made a multitude of converts to the belief; that the Father, Son, and Holy Ghost are three different intelligent agents, and not three intelligent agents making but one intelligent agent; that the Father was before and is *greater* than the Son; that the Son is not the same being with the Father; and that the Father is the *One God*, (as say both the (r) *scripture* and *Nicene creed*) or that there are no other Gods but him; all doctrines contrary to the present orthodoxy. And he has soften'd the zeal of many more, who used to call for fire from heaven, or the sword of the magistrate to defend their sentiments. He has at this time so much credit, that he now says and prints what he pleases, without incurring

U any

(r) Matt. 12. 32. John 17. 3. 1 Cor. 8. 4, 6. 1 Tim 2. 5.

any hazard of persecution from real or pretended zealots; who are forc'd to yield to the superior splendor and power of his honesty, sense, and learning, and fear drawing upon themselves something of more fatal consequence, than the present conversions that he makes. And I am perswaded, that if any country could but furnish twenty such men as he is; that they would, without pay, and with mere liberty to speak their sentiments, put to flight twenty thousand listed to support error.

He is a person, who forms vast projects and designs for the defence of *natural and reveal'd religion*, and for restoring what he calls *primitive christianity* amongst us: as appears by his *Theory of the earth*; his *Chronology of the Old Testament, and harmony of the four gospels*; his *Essay on the Revelation of St.* JOHN; his *Primitive christianity reviv'd*; his *Astronomical principles of natural and reveal'd religion*; his *Essay to restore the true text of the Old Testament*; and his *design* of a new *interleav'd bible* with large additions, and divers particulars *to confirm and illustrate* the same, that *so all honest enquirers may be able to judge for themselves, about the truth of those scriptures, and to understand the greatest part of them impartially, without the danger of imposition from common prejudices; from any later partial expositions or mistakes whatsoever*; to say nothing, or not to enter into the detail of his lesser numerous *projects, essays, designs, suppoſals*, and *theories* in behalf of religion. Nor is he without great *deſigns* for the improvement of philoſophy, and for the welfare and trade of his country: as appears by his attempts to explain the philoſophy of Sir ISAAC NEWTON, and by his other works in *mathematicks* and *phyſicks*, but above all, by his *attempts to diſcover the longitude*, for which he deſerves the *reward* promis'd by *parliament*, tho' he ſhould not ſucceed. But the greateſt good, that he promotes, ſeems, to me what he does *not deſign*; and that is, by putting men upon enquiries, to make them ſee further than himſelf, and to reject his narrow opinions.

He is a very ſerious and grave perſon, but yet chearful, and no enemy to innocent mirth; and he is, even, capable of laughing (*s*) heartily at egregious nonſenſe, ſtupidity, and folly in the moſt *ſolemn perſons*, when they ſpeak about the moſt *ſolemn things*.

I will conclude this account of him, with obſerving, that all the reform'd churches, and eſpecially your *church of Scotland* (which is in a peculiar manner the object of theological ſpite among us) are highly oblig'd to him for a moſt ingenious defence of the validity of their miniſtry in his *Argument to prove that*
either

(*s*) See one of his printed *Letters about Doxologies*.

either all persons solemnly, tho' irregularly set apart for the ministry are real clergymen, and all their ministerial acts are valid; or else there are now no real clergymen or christians in the world. Wherein your ministry, which is so undeservedly contemptible in the eyes of our clergy, who do not make a just comparison between themselves and their neighbours, is, as it ought to be, set upon as good a foot as any ministry whatsoever.

I have nothing further to add, but that I hope this letter, tho' long delay'd, will not be unacceptable to you, from,

Reverend SIR,

Your most humble Servant.

www.ingramcontent.com/pod-product-compliance
Lightning Source LLC
Chambersburg PA
CBHW071227230426
43668CB00011B/1341